*Customer Loyalty Programmes and Clubs*

# Customer Loyalty Programmes and Clubs

## Second Edition

STEPHAN A BUTSCHER

Gower

Published by
Gower Publishing Limited
Gower House
Croft Road
Aldershot
Hants GU11 3HR
England

Gower Publishing Company
131 Main Street
Burlington VT 05401–5600 USA

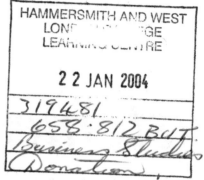
British Library Cataloguing in Publication Data
Butscher, Stephan A.
    Customer loyalty programmes and clubs. – 2nd ed.
    1. Customer clubs    2. Customer loyalty programs
    I. Title    II. Customer clubs and loyalty programmes
    658.8' 12

ISBN 0 566 08451 1


US Library of Congress Cataloging-in-Publication Data
Butscher, Stephan A.
    Customer loyalty programmes and clubs / Stephan A. Butscher. –2nd ed.
        p. cm.
    Rev. ed of: Customer clubs and loyalty programmes, 1998.
    Includes bibliographical references.
    ISBN 0–566–08451–1
    1. Customer clubs. 2. Customer loyalty programs. I. Butscher, Stephan A. Customer
clubs and loyalty programmes. II. Title

    HF5415.525.B87 2002
    658.8'12–dc21                                                2001040992

Typeset in 9 point Stone Serif by IML Typographers, Birkenhead, Merseyside and printed in Great Britain by T J International, Padstow.

319481

# Contents

# List of figures

# List of tables

If you want to build a ship, do not send your men out to get wood and tools ... but teach them the longing for the wide open sea.

A. de Saint-Exupéry

# Preface to the second edition

Who would have thought that the first edition of *Customer Loyalty Programmes and Clubs* would be so successful? It was lucky to be published in the beginning of the second wave of loyalty programmes' popularity boom, which holds until today, driven by Customer Relationship Management (CRM) and the new possibilities that the Internet and modern technology place in the hands of loyalty managers. Every month I read about new loyalty initiatives and companies contact me with their loyalty ideas. Customer loyalty marketing has become an important pillar of corporate strategy in all industries.

The original edition has been published in three languages (English, German and Swedish), and from the feedback I have received over the last three years, has helped many managers to build or refine successful loyalty programmes. Consequently, it seemed logical to start working on a second edition, to update the book with regard to all the key developments of the last few years. All chapters of the book have been reworked, and two new chapters on 'Pricing for Customer Loyalty' and 'E-Loyalty – Customer Loyalty on the Internet' as well as several new case studies have been added. The most important result of the work put into this second edition is that most of the key points we developed in the original book still hold true today, mostly more than ever. We were able to add many new examples, an indication of how more and more companies have begun developing smart and value-oriented loyalty programmes and are becoming more and more adept in loyalty issues.

Again, this edition would not have been possible without the help of many, most notably Verena Burger, Lindsey Clark, Petra Dietz, Julia Goldenbaum, Kerstin Hammel, Christian Müller and Pamela Rathgeber-Zack, all with Simon, Kucher & Partners.

I also thank Jo Burges and Celia Hoare at Gower Publishing for their professional guidance through the publication process of this book.

I am deeply indebted to my wife Susanne for her never-ending love, patience, support and encouragementwhich have made it all possible. It is to her that this book is dedicated.

STEPHAN A. BUTSCHER

# *Preface to the first edition*

When I started studying customer loyalty programmes, and especially customer clubs, in depth in 1992, I tried to identify the source of these clubs. As I had been taught in business school, I first turned west and browsed plenty of American literature. Typically, marketing trends emerge in the US and German marketers adapt them several years later. The UK is mostly a little faster and always among the first European countries to put new findings into practice. But in the case of customer clubs the situation is different. Customer clubs and the idea they represent (customer loyalty programmes that build up real relationships based on a value-oriented benefit package) are one of the few examples where the knowledge transfer can go the other way, from Germany to the UK and the US.

With this book I would like to support this knowledge transfer and open the minds of marketers and professionals around the world to a more value-oriented approach to customer loyalty programmes. Customer loyalty programmes have become a more and more important component of many companies' marketing activities. This importance will certainly increase over the next few years, creating an even larger wave of new programmes than we have seen recently. However, this wave will lead – and already is leading – to a situation in which these programmes become a commodity, in the main because they are all alike. With the value-oriented approach presented in this book, I hope to widen the thinking and planning horizons of those who are responsible for developing a customer loyalty programme for their company or client. A wider horizon is necessary to avoid more 'me too', add more 'just me' and increase the effectiveness of such programmes.

As usual, this book would not have been possible without the help of several people, to whom I would like to express my deepest gratitude.

I thank Dr Klaus Hilleke and Hans O. Schumann, PhD, both colleagues at Simon, Kucher & Partners, and Jon P. Haase for reviewing the manuscript and for their numerous new ideas and insights that I am privileged to have been able to include in this book.

I am deeply indebted to my wife Susanne, not only for her translations of several of the chapters in Part III of this book and her assistance while I was researching the book, but mostly for her never-ending love, patience, support and encouragement that have made it all possible.

I further thank Caroline Carlson, Manoj Garg, Markus Kreusch, Stefanie Lörinczy, Emilia Mota and Vicki Sherwood for their assistance in research, chart design and meticulous proof-reading.

I am also grateful to Patrick Ashworth (Swatch), Reiner Blau (Bates Dialog), Thomas Brinckwirth (SWF3 Radio), Mary Carse (International Customer Loyalty Programs – ICLP), Paul Farmer Roger Burnett Promotions), Dr Ralf Kreutzer (Kunden Club GmbH of the Volkswagen Group), Raimund Petersen (Friedrich Grohe AG), Hans O. Schumann, PhD (Simon, Kurcher & Partners), Prof. Merlin Stone (European Management School, University of Surrey) and Matthias Thieme (Microsoft GmbH) for their practical insights into the customer loyalty world in their respective companies or countries.

I also thank Jonathan Norman (Project Director) and Solveig Gardner Servian (Managing Editor) at Gower Publishing for their professional guidance through the publication process of this book.

Last but not least, I would also like to express my gratitude to the countless managers, professionals, academics and marketers around the world, discussions with whom have strongly inspired my thinking.

This book is dedicated to my parents Barbara and Erwin Butscher, my wife Susanne and my grandmother Charlotte Kolbe. This book is also in memory of my aunt Jutta Kolbe. All of them have shown me the importance of courage and optimism and that love and friendship have the highest value of all.

Diamonds are for ever!

STEPHAN A. BUTSCHER

# PART 1

# *Customer Loyalty Programmes and Clubs*

*Changes in the market environment can quickly alter prices and technologies, but close relationships can last a lifetime.*

(Regis McKenna)

# 1 *Why you should read this book!*

Most customer loyalty programmes offer primarily financial (hard) benefits. In essence, they provide price discounts – and discounts are the last thing that creates loyalty among customers. Customers who buy your product or service merely because of its price will not continue to do so if they can find a better price elsewhere. The only way to create long-term customer loyalty is to establish a true relationship with your customers which is based not on financial incentives, but on emotion, trust and partnership.

This book presents a new approach to customer loyalty programmes. Step by step, it will help you create a benefit package that has a high perceived value for your customers, show you ways to quantify the value of potential benefits, and explain how to find the right combination of financial and non-financial benefits.

Customer clubs, the synonym for such value-oriented loyalty programmes used in this book, began in Germany, where they have been extremely successful since the mid-1980s. Until recently, German law forbade selling the same product to different customers at different prices, for example depending on whether or not they were members of a customer loyalty programme. Therefore, German marketers were forced to develop programmes that created loyalty without financial incentives. The biggest clubs have several hundred thousand members, yet manage to treat everyone as an individual – a step towards mass customization in customer contact. The success of customer clubs in the UK, Australia or the USA has proved that they can work all over the world. We will show that what makes clubs so successful is the creation of a powerful, value-oriented loyalty programme that aims to create a strong emotional relationship with customers and gives them real benefits.

For many years, organizations have tried to attract customers by such slogans as 'The customer is king', 'The customer comes first', 'We guarantee total customer satisfaction' or 'We offer the best service'. This kind of attitude is extremely important for success in an environment of increasing competition and ever more demanding customers – but surprisingly few companies live up to their promises or to their customers' expectations. They may only still be in business because their competitors are not doing any better.

A similar situation exists with customer loyalty programmes. Although there are thousands of programmes in existence, very few create real loyalty and devotion. About 90 per cent of the customer loyalty programmes we analysed while researching the first edition of this book were built on price-related benefits such as discounts, rebates and special offers. These programmes are nothing other than price cuts. During our research for this edition, we revisited many of these programmes, only to find that just a few had learnt their lesson. But those who did had shifted their focus to service elements, special treatment and other soft benefits. They understood that if any customer loyalty was built in the short term it was mostly a result of the discounts offered, rather than stemming from a strong emotional relationship to the product or service. In this book, we shall show that such an approach does not create the bond between the customer and the product, brand or company that is necessary for long-term loyalty. The only way to build long-term loyalty is to establish real relationships based on emotions and trust, by offering uniqueness and high perceived value in your loyalty programme. Financial benefits may be part of this, but they are not enough on their own.

This book will show, step by step, how a customer loyalty programme should be set up in order to create true relationships between seller and buyer. These steps include definition of target groups and goals, choice of programme type, internal and external communication, organizational structure and service centre, using the Internet, setting up and using a database, integrating the programme into the sponsoring company's structure, and measuring the club's success. We will show in detail how to filter out the most highly valued benefits from a wide range of possibilities, which methods can be used to quantify value, and how to find the best combination of non-financial (soft) and financial (hard) benefits. In addition, we will explain that a customer loyalty programme does not necessarily have to be a large drain on the marketing budget, but can be at least partly self-financing.

Part III is devoted to case studies from companies such as Swatch, Volkswagen and Porsche which explain how the concept has been put into practice. Each of the case studies has been written by a specialist from the sector or by the manager who was responsible for planning and launching the customer club and making it successful.

This book is for practitioners, for marketing professionals and managers who want to improve their company's competitiveness by developing a customer loyalty programme that really works. It will also provide fresh ideas and approaches for those in the business or academic world who are concerned with relationship marketing, retention marketing, customer loyalty and other related subjects.

# **2** *Executive summary*

Numerous forms of customer loyalty programmes have resulted from the efforts of countless companies, institutions and non-profit organizations to retain customers. Each of these types of programme has certain characteristics that distinguish it from the others. A customer club is only one type of customer loyalty programme; and even within the family of customer clubs there are several different types, such as end-user clubs, business-to-business clubs and so on. In general, the title of the loyalty programme is irrelevant. What counts is that it achieves its goal of increasing customers' loyalty by offering true value. This book describes how to set up successful loyalty programmes in general – the term 'customer club' is simply a synonym for value-oriented loyalty programmes.

## What is a customer club (value-oriented loyalty programme)?

A customer club can be defined as an at least communicative union of people or organizations, which is initiated and operated by an organization in order to contact these members directly on a regular basis and offer them a benefit package with a high perceived value, with the goal of activating them and increasing their loyalty by creating an emotional relationship.

The most important special characteristics of customer clubs and other value-oriented loyalty programmes are as follows:

- They are initiated, planned and managed by an organization, and not by the customers themselves.
- They offer real and perceived value to their members by optimizing the combination of financial (hard) and non-financial (soft) benefits.
- They provide opportunities for members and the sponsoring company to talk to each other.
- They can collect data which will help other departments of the sponsoring company improve their performance.
- They aim to activate customers by encouraging them to buy or recommend a product, communicate with the loyalty programme and so on.

There are several steps involved in establishing an effective customer loyalty programme. First, put together an interdisciplinary project team that is fully devoted to developing a powerful programme. Creating a customer loyalty programme should involve the whole organization, and by drawing team members from different departments, you avoid a one-sided approach. And before starting any work on a programme, answer one question honestly: 'Are our products (or services) worth it?' If your products are inferior or out of date, any investment in a customer loyalty programme will be a waste of time and money.

## Loyalty programme goals

At the outset, the goals for the loyalty programme must be clearly defined. Only if they are will you be able to measure the loyalty programme's success. The core goal of a customer loyalty programme is, of course, to increase profit, revenue and market share. Other important goals include customer retention, winning new customers, setting up a strong customer database, supporting other departments with information or access to information, and creating communication opportunities between the organization and its customers. A variety of subsidiary goals can be added, such as improving public relations and customer support, increasing usage and achieving more frequent visits to a particular retail outlet. Success measurement has to be considered even at this early stage, defining what scales need to be used to measure success in terms of the defined goals, what levels signify success and failure, and so on.

It is important to be aware that customer loyalty programmes do not create quick results. They should instead be viewed as a powerful retention marketing tool for building long-term relationships.

## Target groups

The primary target group for your customer loyalty programme should be your most important customers, those who constitute the major portion of your business, as securing these relationships is most vital for your future success. Smaller customers and potential customers should not be excluded from the loyalty programme, but the primary focus should be on developing a programme that fits the needs of the top customers. Other customers will still benefit from such a programme, but you will want to target them with concepts that take their particular needs into consideration.

The decision about whether to define your target groups narrowly or broadly depends largely on the goals of the loyalty programme. If you are aiming to set up a complete database of your customer base, then a wide definition of target groups is necessary; if the goal is to secure business from current key accounts, then focus is more appropriate. Another factor to be considered is how potential customers or competitors' customers are to be approached. Sometimes, a loyalty programme can create a wave of new customers for the sponsoring company, but that will depend on the value and attractiveness of the benefit package.

Further segmentation (for example, concentrating on major customers in specific industries) only makes sense if the target groups are not sufficiently homogeneous to be approached through one programme. Customer loyalty programmes are very flexible and can cover several target groups, so it is possible to remain in touch with customers even if their habits change and they move from one target group or segment to another.

## Type of loyalty programme

Customer loyalty programmes can be split into two groups: *limited* and *open*. The most suitable form depends on the loyalty programme's goals, target groups and individual context.

Limited loyalty programmes require a membership fee together with a completed application form, and they try to channel membership towards the primary target groups. Certain criteria often have to be fulfilled in order to qualify for membership. This ensures a better focus on the primary target groups, and helps to keep out freeloaders.

Open loyalty programmes have no entry conditions, but as a result often include many members who are of no benefit to the company. They are ideal if extremely wide target groups have been defined, or if potential and competitors' customers are also primary target groups. The lack of an entry condition will make membership more attractive and easier for a larger number of people.

Loyalty programmes can be further split into end-user loyalty programmes and business-to-business or distributor loyalty programmes, depending on their primary focus and target groups.

## Loyalty programme benefits

The heart and soul of a customer loyalty programme are its benefits. The loyalty programme will only be successful if the right benefits are chosen. Benefits must have a high perceived value for members. To find the right combination of hard (financial) and soft (non-financial) benefits, it is necessary to take a value-oriented approach which consists of three steps.

In the first step, a list of potential benefits is brainstormed, focusing on the needs of the target groups. The only limit to developing interesting benefits is the imagination of the project team.

The second step is a small-scale pre-study which aims to filter out the most and the least interesting benefits from this list by asking a small sample to rate the different benefits. The interviewees are also asked to add new ideas of their own in this phase, in order to make sure that interesting areas are not left out and that the customer's voice is heard.

Some of these new ideas, as well as the best-rated benefits, are taken into the third step, a large-scale survey. Here, a sample of at least 250 people is interviewed for a business-to-customer approach, although fewer interviews are sufficient for business-to-business. Using methods such as ranking scales, constant sum scales or the more sophisticated and very precise conjoint measurement, the value of the remaining benefits is measured.

The result of this three-step approach is that the long list of benefits obtained in step one is split into three groups: a small group of top value drivers, those benefits with a lower value to the customer, and those benefits with no value from the customer's point of view. The final benefits should be selected from the first two groups after taking into consideration factors such as cost, feasibility and competence. These latter aspects should not be considered before this stage, as the value to the customer should be the primary decision criterion. If the value of a benefit is extremely high, it should not be knocked out of contention early on simply because it also carries a high cost; there are many ways to cover the cost of such benefits. Problems of competence can be overcome by co-operating with external partners. However, any partner must be chosen carefully, and must be equal to the loyalty programme and the sponsoring company on factors such as image and quality.

A customer loyalty programme should primarily offer benefits that are related to the core products and services of the sponsoring company. Co-operating with external partners is a good way to expand the loyalty programme's range of benefits by including others that are not product-related and increase the loyalty programme's attractiveness. Other companies are often willing to pay commission so they can approach loyalty programme members with their products in addition to those of the sponsoring company. However, if a loyalty programme chooses to co-operate with external partners, the communication should always be via the loyalty programme and never directly between the external partner and the loyalty programme member.

A customer loyalty programme has a life cycle and must be constantly improved and further developed. Therefore, you should keep some of the top value drivers in reserve for future 'facelifts', rather than offering all of them from the beginning. These facelifts are necessary to keep the loyalty programme dynamic, to constantly improve it, and to make sure it does not lose its attractiveness.

## Pricing for loyalty

No loyalty programme should rely on discounts or other price breaks to create loyalty. Customer loyalty cannot be bought, but must be earned. Consequently, the key benefits should be non-financial and based on service, special treatment, communication and so on (see above). However, discounts are popular, and might significantly increase the value of the programme. If you want to offer discounts, then use one of the several smart pricing strategies that are available that create a win–win situation from which both supplier and customer benefit.

Rather than simply giving away discounts, they should be earned by customers and given to them as a reward. Several sophisticated pricing strategies are available that do this in an intelligent way (such as multi-step discounts, multi-dimensional pricing schemes and so on). Precise analysis is necessary to install these strategies the right way, but the advantages are huge.

## The financial concept

After selecting the right loyalty programme benefits, putting together a sound financial concept is the second most important step in establishing a customer loyalty programme. The annual cost per member of a loyalty programme can range from £5 to £25 for end-user loyalty programmes and £40 to £150 for business-to-business loyalty programmes, depending on type, size and concept. In addition to running costs, the initial cost of developing the programme, including the necessary investments in the technology, personnel and so on, can amount to as much as several tens of thousands of pounds, or even £100 000. The cost largely depends on the quality and size of the loyalty programme, but low-quality, badly performing technology or poorly trained loyalty programme service representatives will strongly limit the possibility of the loyalty programme's success.

A loyalty programme can cover most if not all of its costs by using all possible methods to generate revenue, such as an annual membership fee, sales of loyalty programme merchandise and special products, commission from external partners and/or a credit card, advertising in loyalty programme magazines, or charges for loyalty programme events and benefits. Better cost control can be obtained by limiting membership to a set number. Furthermore, because sales are increased through customer retention, the loyalty programme has an effect on bottom-line profits, and this must also be included in the equation.

In order to prepare for unpleasant surprises, it is recommended that you run through various scenarios concerning how large the loyalty programme might become. These scenarios help to estimate the necessary investments caused by extraordinary developments, for example if membership reaches half – or double! – the expected number.

In general, expenditure on a loyalty programme should not be seen as a 'cost', but rather as an investment in a marketing tool that is a strategic necessity in today's competitive environment.

## Communication

A customer loyalty programme mainly communicates in three areas: with loyalty programme members, with the personnel of the sponsoring company, and with those in its external environment, such as the media. There are a variety of communication methods, such as a loyalty programme magazine, regular newsletters or mailings, a loyalty programme hotline, a Web page, loyalty programme meetings and events, or loyalty programme outlets. Communication with members should not be limited to sales information and special offer brochures. Members will want to know what is happening in the loyalty programme, to receive information on new products, and to read about topics of general interest.

Internal communication with the sponsoring company's personnel and management is important, as they need to be informed about the loyalty programme's existence and its goals in order to support the loyalty programme concept to the full. Internal support is very important, and includes everybody from top management to those at the customer interface. Only if the loyalty programme is supported at every level can it be a success. If, for example, a customer is repeatedly treated badly by service or sales staff, then no loyalty programme in the world can turn them into a loyal customer. Also, a loyalty programme member might expect special treatment at the point of sale. Therefore, all employees who deal directly with customers must understand the importance of the customer loyalty programme, the loyalty effect it is trying to create, and their role in this process.

Finally, the loyalty programme must communicate with those in its external environment to obtain press coverage and to increase awareness of its activities. A great deal of press coverage will not only attract new members, but also enhance the sponsoring company's image as a company that cares about its customers.

## E-loyalty: Integrating the Internet into your loyalty efforts

Online loyalty programmes are generally very effective if your target groups are online. When we talk about customer loyalty on the Internet, we do not want to focus on Internet sites such as *Ipoints* and *Beenz*, which are both pure online programmes that entice visitors to remain logged on for long periods of time by rewarding them with 'Web money' for taking part in certain activities, or other programmes such as *Webmiles* which offer bonus points for online purchases from participating e-commerce sites. In all of these cases, loyalty is primarily achieved through the respective currency, and the focus is on online target groups and activities. We want to focus on 'normal' loyalty programmes that also use the Internet for (some of) their benefits and communication.

The key questions that need to be answered are:

• What basic requirements must we meet before going online with a loyalty programme?

- Should the entire programme be conducted online, or just parts of it?
- Which programme elements should be offered online?
- Do e-programmes generate advantages that traditional loyalty programmes cannot realize?
- What drawbacks do they have?
- What other aspects must be considered when designing an e-loyalty programme?

Companies should be aware that the online elements of loyalty programmes demand a great deal of time and resources. The basic rules for creating loyalty in the offline world apply in the online world as well. But some factors, such as relevant content and individualization, trust, complementarity, community and brand are even more important for online programmes. Communication is cheaper online, and generally better. Online communication also makes it easy to collect customer information which can be used to create new products and services. The success of a loyalty programme depends on the speed at which it is implemented, as well as on the company's capability to realize the right balance of rational and emotional appeal.

## How the loyalty programme is organized

A customer loyalty programme is a complex organization involving many different parties, including the sponsoring company, the loyalty programme management, external partners, financial partners and the members. It also encompasses a variety of processes and tasks, such as distributing benefits, communicating with customers, dealing with financial issues and handling problems. In order to manage the loyalty programme properly and ensure a smooth operation, a loyalty programme service centre should be set up that serves as the hub for all loyalty programme contacts and activities. Because of the complexity and the general goal of increasing customer loyalty, the loyalty programme service centre must be of a very high quality. Therefore, the personnel, technology and other infrastructure must be chosen carefully.

The question of whether to do all these tasks in-house or outsource them to an external agency is difficult to answer, as both alternatives have their advantages. In general, it is a good solution to take care of core loyalty programme tasks within the company, while more routine administrative tasks are outsourced. But the final decision depends on the financial situation of the sponsoring company and the degree of independence it wants to have.

## Integrating the customer loyalty programme into the sponsoring company

One of the questions that needs to be addressed is how to integrate the customer loyalty programme into the sponsoring company's organizational structure. There are a variety of alternatives, from founding a totally independent company to manage the loyalty programme, to integrating the loyalty programme into an existing department, to outsourcing the entire loyalty programme management to an outside agency. There is no best solution, so this decision depends on the individual situation of the sponsoring company.

It is more important to ensure that the customer loyalty programme's enormous support potential is fully exploited within the company. Departments such as market research, product marketing or R&D can use the information in the loyalty programme data members themselves to test new products, to discuss existing products in order problems and areas of improvement, to test new advertising campaigns, and for many opportunities. Loyalty programme members demonstrate more willingness than ordin customers to participate in surveys, as they have a stronger relationship with the products expressed by their membership.

The loyalty programme and the departments need to develop a co-operative attitude, and the company's management must make sure that both sides realize they are trying to achieve the same goals and should help each other.

If the right procedures are implemented, retailers can also profit from the loyalty programme, because it can increase store traffic and improve the relationship between retailers and customers.

## The loyalty programme database

A database that contains detailed and correct information on your customers is a strategic weapon that will have a great influence on the success of companies in the future. Not only since the advent of Customer Relationship Mangement (CRM) must databases be seen from a strategic rather than a tactical viewpoint: without detailed knowledge about its customers, no company will be able to compete.

A customer loyalty programme is the ideal instrument for collecting data of the right quality and quantity on your most important customers. The greater willingness of members to provide information comes from their higher affinity with the loyalty programme and the sponsoring company. This data can be used for loyalty programme activities, but is a valuable source of information that should also be made available to other departments within the organization. A well-maintained database has the potential to move your company one step closer to one-on-one marketing.

In order to reach its maximum effectiveness, the database must be well planned and executed. It is necessary to decide in advance what information the database should contain, how this data could be collected, what technical and human resources are necessary, how the data should be analysed, and for which purposes the data can be used.

## Business-to-business customer loyalty programmes

Customer loyalty programmes are successful not only with end-users, but also in business-to-business environments. The procedure for setting up a business-to-business loyalty programme is the same as for an end-user customer loyalty programme. The most important concern for both types of loyalty programme is to offer benefits that have value for the members.

However, business-to-business loyalty programmes have certain specific characteristics that should be considered. For instance, the target groups in a business-to-business environment are relatively small, consisting mostly of professionals or businesses. These target groups are very clear about what they expect from a customer loyalty programme, and are primarily looking for benefits that help their business, rather than personal benefits. Loyalty programme benefits must be designed accordingly.

cteristic of business-to-business loyalty programmes is that they
ship, as loyalty programme sponsor and loyalty programme mem-
utual goals in the market. Particularly in the business-to-business
d relationships between seller and buyer are extremely important,
ild up the necessary trust and respect. The existing personal con-
ring company and its business customers should not be replaced by
ut should rather be integrated into the loyalty programme concept.
amme can build a supportive benefit package around these personal
sh a further relationship on a company level. Thus, business-to-business loyalty programme members are often more intimately involved in the loyalty programme's management and development.

Business-to-business loyalty programmes can target either professional customers, or
other business partners such as dealers and distributors. Although professional loyalty programmes are more common, some companies have developed loyalty programmes whose
main aim is to support the retailers who sell their products.

## How to measure the loyalty programme's success

The success of a customer loyalty programme must be measured, just as with any other marketing tool. Therefore, indices must be devised for aspects of the loyalty programme's performance that clearly define levels of success, average performance and failure. These indices
must include clearly quantifiable factors that can be measured automatically, such as
response rates to loyalty programme activities, but also more qualitative factors such as brand
loyalty.

The indices chosen depend largely on the importance of each different loyalty programme goal. The more important the goal is, the more important it is to measure how far it
has been achieved. Comparing the results for loyalty programme members with those for a
non-member control group can help isolate the effects of the loyalty programme's marketing
from other influences. Other indicators of the loyalty programme's success are the level of
utilization of its database, the savings achieved by other departments due to the loyalty programme's activities, and the support it has given to other departments in the sponsoring
company.

Empirical studies have shown that loyalty programmes can be very effective: increases in
sales of between 6 and 80 per cent have been achieved. But even with their proven track
record, some customer loyalty programmes need to be ended at some point. Plan the end just
as carefully as the beginning. There are many questions to be addressed. How much cost will
you really save? Who will own the customer database, the infrastrucure and so on in the
future? What will happen with the programme personnel? Are there any assets that can be
sold to cover some of the cancellation cost?

It cannot be said with absolute certainty whether a 'big bang' (simply stopping the programme on day x) is better, or a slower phase-out. This really depends on the specific situation of the programme. A big bang is better if you have no obligations to your members
(such as loyalty points) and you know there will not be a major PR backlash. A slow phase-out
is better if you fear the customers will develop strong feelings about the programme's end or
if you still 'owe them something'.

# The future of customer loyalty programmes

In a market environment characterized by increasing competition, unpredictable and well-informed consumers and lack of growth, customer loyalty efforts are gaining in importance and might come to be one of the most important strategic success factors. It is essential for a customer loyalty programme to function smoothly to achieve its goal of customer retention. While companies are gradually moving towards one-on-one marketing, overlooking the significance of customer loyalty programmes that help to develop strong relationships with individual customers can become an organization's downfall.

Customer loyalty programmes are not easy to develop and manage, but their effectiveness is difficult to match. Set up the right way, a customer loyalty programme can play an important part in your future success. The most important factors to consider are offering real perceived value to members, developing a sound financial concept, obtaining support from the whole organization, from top management to entry-level employees, and fully exploiting the loyalty programme's potential to provide data to support other company departments.

How long will it be before you can say 'Welcome to the club!'?

# 3 *What is a customer club?*

Numerous different forms of customer loyalty programmes have resulted from the efforts of countless companies, institutions and non-profit organizations to retain customers. Each of these types of programme has certain characteristics that distinguish it from the others. A customer club is only one type of customer loyalty programme; and even within the family of customer clubs there are several different types such as end-user clubs, business-to-business clubs and so on. In general, the name of the loyalty programme is irrelevant. What counts is that it achieves its goal of increasing the customers' loyalty by offering true value. While this book describes how to set up successful loyalty programmes in general, we want to use this chapter to introduce 'customer clubs' as a convenient shorthand for value-oriented loyalty programmes.

## Where did customer clubs come from?

Customer clubs are one of the few marketing trends that did not originate in the USA and then sweep the world. Customer clubs are a German invention, primarily driven by two factors. First, Germans are clubbers. Every German is a member of at least two or three clubs, be it a tennis club, a collector's club or a fan club, so it was a natural step to use membership-based, club-like instruments in marketing as well. Second, until the autumn of 2001, German law placed restrictions on the giving of discounts or other financial incentives to particular customer groups. In principle, it was illegal to give a discount to somebody because they belonged to a certain group of customers or had specific characteristics (for example, owned a specific car, were a good friend, were a member of a loyalty programme, or were a regular customer). If a discount was given to some customers, it had to be given to all customers. The only discount allowed was a discount of up to 3 per cent on cash purchases, which again could not be restricted to a specific customer group. However, discounts could be based on performance, such as purchase volume. Of course, this legal restriction did not in practice prevent special pricing for friends or individual customers, but this was mostly because it was impossible to control every transaction that took place. But customer loyalty programmes and their benefits are more in the public view, as they need to communicate their benefits and advertise the advantages of membership. Therefore, it was impossible to offer a 10 per cent discount to the members of your loyalty programme and not give it to non-members if they requested it. Thus, customer clubs are primarily based on non-financial benefits. German law further forbade offering a free product as a gift for making a purchase that was worth more than a small percentage of the purchased product's value. (This law was eliminated by the German Parliament in 2001, but it remains the root cause for the development of this new type of loyalty programme.)

These factors combined to force German marketers to come up with a new type of loyalty programme that does not rely on discounts but still offers value and creates loyalty.

This was at the same time a curse and a blessing. On the one hand, discounts have a high value for customers, so it was certainly a limitation that they could not be integrated into a loyalty scheme in Germany. On the other hand, marketers were forced to develop programmes that offered a high value without relying on discounts, thus avoiding a situation like that in the USA, where 90 per cent of all programmes offer a discount and nothing else. Such programmes may offer value, but the amount of loyalty they can achieve is limited because discounts can easily be matched by competitors. Furthermore, such customer loyalty programmes do not treat special customers in a special way: they merely offer price cuts.

This situation led to the creation of customer clubs, of which there are currently some 400 in Germany. They can be found in every industry (radio and TV, retail, magazines, cars, insurance, banks, toys, watches, computer hardware and software, cigarettes, services, sports and others), come in all sizes (from about one hundred to over a million members) and remain extremely popular.

More and more club schemes can also be found outside Germany, for example in the UK and the USA. In most cases, these have been introduced by a German parent company, though the number of non-German clubs is increasing. However, there is a growing demand for value-oriented loyalty programmes, so their development in other areas will inevitably increase.

## Characteristics of a customer club

A customer club has certain specific characteristics. While a customer club might share some of these characteristics with other customer loyalty programmes, it is the combination of these characteristics that clearly distinguishes a customer club:

- A customer club is initiated, planned and managed ('sponsored') by an organization. This implies two important aspects. First, the organization does not have to be a typical profit-oriented business, but could also be an academic institution, a non-profit organization such as a museum, or any other form of organization (for simplicity's sake, we will refer to the sponsoring organization as the 'sponsoring company' in this book, as more than 90 per cent of customer clubs are sponsored by a company). Second, this organization is the initiator of the customer club, and is also involved in its operation. This is important in order to differentiate customer clubs from other programmes that are initiated by customers, such as fan clubs or owner initiatives, or by an external company, for example programmes such as 'Hotels for Half Price' or 'Travel Discounts'. In the latter case, an agency puts together a programme that offers hotel or travel discounts to everybody who joins. Hotels, airlines, car rental companies, theme parks and the like can participate in such a programme by offering coupons or special offers, but these programmes are not those companies' customer loyalty programmes. Of course, outside agencies or consulting firms may be included in the process of planning and also running the customer club, but the company itself has a significant and active part to play in the club business.

- Customer clubs aim to create communication opportunities on a regular basis. This not only includes communication from the sponsoring company directed at the members, but also the other way round. Customer clubs want to encourage members to communicate actively with the club, since more data can then be obtained which is of much better quality. The concept behind communication in customer clubs is to establish a dialogue between the company and the club members.

- A customer club offers real and perceived value to its members. The club benefits, special services, the different ways of communicating or special pricing aim to create value on top of the actual products the sponsoring company sells. Creating value for members is the principal idea behind a customer club, and is best achieved by offering a unique combination of financial and non-financial benefits exclusively to members. We see 'customer clubs' as a synonym for such value-oriented programmes, although unfortunately, not all customer clubs reach this standard.

- The last two points – dialogue-oriented communication and exclusive value-driven benefits – are the pillars of the club's aim of establishing an emotional relationship with members. It is the emotional relationship, and that alone, that will make loyal customers out of your current customers and will ensure that your customers are immune to competitors' poaching attempts. Discounts and services are fine, but they will only create loyalty if they are of value to members, are offered exclusively to them, and are combined in the right way.

- A customer club is a marketing instrument. Although in some cases a customer club might be a legal organization separate from (but not independent of) the sponsoring company, it is oriented towards a particular purpose: fulfilling certain marketing goals, rather than financial or membership goals.

- Membership of a customer club necessitates activity from the potential member, in the form of paying a membership fee, filling in an application form and so on. In the rare case when there is automatic membership through the purchase of a product, the purchase serves as the activating factor.

- Customer clubs are aimed at customers. 'Customers' in this sense must not be interpreted narrowly as current end-users only, but must include potential customers, business customers, and also retailers or other distribution partners of the sponsoring company. Depending on its goals and the way it is set up, a customer club can focus on one or several of these customer groups, or even on certain segments within them. It is not important that somebody has actually bought the product, but rather that they belong to a group of people or organizations that have similar interests and needs, and thus might be encouraged to join the customer club (Diller, 1996, p.6).

- Customer clubs organize their members to a certain degree. This can range from a very loose, no-obligation type of organization, to a structure where the members have strong obligations to contribute to the club organization. The degree of organization is determined by legal obligations according to the membership contract, through the structure of the club and its internal organization, the club's activities and the resources provided by the sponsoring company (Diller, 1996, p.9). This leads to a large variety of possible club types that will be discussed in more detail in Chapter 8.

## Differentiating customer clubs from other forms of customer loyalty programmes

The above characteristics help to differentiate a customer club from other forms of customer loyalty programmes or clubs (Butscher, 1995, p.10; Holz and Tomczak, 1996, p.8):

- Book and music clubs are revenue- and profit-oriented, rather than offering exclusive benefits to their members. The members are obliged to buy a certain number of products, mostly at no better prices than elsewhere. Book and music clubs therefore serve more as alternative distribution channels. Examples are Bertelsmann Bookclub or Life Club.

- Fan or user clubs are mostly initiated by a group of people with common interests, such as fans of a specific sports team or car. They are not initiated by an organization, and are at most supported by one. Examples are fan clubs of sports teams, Jeep Club Germany, and the Apple User Group. However, depending on the degree of involvement and support of the sports team or organization, such clubs can also be very powerful loyalty instruments.

- Consumer clubs organize consumers in order to increase their ability to promote and voice their interests to industry, other associations and companies. They represent the consumer, not the company. In addition, they are not a marketing instrument that helps support other goals, but are founded in order to serve a very specific purpose of their own. In some cases, they can be seen as a consumer lobbying organization. Some examples are the German ADAC or the American Automobile Association.

- Bonus and frequency programmes can be included in a customer club as part of the benefit package, but as stand-alone programmes they do not offer exclusive benefits to their members to the same extent as customer clubs. Points, rewards and bonuses can be accumulated through purchases, which basically results in no benefits if there are no purchases. Members of a customer club receive the benefits regardless of their current purchase level. Examples of bonus or frequency programmes include most airline, hotel and car rental programmes, as well as those offered by many restaurants, bookshops and so on, where customers collect a stamp for each purchase, and after having collected perhaps ten stamps get a free pizza or 15 per cent off the next book purchase.

- Discount clubs are purely discount-based. Sometimes an annual membership fee guarantees a 10 per cent discount on all purchases for one year, sometimes discount clubs send out a special catalogue with discounted products to selected households. They do not offer any additional benefits, have no organizational structure, and sometimes not even an official membership.

- Warehouse clubs are a relatively new distribution channel. An annual membership fee of about £5 to £25 allows members to buy at the warehouse club, which mostly offers quality products, in large units, at competitive prices and with minimum service. This is not a programme sponsored by a company, but rather a special form of distribution and a company in its own right. Examples are Sam's Club and Price/Costco.

It is important to note that a customer club does not necessarily exclude all of the features of these other kinds of programme. A customer club can offer discounts and allow the collection of air miles, for example. But these elements would only be part of the wider range of benefits and communication opportunities that a customer club offers.

## Defining a customer club

Based on the above, we can define a customer club as follows:

> **A customer club is an at least communicative union of people or organizations, which is initiated and operated by an organization in order to contact these members directly on a regular basis and offer them a benefit package with a high perceived value, with the goal of activating them and increasing their loyalty by creating an emotional relationship.**

Let us look at the different parts of this definition in more detail:

- *People or organizations* – Not only individuals, but also groups such as families or companies (for example, in a business-to-business environment) can join the club.

- *An at least communicative union* – A customer club can have different degrees of organization and different forms of contact, ranging from mere communication to physical contact through club trips and the like.

- *Initiated and operated by an organization* – The club must be established by an organization, as opposed to an individual or consumers. The club must also be operated by this organization, which does not mean that all club activities and administrative work have to be done by the company. While many of these tasks can be outsourced to external service companies, the organization must be responsible for the club and be involved in its management and conception.

- *Contact these members directly on a regular basis* – The club seeks to communicate with members on a regular basis (for example, once a month) and does not use mass communication channels (for example, television advertising), but personalized means of communication to do so (for example individual mailings, a telephone hotline, interactive communication via the Internet).

- *Increasing their [the members'] loyalty* – To achieve this goal, customer clubs offer them a benefit package with a high perceived value. The benefits a club offers must have a perceived value for the member. If only the club management thinks that the benefits are good, they will not work. These benefits are the main loyalty-creating element, and can include the communicative activities mentioned above.

- *With the goal of activating them* – The activities desired include further purchases, increased usage, more word-of-mouth advertising, active communication with the club, provision of data and so on. The club aims to activate members in order to reach its ultimate loyalty goals.

- *Increasing their loyalty by creating an emotional relationship* – Obviously, the ultimate goal is to create loyalty among members. Customer clubs try to achieve this goal by establishing an emotional relationship with their members, rather than relying on financial incentives alone. Emotional relationships are a much stronger and more durable loyalty driver than discounts or other financial benefits will ever be. Customer clubs should offer a well-balanced benefit package consisting of financial and non-financial benefits.

## Summary

A customer club has several characteristics, such as dialogue-oriented communication, a value-oriented benefit package consisting of financial and non-financial benefits, a goal of establishing an emotional relationship, necessary activity from the members' side and so on, that help to differentiate it from other forms of club and customer loyalty programme such as fan clubs, consumer clubs, warehouse clubs, discount clubs, bonus programmes, reward programmes or frequency programmes. A customer club is defined as an at least communicative union of people or organizations, which is initiated and operated by an organization in order to contact these members directly on a regular basis, with the goal of activating them and increasing their loyalty by creating an emotional relationship.

# 4 *The retention marketing trend*

Loyalty marketing, relationship marketing, retention marketing, customer bonding, partnership marketing, and lately, Customer Relationship Management (CRM) or one-to-one marketing – regardless of what you call it, all these names and what they stand for have two major things in common. First, they describe efforts to establish loyalty among your customers towards your product, brand or company. Second, they are increasingly influencing strategies and industry developments. In all markets and industries, marketing efforts increasingly aim to bring companies close(r) to the customer, offering customized products and services, or listening to the marketplace and extracting valuable information. The importance of such loyalty efforts has increased significantly over the last few years, and is increasingly expanding from companies to non-profit organizations (which focus on retaining donors) and governmental institutions (for example, state health insurance trying to dissuade customers from switching to private health insurance). Even investors have become the target of loyalty activities (investor marketing), as companies realize how important it is to keep (especially institutional) investors' money invested to avoid major downward shifts of the stock price.

Customer retention marketing has never been more popular than today, partly due to the New Economy, which has given the customer additional power. Never were there more people participating in customer loyalty programmes. In Europe, the number of members in retail loyalty programmes has increased from 309 million in 1998 to 453 million in 2001 according to a Datamonitor study. The UK has the most members (125 million in 2001), followed by France, Italy, Spain and Germany. Of course, many members are registered in more than one programme.

In the USA, ACNielsen found that in 1998 55 per cent of all households had at least one grocery store loyalty card, up from 35 per cent in 1997 (ACNielsen, 1998, p.1). This proportion will be much higher today.

## The current market situation

This trend towards becoming closer to the customer is not being initiated by companies, it is forced on them by a market environment that is characterized by factors such as:

- growing competition from a smaller number of stronger and bigger competitors resulting from mergers and acquisitions
- increasing competition through the Internet, as regional boundaries fall and customers' access to information and alternative suppliers is becoming more and more easy
- new competition from low-cost producers from the Far East, South America and India
- a focus on core competences, forcing companies to develop or strengthen strategic competitive advantages (Simon, 1988, pp.461–80; Porter, 1980; Porter, 1985) in order to remain competitive

- the shareholder value-driven company strategies and the resulting constant pressure for growth, which has to come from new as well as existing customers
- companies' realization that it is more profitable to keep current customers than constantly trying to find new ones
- downsizing, forcing companies to use limited resources in an increasingly efficient way
- large, diversified corporations splitting into smaller, more homogeneous units
- the realization that the billions of dollars spent on TV, radio or print advertising are not necessarily spent to maximum effect. People are reacting more and more negatively to constant advertising for products they do not need, and they tend to tune out or turn the page. Spots for products aimed at a particular target group are also being aired in the wrong environment, as the advertisers' influence on spot time and place is limited
- 'nomad' customers who no longer fit into a specific target group – the kind who drive to WalMart in their BMW, have breakfast at McDonald's and dinner at an exclusive French restaurant downtown
- consumers that are becoming smarter and better informed about product alternatives
- consumers with increasing demand for individualized product and service offers
- products that have become more and more similar in their basic features, and call for differentiation on the service level
- stagnation or even negative market growth.

Of course, not all these factors apply to all markets and industries, but there are no longer any easy markets. Even in new or fast-growing industries such as software, tourism, logistics, and so on, the competition between the various service providers is fierce. Thus, even in such markets customer loyalty is an issue, and companies soon learn that customer acquisition is not the only issue they need to be concerned with.

## Customer loyalty efforts as a success factor

Being close to the customer and running a successful customer loyalty programme is not only important, it is also a key success factor for many companies. The 'Hidden Champions', small- to medium-sized companies that are unknown to the public but are world market leaders in their area, were analysed by Professor Hermann Simon, who found that one of their strategic competitive advantages is their closeness to the customer. This factor, combined with excellent product quality and a perception of good value for money, forms the foundation of their market leadership (Simon, 1996, pp.134 or 157). This closeness to the customer is also a major market entry barrier for new companies, as they not only have to match the Hidden Champions' products in terms of quality, but also have to break into a strong system of personal relationships, trust and respect that has developed over time. Figure 4.1 shows the matrix of competitive advantages for Hidden Champions.

Another issue is the trend towards service automation. In the 1980s and 1990s, services became a tool for differentiation. Services are often the only distinguishing factor separating one company from another whose products both offer the same solutions, quality and performance. Over time, these services have come to represent a significant cost, forcing managers to think about how to improve their cost–value ratio. In many cases, service automation was the answer. Today, automated answering systems guide you through endless menus to get the answer to a question that a customer service representative previously could

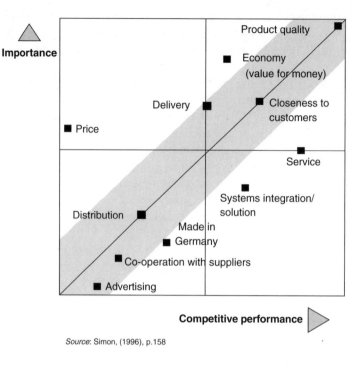

Source: Simon, (1996), p.158

**Figure 4.1**    Matrix of Hidden Champions' competitive advantages

have answered in less than a minute. Company information is no longer sent out to callers by a public relations person. Instead, the central switchboard tells them to visit the company's Web site. Several industries, such as airlines, have received steadily decreasing customer satisfaction ratings for years in a row, as their service grows worse and worse.

The resulting decrease in personal contact, relationship and affinity with the company eventually leads to lower customer loyalty, as shown in Figure 4.2. Customer loyalty pro-

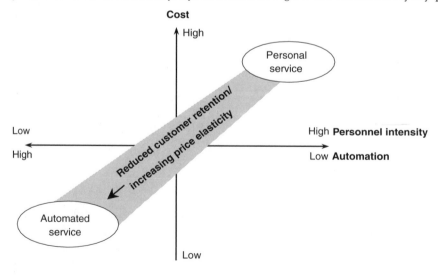

**Figure 4.2**    Service automation: Cost saving v. reduced customer retention

grammes emerged as an attempt to repair the damage. A better idea in many cases would have been to integrate personal services into a customer loyalty programme, rather than automating them (Butscher and Simon, 1997, p.46; Butscher, 1997c).

## The next marketing generation

All these factors indicating the increasing competitiveness in today's markets and the limits of current marketing have forced marketing to move forward with a creative and innovative perspective. Figure 4.3 shows the different steps of marketing's evolution and indicates that we are currently moving towards the next marketing generation: *individual relationship marketing*.

Individual relationship marketing in its ideal form means one-on-one marketing. This concept is realized when every individual person is approached with products and services, communication and marketing activities that are entirely customized to meet their personal needs and tastes. But this is in the future. In current relationship marketing, individuals are still grouped together in segments. These individuals are offered what seems to be personalized service, but is actually an offer designed for a group of individuals with a similar demand structure. These segments will become smaller and smaller as we approach the peak of relationship marketing, but real one-on-one marketing on a broad scale is still many years away. Technology and marketing know-how are not yet sufficiently developed to make production, sales, distribution and so on cost-effective in that context.

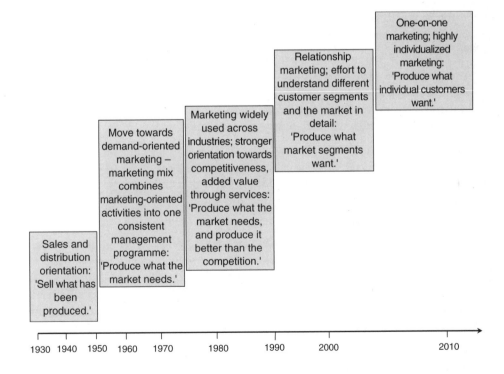

**Figure 4.3**    Different evolutionary steps of marketing

However, individual relationship marketing does not mean bombarding the customer with offers. Most customers are actually turned off by too much closeness to their suppliers, and have developed an allergy against the empty phrases they hear day after day ('Your call is very important to us, the next customer service representative...' or 'We truly value your business...'). You need to come up with something better than that, and customer loyalty programmes are just the right thing. The customer joins voluntarily, and the amount of interaction is well judged.

## The bottom-line impact of customer loyalty

In addition to the external pressure that forces companies to develop appropriate customer loyalty programmes, companies are beginning to realize the positive effect that retention marketing can have on their bottom line. Studies into this factor have been widely publicized, therefore a short summary of the most significant results should suffice:

- A 5 per cent decrease in customer defection can increase profits by between 25 and 85 per cent, depending on the industry (Reichheld and Sasser, 1990, p.110 or 113).

- This profit increase is based on the fact that the profitability of a customer increases over time due to revenue growth, cost savings, referrals and price premiums. These customer life cycle patterns differ from industry to industry, but all show significant increases in profit as early as the first five years of the relationship (Reichheld and Teal, 1996, p.38).

- Customer satisfaction is not a replacement for customer retention, although this might appear plausible. Between 65 and 85 per cent of customers who defect say they were 'satisfied' or 'very satisfied' with their former supplier (Reichheld, 1993, p.71 or 112).

- Customer loyalty programmes could help to detect satisfied customers who, despite their satisfaction, still cover part or all of their demand with competitors' products. Customer loyalty programmes can help to win these sales back and, by offering extra value, turn customer satisfaction into customer loyalty.

- Following the 80:20 rule, 20 per cent of your customers account for 80 per cent of your business. This 20 per cent must be identified and, in order to attain the maximum effect on your bottom line, resources must be focused on these best customers. Customer loyalty programmes not only help to identify but also help to court these customers so that they remain top customers.

- Only around 5 per cent of all unsatisfied customers complain to top management/head office. The other 95 per cent either complain to the branch or a local employee, or do not complain to anybody, but simply go elsewhere (Maszal, 1996, p.10). In order to increase the frequency of communication with customers and identify dissatisfaction earlier and more easily, customer loyalty programmes play an important role by creating opportunities for both the company and the members to communicate with one another.

- It is four to six times more expensive to make a sale to a new customer than to make an additional sale to an existing customer.

Responding to the findings described above and to increasing pressure from the market, companies around the world and in all industries have developed or are developing different loyalty schemes. Companies that are left behind will sooner or later run into trouble. A good example is the UK retailer Sainsbury's, whose share price and performance have dropped continually over the last five years. The *Economist* Magazine wrote: 'Mr Sainsbury's biggest missed opportunity was his failure to spot the significance of customer loyalty programmes' (*The Economist*, 1997).

Apart from developing specific loyalty programmes, companies also try to include retention-oriented thinking in other areas. Telecommunications company MCI is basing the compensation of its 1000 long-distance service telemarketers not only on the number of customers who sign up, but also on the number of customers who stay signed up. Staff will now be rewarded for spending time with customers, learning which services they want, and devising ways to keep them on the MCI roll after the initial sale (*Marketing News*, 1997). In an interview with *Management Review*, Frederick Reichheld of management consultancy Bain & Co. demanded more loyalty-based key statistics in companies' annual reports, such as 'What percentage of our customers' business are we getting?', 'Of all the new customers we brought in two years ago, how many are still with us?' or 'What percentage of the prospective customers we pitched actually gave us a try?' (*Management Review*, 1997, p.17). Another example is Southwestern Bell's volunteer ambassador programme. Employees volunteer as 'ambassadors' and establish relationships with their designated customers. This puts a human face to the company and lets these customers know that the company cares about them (Long, 1997).

## Key considerations for customer loyalty programmes

Not all programmes that are introduced to the market work. In order to increase the probability of success, there are certain factors that must be considered when setting up a customer loyalty programme:

1. You must offer the members true value. The 1990s have repeatedly been named the 'value decade'. Buyers compare different alternatives, decide what has the greatest overall value for them and then go with that choice. In order to rank high on the value scale, a company must not only offer what its customers expect, but also something they do not. This unexpected value can be the decisive factor in their decision. The 2000s will be even more value-driven than the last decade.

2. You must give the members as much as possible of what they want and reduce the components that they do not want. This requires measuring precisely what value different alternatives have.

3. You must offer the members the little 'extra' that they cannot get anywhere else and that makes them feel special. No single element such as a free newspaper will make the difference, but rather the combination of listening to the customer and giving them the little extra. Currently, most markets are driven by demand, so that customers will go where they feel best treated, expect to get the best price or receive the best service, whatever is more important for them.

4. Cost and additional profit created by the customer loyalty programme must be weighed in order to find the right degree of closeness to the customer. If it costs you £100 to make

an extra £100 revenue, then this situation is not optimal. Figure 4.4 shows the optimal closeness to customer, in relation to cost and profit.

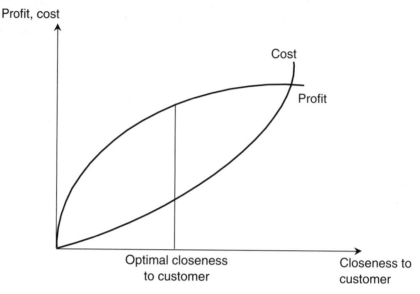

**Figure 4.4**  Cost v. closeness to customer

*Source*: Simon (1991), p.23

5. Retention marketing includes closeness to the customer and customer satisfaction for more than an isolated purchase. Retention marketing is a long-term way to approach the challenges in today's markets. Because the market environment changes quickly due to new products, competitors and technologies, close relationships that endure (preferably for ever) have become crucial to future market success.

6. Customer loyalty programmes involve more than the customer service department or the marketing department. All departments of a company should be involved, including those without customer contact. Relationships with all partners on both horizontal and vertical levels must be included in order to make the retention marketing efforts more effective. The more departments and parties are involved in the programme, the greater its acceptance within the company and the greater its chances of succeeding.

7. The customer loyalty programme must be integrated into your existing marketing plans. By doing so, you will effectively support your company's departments, other marketing efforts and overall strategy.

8. Integrating the customer loyalty programme includes setting up a database of members and customers, and utilizing this information in more individualized marketing approaches. Integrate your programme into your CRM initiatives, and use the IT infrastructure CRM projects usually contribute.

9. Use the programme to listen to your customers. Find out what services they want, how new product ideas are perceived, how your current service level is seen, and so on. The available data is a goldmine.

10. Make use of modern technologies and the Internet to maximize the performance of your programme.

11. The programme must blend well with and express your corporate culture.

12. In order to establish a quantitative base for the evaluation of the customer loyalty programme's success, you must define the goals of the programme precisely and measure all related factors.

13. All this means that a customer loyalty programme must be well planned and managed.

Formal customer loyalty programmes are an effective tool to create loyal customers, offer them true value, communicate with them on a personal and individual level, and create true relationships. Use customer loyalty programmes to:

- build emotional relationships
- involve customers and become involved with them
- reward loyal customers
- help build your brand (Joachimsthaler and Aaker, 1997, pp.44–5)
- shift communication expenses to more effective areas
- collect free data on your customers, their demands and perceptions (Hagel and Rayport, 1997, pp.53–5)
- support the different company departments
- ultimately, create loyalty.

In Part II of this book, we will describe in detail how to set up a customer loyalty programme and then, in Part III, look at several examples of successful programmes in different countries.

## Coalition programmes

The latest development in the loyalty arena is the increasing number of coalition programmes: customer loyalty programmes that are not managed by one single company, but combine the retention efforts of several companies from different industries. Air Miles in the UK, UPromise and the Air Miles relaunch in the USA, Equity and Air Miles in Canada, Loyalty Partner in Germany – such programmes are centrally managed by an independent organization, and lift increasing customer loyalty marketing to the system level, rather than keeping it on the individual company level. Figure 4.5 shows how this achieves a stronger loyalty effect. Many experts expect this form of loyalty effort to be the 'next wave'.

## Summary

Most industries are extremely competitive, and customers and sales must be fought for. Over recent years, retention or loyalty marketing has become an integral factor in companies' strategies and marketing efforts. Numerous studies have shown that making an effort to keep your customers pays off on the bottom line, for example because profitability increases with the length of a customer relationship. Furthermore, customer satisfaction with the product is not on its own a guarantee of customer loyalty. It takes an extra effort to create true loyalty.

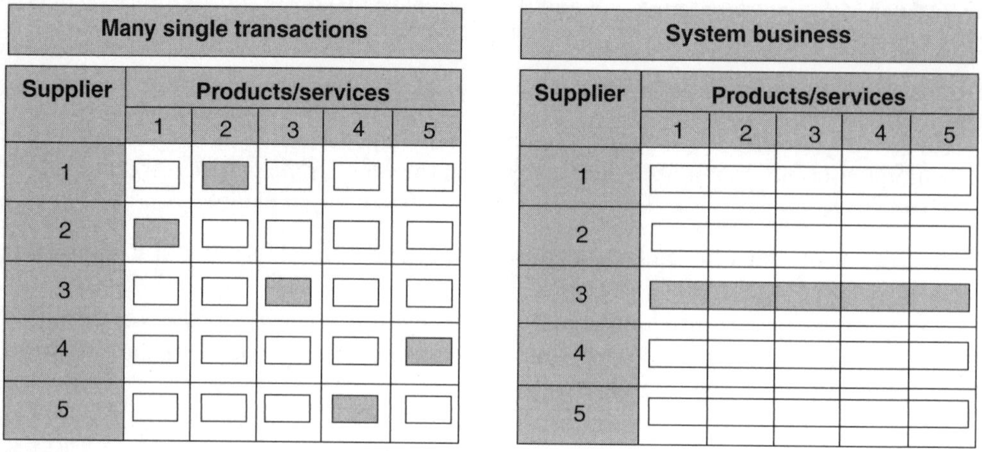

| Many single transactions | | | | | |
|---|---|---|---|---|---|
| **Supplier** | **Products/services** | | | | |
| | 1 | 2 | 3 | 4 | 5 |
| 1 | ☐ | ▨ | ☐ | ☐ | ☐ |
| 2 | ▨ | ☐ | ☐ | ☐ | ☐ |
| 3 | ☐ | ☐ | ▨ | ☐ | ☐ |
| 4 | ☐ | ☐ | ☐ | ☐ | ▨ |
| 5 | ☐ | ☐ | ☐ | ▨ | ☐ |

| System business | | | | | |
|---|---|---|---|---|---|
| **Supplier** | **Products/services** | | | | |
| | 1 | 2 | 3 | 4 | 5 |
| 1 | | | | | |
| 2 | | | | | |
| 3 | | | | | |
| 4 | | | | | |
| 5 | | | | | |

**Figure 4.5**   System effect

In order to make a customer loyalty programme effective, several factors must be considered, such as offering real perceived value, viewing loyalty from a long-term perspective, making cost–benefit calculations to measure the financial effect of a loyalty programme, involving the entire company in the programme, integrating the programme well into current marketing plans and the corporate culture, and setting clear goals whose achievement is measured. Customer loyalty programmes are an ideal way to create true loyalty, to become involved with and reward customers, to extract a large amount of high-quality data, and to build true relationships.

# 2 *Setting up a Customer Loyalty Programme*

*The value decade has already begun!*

(Jack Welch, General Electric, 1995)

# 5 How to develop a customer loyalty programme that offers true value

Developing a customer loyalty programme is very similar to developing a new product: it requires detailed planning, concentrated work and must be taken very seriously. Not only the people directly involved in creating the concept, but also those backing it – such as top management – must be committed to the project.

Although relationship marketing has been a major marketing trend for many years now, many companies have yet to comprehend its fundamental ideas. The goal in relationship marketing is to establish a relationship between company and customer that is not only built on such factors as good prices, but also on emotions. The emotional connection manifests itself in aspects such as the feeling of being treated as a special customer, the knowledge of getting better deals, and trust being built up by successful projects. This idea is nothing new: think of a healthy personal relationship between husband and wife or between friends. These relationships last because there is an emotional link in the form of trust, affection and pride that is reciprocal. Not all relationships last for ever. Generally, they end because the emotional connection is broken off by one or both sides. Why do you no longer know the whereabouts of some of your best college friends? Probably because one of you stopped writing or calling. Or why does a wife seek a divorce from her husband? Because, over time, the deep bond has faded.

This is what relationship marketing is all about. In a business world where there are battles for every customer and every sale, ignoring the customer will contribute to a company's demise. The customer must be worshipped, communicated with and given the 'extra treat' that makes them feel special. There is no room for ignorance, or for a poorly set up and badly performing customer loyalty programme. If you do not take the time and the effort that is necessary to develop a detailed, customer-oriented loyalty programme that offers real value to its members, you are probably better off without one. The result would be the same – no effect at all – and you would have saved the investment. The famous quote from Henry Ford referring to his early car models, 'The customers can have any color they want as long as it's black', certainly does not hold true in today's business world.

Unfortunately, most programmes underperform or do not realize their full potential. One of the reasons there are so many underperforming programmes is the new relationship marketing frenzy. As an abundance of loyalty programmes spring up, more pressure is put on those companies that do not have a programme of their own. Another source of pressure is the Internet, which gives the customer access to a wider range of alternatives, and forces companies to intensify their customer retention efforts. Obliged to come up with a loyalty scheme, in many cases quality is sacrificed for speed, and that is not a good trade-off. Just as a poor-quality product eventually will not sell, a poor loyalty programme will not create long-term loyal customers.

The secrets of successful programmes are that they are well planned in detail, include the customer's point of view, are thoroughly tested and the company developing the programme takes it very seriously. Taking it seriously means being aware of the time, effort and financial investment required. Above all, setting up a loyalty programme means entering into a long-term commitment. Loyalty programmes do not produce results within the first weeks or months. Depending on the industry, it can take several years before they start to show how successful they are. For example, compare a petrol company with an automobile manufacturer. Within a few months the petrol company can measure whether its loyalty programme has increased the frequency with which the members fill up their cars at the company's petrol stations. The car manufacturer, however, will not see any results until the member wants to buy a new car, which might not occur for two, five or even ten years. Therefore, proof of loyalty will take longer to materialize.

Examples of lack of professionalism can be found in all types of loyalty scheme, be they frequency programmes, reward programmes, customer cards or customer loyalty programmes. This part of the book will outline the different elements of the development of a successful customer loyalty programme. All the various steps, aspects or difficulties we will discuss are applicable to any type of loyalty programme. It is not the name of a programme that is important, it is the idea, concept and philosophy behind it. Call it loyalty programme, card, preferred customer programme, frequent user programme or whatever you want, as long as the development of the loyalty scheme is value- and customer-oriented.

Figure 5.1 shows the elements of a customer loyalty programme concept, which will be discussed in more detail in the following chapters, with each chapter focusing on one particular part of the process. During each stage, remember that the customer loyalty programme should be sustainable and manageable by your employees. If the loyalty programme is too complex to be understood and managed, it will be counterproductive and create hostility, both from your customers who do not understand the loyalty programme and your employees who cannot run it. A programme does not have to be overloaded and complicated to be value-driven.

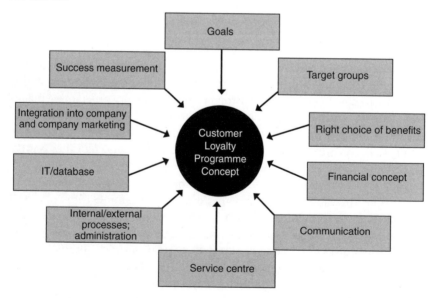

**Figure 5.1**    Elements of a customer loyalty programme concept

## The elements of developing a customer loyalty programme

The first step is always to answer the following questions honestly:

- Is my product good enough?
- Is my product worth the investment?

If the product does not sell because of a significant quality, distribution, design or price problem, then a customer loyalty programme will not be able to salvage it. Only if the product is already competitive does a customer loyalty programme make sense. The foundation of customer retention is customer satisfaction, as Figure 5.2 shows. However, customer satisfaction alone is not sufficient for customer retention. If the objective of the customer loyalty programme is to support a whole product line or even the entire company, then of course these questions must be answered on a corporate rather than a product level. A thorough analysis of the current situation of the company and/or the product is necessary. You must clarify how sales have developed to the current level, and why they have developed that way. You must know the value of the product in the customers' eyes, and what features drive its sales. Likewise, you must identify the main problems you are currently encountering in the market.

Only after a picture of the present situation has been painted can you move to the next two steps: to identify distinctly the loyalty programme's goals and target groups. Although this sounds trivial, the importance of these steps should not be underestimated. The defini-

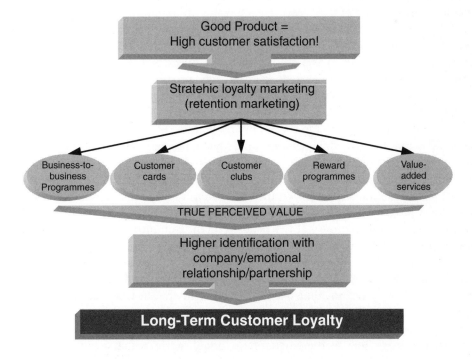

**Figure 5.2**   Loyalty is based on satisfaction and value

tion of the goals and target groups largely influences the type of loyalty programme you will produce. More importantly, the choice of target groups is directly linked to the benefits the loyalty programme must offer, as each target group has its own preferences and demands different benefits. The selection of the right benefits is the most intricate and most important part of the customer loyalty programme concept. The benefits are the heart and soul of the customer loyalty programme. They are almost solely responsible for its success or failure. The link between target groups and benefits shows the importance of an exact definition of goals and target groups.

A loyalty programme concept will only work if the benefits offered have a high perceived value for the customers. The main reason for a customer signing up for the programme will be that they perceive the benefits to have a high value, and only if customers join the loyalty programme can it reach its loyalty goals. Considering the importance of the right choice of benefits, it is surprising how many firms neglect this issue while developing their concept. Very often, the benefits are not determined empirically, but on a purely internal, ad hoc basis. No customers are asked, no value is measured, and no study is run. Often, the managers' gut feelings or personal preferences and experiences are the basis for deciding on the benefits. But normally, their only experience with customer loyalty programmes has been hotel and airline frequency programmes, neither of which is the optimal model for the company's own customers. And be honest: which manager would dare introduce a product to the market whose design, features and price were purely determined by an internal team that never talked to a customer?

Another important issue is finance. Customer loyalty programmes can be expensive to maintain. One of the main reasons for the demise of loyalty programmes is that they fail to maintain tight control of their costs. Therefore, it is important to set up a detailed long-term financial concept that covers the probable cost factors as well as the possibilities for covering these costs. Although this is very difficult, with the right financial concept the loyalty programme could even be run as a profit centre. However, the main benefits of a loyalty programme come from the (increased) sales for your products. Together with controlling, a system must be in place that allows you to measure these effects and tries to determine how much of these is attributable to the loyalty programme.

The next step is to develop the loyalty programme communication plan. First, decide how often and through which channels the loyalty programme should communicate with the members, and how they will be able to contact the loyalty programme. Then plans should be made for communicating the loyalty programme externally. Another important aspect of the communication plan is internal communication. Providing information about the loyalty programme to gain the support of employees is crucial, as the overall success of a customer loyalty programme is also dependent on the commitment of the sponsoring organization and its staff. Therefore, the employees of the sponsoring company must be involved in the development of the concept. You must explain to them why the programme is being set up, how it works, what the goals are and so on. Employees will not be able to support the programme if they do not understand or believe in the idea of a customer loyalty programme.

Next, you have to decide how the loyalty programme should be organized and managed. This covers aspects such as the programme's service centre, which activities should be outsourced, what resources are required (organizational, technological, personnel) and the logistics of the loyalty programme benefits.

Finally, you need to determine how to set up and use the database most effectively, how to integrate the loyalty programme into the company and fully capitalize on its potential to assist other company departments, and how to measure the loyalty programme's success. A well-organized database is one of today's most powerful marketing tools, and has a high strategic relevance. The set-up of the database must be planned carefully in order to exploit its full effectiveness. A customer loyalty programme can be a very valuable partner for many other departments in the sponsoring company, such as R&D, product management or market research. This potential should be used fully, both to help increase the performance of these departments and also to increase the value of the loyalty programme to the sponsoring company. Achievement of the loyalty programme's objectives and goals needs to be measured on a regular basis in order to determine how successfully the customer loyalty programme is working and in which areas it needs to be improved.

## Project team

In order to guarantee a smooth development of the loyalty programme concept and its implementation, the sponsoring company's management should put together a project team of people from different departments (marketing, sales, IT, market research, finance and so on) and management levels (from top management down to customer service representatives). Developing a customer loyalty programme is impossible without focus. By including different departments in the team, a one-sided approach can be avoided. This diversity also ensures the acceptance of the final concept throughout the company, for every department's view will have been included. By involving different management levels, you make sure that top management supports the final concept, that the people who have to manage it are satisfied with the programme for which they are responsible, and that the employees at the customer interface who have to promote and sell the loyalty programme support the idea. A steering committee should be set up whose members are from a high management level of all relevant departments. Finally, if there is diversity in the team, it will be easier to integrate the loyalty programme into the company organization and the existing marketing plan. Instead of representing a top-down decision, the loyalty programme will be supported on all levels.

## Research

To enable the task of developing a customer loyalty programme to be approached from a broad perspective, it is worthwhile carrying out some research. Consider the following questions:

- How do competitors organize their customer loyalty programmes?
- How are loyalty programmes set up in other industries or in other countries?
- What can we learn from other successful customer loyalty programmes?
- What can we learn from loyalty programmes that have failed?
- Is there any specific literature (for example, case studies) on this subject?
- Are there outside specialists whom we can consult?

This research will allow proper benchmarking and inspiration in 'best practice'. In general, the development of such a programme from the moment of the first idea to its full implementation will take six to twelve months. Again, attempting to save time by copying other programmes or sacrificing research and analysis investment will never pay off. The overall investment in such a programme and its importance to the company can be enormous, so it should not be rushed. It is always better to introduce a perfect programme one quarter later than to rush into a poor one. Table 5.1 summarizes the most important questions to be answered, and gives a brief overview of what follows in the next chapters.

**Table 5.1**   Checklist for the development of a customer loyalty programme concept

1   **Is my product good enough?** Does it have a sufficient well-perceived quality or what are the main problems? Does it have a value to the customer, and does it meet the customers' expectations? How high is the customer satisfaction? Is this product worth the investment?

2   **Which primary goal does the loyalty programme pursue?**

- keep customers/reward loyal/important customers
- find new customers
- support other company departments
- build up a database
- create communication opportunities
- other/secondary goals

3   **Which are the target groups?**

- regular customers
- VIP customers
- A, B or C customers ⟶
- occasional customers
- potential customers
- retailers/distributors

- All target groups
- Some target groups
- Selected segments of a target group

**Between which parties should the loyalty programme help establish a better relationship?**

- manufacturer–retailer
- manufacturer–consumer
- retailer– consumer

4   **Which loyalty programme type would best help to achieve the goals?**

- customer club, customer card, bonus programme, community or other
- open loyalty programme
- limited loyalty programme
  - conditions for membership
  - differentiation of membership (for example, special VIP membership)
  - possible focus of loyalty programme (for example, special interest, lifestyle, and so on)

5    **Which benefits should the loyalty programme offer?**

- hard benefits:
  - rebates, discounts, two-for-ones and so on.
  - special prices
- soft benefits:
  - special services
  - insurance policies
  - travel and entertainment
  - seminars, conferences
  - loyalty programme merchandise
  - culture and sports, and so on
- in principle, whether product-related or not
- value measurement
- with or without extra payment
- self-organized or in co-operation with external partners
- cost, practicability, legal issues, and so on

6    **Long-term financial concept:**

- What costs will occur?
  - human, technological, logistical resources?
  - run through different scenarios to prepare for unexpected developments.
- How can the costs be covered?
  - in case of a membership fee, amount and period of validity
  - co-operation with external partners, commission, merchandise
  - loyalty programme benefits liable to fee
- budget out of the overall marketing budget
- close co-operation with controlling to measure programme's effect on sales, revenue, profit

7    **What should the communication concept of the loyalty programme look like?**

- concept and design of loyalty programme magazine, mailings, hotline, meetings, Web page and so on
- How can the members actively communicate with the loyalty programme and among each other?
- How can the loyalty programme be advertised in the loyalty programme environment? How can it support the company's PR (for example, point-of-sale promotions, members bring in members, ads in specialized media of the industry, and so on)?
- How must the loyalty programme and its activities be communicated internally to have the full support of management and employees (for example, training of workforce, briefing of sales reps, company internal media, and so on)?

8    **How should the loyalty programme be organized?**

- internal or external loyalty programme service centre
- personnel (number of employees, training, and so on.)
- technology (computers, database, telephone system, and so on.)
- logistics of the loyalty programme benefits (storage, shipping, co-operation with external partners)
- co-operation with external service providers
- definition of processes for all relevant activities
- online v. offline activities

**9   How should the database be set up?**

- What data should/will be collected, and in what quantity?
- How must the data be analysed (which results must be able to be obtained from this analysis, information demand from other departments, detailed analysis of certain segments, and so on)?
- What are the hardware and software requirements for that?
- Should a loyalty programme card with a magnetic stripe or chip be offered in order to have better access to purchasing data and so on?
- If yes, what kind of card?
  - with or without credit card function?
  - co-operation with which financial service/credit card company?

**10   How is the loyalty programme best integrated within the organization of the company?**

- To whom does the loyalty programme management report?
- How do you ensure that other company departments can co-operate closely with the loyalty programme and can contribute to/benefit from its performance?

**11   How can the success of the loyalty programme be measured?**

- Which factors can be used to measure success?
- Which scales must be used to measure these factors, and which levels on these scales indicate success/lack of success?
- How can these factors be recorded? How must they be interpreted?
- Who is responsible for success measurement?

*Source:* Butscher (1996c), p.46; Wiencke and Koke (1994), p.91.

# 6 *The loyalty programme goals*

The ultimate goal of every customer loyalty programme is to increase profit, revenue and market share, thus securing the company's stability and existence. But these are often mid-term or even long-term goals which can only be achieved if other intermediate goals are reached first. Figure 6.1 shows the typical five main goals of many customer loyalty programmes.

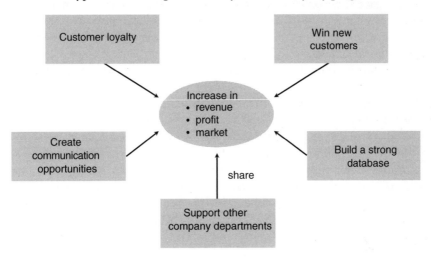

**Figure 6.1**  Main goals of customer loyalty programmes

## Primary loyalty programme goals

A customer loyalty programme's primary purpose is to build a relationship with the customers that turns them into long-term loyal customers, who ideally will obtain their lifetime demand for a specific product or service from the company sponsoring the loyalty programme. It is not the best idea to try to be everybody's darling. In some cases, the demand of certain customers is so small, even after a lifetime, that the cost and effort of turning them into loyal customers are out of proportion to the revenue they could generate.

The second main goal is to attract new customers through the loyalty programme. This happens in two ways. First, satisfied loyalty programme members increase their word-of-mouth advertising because of the loyalty programme's activities. The programme's benefits give the customers something to talk about, and the increased number of contacts between customer and manufacturer or dealer through the loyalty programme communication ensures that the product has a higher profile in the members' minds. This may well increase the number of times they refer to the product or recommend it to friends. The other way a customer loyalty programme can lead to new customers is that the value of the loyalty programme benefits themselves is so attractive that non-customers join the loyalty programme. These new members will eventually try the product, and will continue using it after a satisfactory initial experience.

A third main goal is the creation of a customer database. A well-maintained database that is constantly loaded with up-to-date information is one of the most powerful marketing tools a company can have, and can be used for a large variety of marketing activities. Many companies have volumes of data available from sales, advertising with response elements, direct mail and so on, but they simply do not use it. This data also tends not to be very detailed at the individual customer level. Take the hotel industry as an example. Many 'frequent sleeper' programmes have celebrated their tenth anniversary, and an unbelievable mass of data has been collected so far. But hardly any of it is being used for customized service offers, individual booking profiles or similar activities. Or have you ever made a reservation and the hotel automatically gave you your preferred type of room (non-smoking, not next to the elevator or ice machine, on one of the higher floors – basically, the one you had on the last ten stays), had fresh fruit ready (that you ordered the last ten times) and remembered your preferred newspaper in the morning?

Using the data from the loyalty programme database in a professional way is a strategic weapon. Ideally, the database not only contains socio-demographic data, but also detailed information on purchase behaviour (for example, brand usage, purchase frequency, purchase volume or switching between products) and preference data. This information is normally difficult to obtain, and can only be collected if customers use a company's own credit card or identify themselves in some other way at the point of payment, for example by giving the cashier a membership number. In both cases, the purchase details can be linked to a name or household and used for further analysis and marketing activities. If the credit card is not only accepted at the company's own points of sale but is also accepted in other stores, an even more complete picture of the customer's purchasing behaviour is painted. Data on purchases of competing products, related products and so on is available. In the case of a customer loyalty programme, such a card would be the membership card, enhanced with a credit function.

A customer loyalty programme has an advantage over other loyalty programmes in that it achieves the goal of data collection more effectively. By joining the loyalty programme, the members have already identified themselves as having a special interest in the products or services that the loyalty programme represents. In most cases, a joining fee has to be paid or a similar hurdle has to be overcome to join the loyalty programme – an effort that non-interested customers would probably not invest. In many other loyalty programmes, membership comes automatically with a product purchase or is granted without any formal process. The existence of this special interest means that the sponsor of a customer loyalty programme can therefore easily approach its members with detailed surveys concerning their purchase behaviour, purchase motivation, related attitudes and beliefs, product perception and so on. All this detailed information can be entered into the database. The members are in many cases delighted that finally somebody, whom they know and whose products they care about, shows interest in and concern for their opinions (see Chapter 16 for further details).

This also supports the fourth main goal of a customer loyalty programme, which is to assist other departments such as R&D, product marketing, or market research. The loyalty programme offers a unique opportunity for these departments to communicate with customers who are certainly more willing to share information and opinions with the company than mall-intercept interview recruits will ever be. Why not use this potential to find out about market trends, consumer demands or to test new products? Nowhere else will you find a group of consumers with more interest in the product and all related issues, and whose opinion could be more valuable. A dialogue with these customers can help to identify problems with the use of existing products, possible areas of improvement, ideas for new products, and many other issues.

Nevertheless, you should be aware that despite its quality, such a sample will not in all cases be representative of the entire market. Therefore, these contacts should not replace full-scale market studies that include competitors' customers and non-users of the product and that should precede any major marketing decision. But loyalty programme members do represent a perfect solution for quick, small-scale research (see Chapter 15 for further details).

The fifth and final main goal is to create communication opportunities that can be used to intensify contact with the members. This not only leads to more regular contact with the members, which is initiated and thus controlled by the manufacturer or dealer, but also leads to direct and personalized communication. In contrast to mass communication through advertising and direct mail – which even today is far from being truly personalized – this ensures more efficient use of the communication budget, and a much more positive effect (see Chapter 12 for further details).

## Secondary loyalty programme goals

Apart from these main goals, a customer loyalty programme can pursue further goals, such as:

- increasing product, brand and company image through the positive effect of the loyalty programme and its activities
- increasing visit frequency by attracting customers to points of sale through special promotions, sales or events
- increasing usage frequency by ensuring that the product is constantly in the minds of the users
- developing solutions for members' problems (especially in business-to-business loyalty programmes)
- supporting the company's public relations activities through reports on the loyalty programme's activities in the media
- adding customer support capacity which is qualitatively superior to the support a customer could receive from a dealer (especially for more complicated products or products that need more intensive explanation, such as high-tech products)
- supporting the dealer network (if the customer loyalty programme is sponsored by a manufacturer) by developing special displays, assisting with the development of local advertising campaigns and so on
- other case-specific goals.

Figure 6.2 summarizes this hierarchy of goals. The goals can differ in content and importance depending on the industry, the company context and so on, but in most cases they are closely related to the product's, product line's or company's situation. For example, a new cable channel will primarily aim to win new customers and increase awareness, while the customer loyalty aspect will be more important for an established carrier in the highly com-

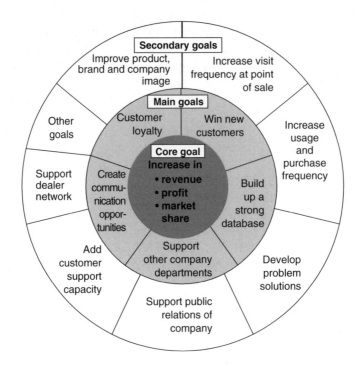

**Figure 6.2**    Hierarchy of goals of customer loyalty programmes

petitive airline industry. A non-profit organization is more likely to aim to increase the value of the membership in the organization, to develop a stronger commitment to the organization, and to achieve broader media coverage of the organization and its activities. A retail chain will try to initiate purchase activities, to increase the frequency of purchases and store visits, and to strengthen its position in relation to manufacturers.

## Prepare success measurement at an early stage

Although the definition of the goals (and target groups) is the first step in developing a loyalty programme, you need to already have one of the last steps in mind – success measurement. The success of a loyalty programme ultimately means achieving the defined goals. In order to be able to measure whether the goals have been achieved or not, several aspects need to be defined at this early stage, which we will summarize briefly at this point (please refer to Chapter 18 on success measurement for further details).

First, you need to formulate your goals precisely. 'We want to increase the loyalty of our customers' is not detailed enough. Let us take the example of a radio station: 'We want to increase the loyalty of our regular listeners, which we define as listeners between the age of 17 and 29 who listen to our station for more than 10 hours a week, by increasing their average listening time by 20 per cent over the next 24 months' reflects the degree of detail you need in defining the goals.

Second, you can now easily measure the success, because you know which scale to use (listening hours per week), and how and when to measure it. Once the scales have been defined, the levels on these scales that represent success (for example, an increase of 20 per cent or higher) or failure (for example, an increase of 5 per cent or less can be established). And once these levels have been defined, future discussions about whether the loyalty programme justifies the investment, or even additional funding, can be (at least partially) de-emotionalized, because you have clear results that prove its success or justify any criticism and show which areas you need to focus on in the future to increase the programme's performance.

Third, in order to make the success measurement work, all parties that will be involved in judging the programme's performance need to be involved in the goal-definition process. This is especially true for those in charge of freeing or cutting the programme's budgets.

## Loyalty programmes have a long-term effect

A closer look at the list of goals discussed in this chapter reveals the fact that the loyalty programme concept mainly aims to achieve a strong long-term effect. A customer loyalty programme does not create the same short-term results as does an enticing special offer via direct mail or heavy local advertising. Even so, certain results can be seen rather quickly. In particular, the secondary goals can be achieved in the short term. However, the primary goals are of a long-term nature, and only if customers are committed to the loyalty programme, and thereby to the company, is the true profit potential of a customer loyalty programme realized over time. It can take several months or years to set up a database that is complete and detailed enough to be used for large-scale marketing activities. In order to be able to measure the achievement of the overall loyalty goal, a customer must be observed for a longer period before being able to say that they have stopped using competitors' products and have limited product usage to your brand.

A customer loyalty programme does not lead to immediate business improvement and success, but gradually works towards all these goals over the months and years of the relationship with its members. No loyalty programme will double profits within a few weeks. However, the relationships that a loyalty programme helps to build are very strong and productive. From a long-term perspective, there are few other instruments as powerful as a well-planned, value-oriented customer loyalty programme. This must be clearly understood, both so that adequate indicators are used to measure the loyalty programme's success and so that the substantial investments made in this loyalty tool are not prematurely considered to be wasted.

In general, it is difficult to measure the isolated economic effect of a single marketing tool or initiative. This is the case for advertising campaigns and direct mailings as well as for customer loyalty programmes or any other loyalty programme. The long-term perspective increases the difficulty of measuring the degree of economic success purely related to the loyalty programme. But if results can be broken down to an individual level – and that is what makes a customer loyalty programme and its database such a powerful tool – a significant step towards one-on-one communication can be taken, which is the ultimate communication goal.

Three other considerations must be pointed out:

- In order to plan and manage a customer loyalty programme properly, you must realize that loyalty programme membership is never a goal in itself, but is always a means of achieving the other marketing goals described above.

- No loyalty programme can be successful if the product behind it is no good. A loyalty programme is not a cure for price, distribution or quality problems. A customer loyalty programme can add value to a product, but cannot *be* the value. Likewise, the loyalty programme cannot overcome significant discrepancies on other decisive factors.

- Looking at the loyalty programme goals we discussed in this chapter, you might gain the impression that members are merely used to provide information. Of course, you must give something to the members first in order to be able to take something from them. The value of what you give to them must be significant, and will be discussed in detail in Chapter 9 on loyalty programme benefits.

## Summary

The overarching goal of customer loyalty programmes and other loyalty programmes is to increase profit, revenue and market share. The five main loyalty programme goals are: customer retention, winning new customers, setting up a strong customer database, supporting other company departments with information or information access, and creating communication opportunities between company and customer. Define the goals precisely, including which scales to use for measurement and which levels on these scales are judged a success or failure. A customer loyalty programme does not create results immediately, but is one of the most powerful retention marketing tools that builds strong long-term relationships. As powerful as loyalty programmes can be, as with any other loyalty programme they cannot work if the product or company supporting the loyalty programme does not deliver a minimum level of quality. Loyalty programmes add value to a product; they do not represent the sole source of value.

# 7 *The loyalty programme's target groups*

The target groups for a customer loyalty programme consist of those customers with whom the sponsoring company primarily wants to develop long-term relationships. Defining these target groups for your customer loyalty programme might seem easy, for example 'our customers', but in fact, it is not that simple. It is also a very important issue, as it is (together with the programme goals) directly linked to the question of which benefits to offer.

Each target group has its own preferences and specific value-driving factors. This connection leads to two consequences:

- Even a slightly different definition of the target groups, for example by specifically including another segment, can lead to a different list of benefits. This could mean that the loyalty programme service centre has to be set up differently. Perhaps other external partners will have to be found. All these aspects eventually drive up the cost and make a different loyalty programme concept necessary.
- The more broadly the target groups are defined, the larger the number of benefits will have to be in order to satisfy all of them. Again, this will strongly influence the cost.

As the correct definition of loyalty programme benefits is the most crucial point of the whole loyalty programme concept, the target groups must therefore be wisely and clearly defined. Although in principle every customer and potential customer is important, it is not possible or efficient to reach everyone with the same means and/or loyalty programmes. Just as with products and services, a segment-specific offering is optimal. Sometimes, membership must also be limited to specific groups in order to achieve a certain elitist character (for example, Porsche would risk much of its special status if it gave the Porsche Card to anybody, rather than only to Porsche owners). In principle, two questions need to be answered:

- Do we want to focus on existing and/or on potential customers?
- Do we want to target all of the existing/potential customers, or only certain segments?

## Existing v. potential customers

When considering whether to focus on existing and/or on potential customers, there are two schools of thought. One opinion is that customers who are with the company already have an established relationship and have proved that they are loyal even without extra incentives such as the benefits of a customer loyalty programme. Therefore, the focus of the loyalty programme should be on low-volume and potential customers, and on trying to increase their purchase volume and usage. In such a case, the main customers will still be able to benefit from the loyalty programme services, as they are, of course, not excluded from membership. But the main attention of recruiting activities and loyalty programme advertising is placed elsewhere.

The other opinion is that these loyal customers are the company's most important customers, and ensure its existence. Following the 80:20 rule, 20 per cent of customers account for 80 per cent of all sales, so that the loss of even one account out of this group significantly affects revenue and profit. From our experience, the 20 per cent figure can actually vary from 10 to 30 per cent, and the sales they account for can vary from 70 to 90 per cent, depending on the company. Nevertheless, this simple rule holds true, and implies that a relatively small group of customers forms the backbone of the company. Therefore, one should focus on these main customers rather than on sporadic or potential customers, and aim to secure their revenue and the profit that comes with it.

Based on our experience, we suggest that your main customers should also be the main target group of the customer loyalty programme. They keep your business alive. Not only do they account for the major part of your revenue and profit, these established relationships are the ones you can learn from most. Heavy users have the most to say about the performance of your product, the quality of your service, possible problems that have to be solved, improvement potential and so on. A dialogue with these customers will enable you to improve the competitiveness of your products significantly. The fundamental relationships that your company needs for long-term survival must be secured for ever.

Depending on the definition of the loyalty programme goals, there are exceptions to this rule. If one of your main goals is to attract new customers, then the target group must also include potential customers. If one of your goals is to set up a complete customer database, regular high-volume and sporadic small-volume customers both have to be targeted. It is also plausible to set up a multi-layer customer loyalty programme with different membership levels. The top level would be for today's most important customers, the medium level for sporadic customers, and the bottom level could target mainly potential customers. The higher the level, the more benefits are offered and the more valuable the membership is. Many airlines offer a similar approach in their frequent flyer programmes. For example, British Airways' Executive loyalty programme starts with a Blue tier status and continues with Silver and Gold tier status. US Airways (formerly US Air) has introduced a redesigned frequent traveller programme, known as Dividend Miles, that has three levels plus a Chairman's Preferred level for those who fly more than 100 000 miles annually. With most airlines these levels have to be earned through flight activities. One exception is Lufthansa's Hon Card, which is given to celebrities. In a customer loyalty programme, the different customers could be given different loyalty programme membership levels according to their current status, rather than having to earn it over time. Status upgrades could, of course, be possible.

Special promotions and programmes or discount pricing strategies aimed at acquiring new customers often backfire, because these new customers accept the offer but move on to your competitors' special promotion the next time. Cable television and telecommunications companies have been trying for years to increase retention rates but at the same time recruit new customers with price promotions and free sampling. These techniques draw out of the woodwork precisely those customers who are hardest to keep (Reichheld, 1993, p.66 or 108). Instead of focusing on these customers, the main effort should be on filtering out customers unlikely to be loyal, and courting the remaining ones. This does not mean ignoring these 'promotion jumpers', as that could lower your customer base significantly. But these segments have to be approached with other programmes and marketing activities that are more customized to their behaviour and needs.

A study conducted at the University of Nuremberg-Erlangen in Germany showed that most of the members of the analysed programme already had a strong affinity with the company or product before joining the loyalty programme. In addition, they mostly also belonged to the group of customers with higher-than-average annual purchase volumes. A form of self-selection process brought a higher number of heavy users to the loyalty programme compared to a smaller number of non-regular customers. This indicates that a customer loyalty programme can successfully help to identify and approach these vital customers and start an individualized dialogue with them, without overlooking the large number of medium- and small-volume customers. All can benefit from the loyalty programme, but it is primarily the heavy users who join (Diller, 1996, p.37).

Focusing on certain target groups could mean specifically excluding other customers, for example, by defining certain conditions for membership or hand-picking the members through personal direct communication. As stated earlier, totally different marketing activities might be necessary to approach these other segments successfully.

Potential customers might be attracted to the loyalty programme, but new customers are mainly won because of a strong product, excellent service, superior brand image, low price or other competitive advantages. A customer loyalty programme will be able to provide support for most of these factors. The loyalty programme might even help to build them, or lead to an initial contact by potential customers with the company or product. Yet the loyalty programme alone will never lead to a dramatic increase in customers. That is the product's job. If the product does not offer value, the loyalty programme cannot perform miracles.

Strangely enough, many companies that run customer loyalty programmes have not yet realized this need for focus. Two studies on customer loyalty programmes in Germany show that a large majority of loyalty programmes (44 and 52 per cent respectively) approach customers and potential customers simultaneously and with the same effort, not differentiating at all between the importance of different target groups (Holz and Tomczak, 1996, p.33; Kirstges, 1995, p.8). This is also the case for many other loyalty programmes in Europe and the USA, despite the fact that they claim to target frequent customers and are consequently called 'frequent flyer or buyer programmes'. More recently, however, companies have started to target smaller segments with more exclusive approaches (for example, T-D1 Company Class, Porsche Card, D2 Platinum Club).

## Whole target group v. selected segments

The second question is whether to target the entire target group, or only selected segments (for example, major customers in specific industries, customers of a specific age or certain income groups). If the target groups themselves are small, it does not make sense to reduce them further. In addition, in many cases a loyalty programme must reach a high critical mass to be sufficiently effective. In such a case, targeting only a few segments might be counterproductive. Another reason to focus on the entire target group is when it is very homogeneous. Here, further segmentation would not make sense, as the entire target group can be addressed with the same effort and benefits.

However, if the target groups are either extremely big or heterogeneous, it is often better to identify the most important segments within them (for example, the heaviest users, the users with the highest affinity to the product, the users that are most vulnerable to competitors' approaches), and focus on them. Other reasons might be small budgets or lack of resources to set up a larger loyalty programme infrastructure.

It is possible, but not very probable, that a customer loyalty programme or any other customer loyalty programme will lead to a lifelong relationship with its customers. First, most consumers cannot be allotted to a single, clearly defined target group. Today's 'nomad' customers either belong to several target groups simultaneously, or continually move from one group to the other. In the 1990s and 2000s, a person who eats at a five-star restaurant and yet shops at a discount store is a common phenomenon, or the businessperson wearing a £1000 suit who changes into torn jeans and T-shirt after work, or the computer freak who previously used their PC mostly for games, but then expands their interests and turns into a programmer.

Second, in most cases in typical consumer markets, interest in the product or the loyalty programme crumbles after three or four years (Zorn, 1991, p.15). People move to other cities or countries where your airline does not offer a service, they grow older and out of the age group that uses a specific product, or they have a family and their interest moves away from former hobbies to more family-oriented activities. There is constant change everywhere, and consumers' habits change accordingly. In industrial markets, or in business-to-business relationships, this period may be several years longer, but so far, eternal relationships are rare. Changes in management, a new product generation that no longer meets a particular customer's expectations or a new strategy that focuses on other industries or markets are only some of many possible reasons for a relationship ending or turning bad. In order to prolong the length of membership, it is extremely important constantly to improve and update the loyalty programme's performance and benefits in order to maintain a high quality level and keep membership attractive. At the same time, the sponsor's product must continue to develop further to retain its competitiveness.

In order for a loyalty programme to be able to infiltrate its target groups sufficiently, these target groups must exist for long enough. This is especially true for loyalty programmes that try to establish or support a certain lifestyle that is related to the sponsor company's products, as they tend to set up on fashion and lifestyle trends that are mostly only temporary. But even for very stable target groups, the loyalty programme's penetration will never be 100 per cent, and even the best customer loyalty programme will only reach 20, 40 or at the very best maybe 80 per cent of the target groups.

One big advantage of a customer loyalty programme is that it can cover several target groups. So even when consumers move from one segment into another, a customer loyalty programme may be able to follow them. Some companies have even started to set up a system of customer loyalty programmes, in order to be able to address their different target groups and segments with more customized benefits and be relevant to members for longer, even when they change habits. A good example is the Hidden Champion Gebrüder Märklin & Cie. GmbH, the world leader in model railways. Märklin has two customer loyalty programmes. 1.FC Märklin aims at children up to the age of 16. When they are older, they become part of the target group of the adult loyalty programme, Märklin Insider. The latter has a US branch called the Märklin Loyalty Programme, located in New Berlin, WI. (Märklin also has the Märklin Dealer Initiative that supports smaller and medium-sized speciality dealers, which account for about 90 per cent of Märklin's sales. The Märklin Dealer Initiative is described in more detail in Chapter 17.)

Another good example is Delta Airlines. Delta has developed a system of loyalty programmes that target different, clearly defined target groups. Senior Select targets senior citizens aged 62 and older; Executive Women's Business Travel aims at businesswomen in management positions, and the Fantastic Flyer Loyalty Programme has over 600 000 members aged 2–12. Further programmes include the Extra Credit College Program and the Escape Plan.

Thus, the most important customers should be identified, pursued and rewarded. This aspect is not as trivial as it might seem. To achieve this goal, it is necessary to offer something out of the ordinary to the customer: something of high value from that customer's point of view. Only if this can be done will customers develop a stronger identification with the product, the brand or the company. This, in turn, leads to a higher repurchase rate or purchase volume, and increases revenue as well as profit. A customer loyalty programme aims to offer this necessary added value by building an emotional relationship with its members. It is this emotional link that makes the bond between company and customer unique, strong and long-lasting. It does not purely rely on hard financial benefits, but builds on soft benefits that make the loyalty programme membership valuable and its members privileged. By building this emotional relationship, the loyalty programme creates a competitive advantage that at least partially immunizes the members from competitors' poaching activities.

## Summary

The most important and in the main also the most profitable customers for a company are those 20 per cent that account for 80 per cent of the sales (the 80:20 rule). These should also be the primary target group for a customer loyalty programme, as securing these relationships is most important for the company's future success. Thus, the primary focus should be on putting together a programme that fits the needs of the top customers. Other customers can still profit from these benefits, but in many cases it is better to explicitly exclude them and approach them with other concepts specifically targeted at them. Further segmentation makes most sense if the target groups are not homogeneous enough to be approached with one programme, and instead require different approaches. A multi-tier membership approach has proven very successful in many cases.

# 8 *The type of loyalty programme*

Depending on the selected target groups, one particular type of customer loyalty programme might be more suitable for achieving the desired goals than another. In principle, there are two different types of customer loyalty programmes: *limited* and *open*. A limited loyalty programme cannot be joined by just anybody. You must go through a formal procedure in order to become a member. This process might include paying a joining fee and/or an annual membership fee and filling out an application form. In some cases, certain criteria must be met in order to be admitted as a member (for example, a certain purchase volume per year, subscriber of a magazine, user of a specific software, or a minimum length of customer relationship). By applying these membership conditions, the loyalty programme has a better influence on filtering out unwelcome members and making sure that the members who join the loyalty programme belong to the primary target groups.

In contrast, open loyalty programmes can be joined by anybody, and usually do not have such a formal application process. Sometimes, the emotional base of a product is not strong enough to develop a limited loyalty programme around it. In such a case, a limited membership would not attract enough members, as the entry hurdle would be too high for a product that does not reciprocate. If an open loyalty programme is established, a broader membership base can be built up, because open loyalty programmes have no joining or membership fee, and in some cases not even an application form (the buyer of a product automatically becomes a member by making the purchase). Open loyalty programmes also address potential clients and clients of other brands in order to start a dialogue and bring them into contact with the company's own brand.

Whether you call your loyalty programme a 'customer card', 'customer club', 'frequency programme', 'bonus programme' or 'VIP programme' does not really differentiate the type of programme. The key differentiators are the type (open v. limited) and, of course, the benefits a programme offers. A customer club can offer bonus points, while a bonus programme can also use a card as an ID vehicle. Therefore, the name is no more than that: a name.

## Open v. limited loyalty programmes

Both open and limited loyalty programmes have their advantages and disadvantages, and these are shown in Table 8.1. The concept chosen mostly depends on the goals of the customer loyalty programme.

**Table 8.1** Advantages of limited and open loyalty programmes

| Limited loyalty programme | Open loyalty programme |
| --- | --- |
| • Membership fee helps cover costs.<br>• Membership prerequisite helps channel membership/focus on target groups.<br>• Limited access makes membership more valuable.<br>• Clearly defined membership structure makes communication more effective.<br>• Membership prerequisite keeps number of members, and thus cost, down.<br>• Database includes only members with an above-average interest in the product.<br>• Membership payments raise expectations, so the loyalty programme management is constantly forced to improve value. | • A wider number of customers can be reached.<br>• Database more complete.<br>• Potential customers and competitors' customers can be reached more easily.<br>• Completeness of database could, after further analysis, lead to segmentation and segment-specific communication.<br>• Larger number of members helps to reach critical mass, which makes loyalty programme become more cost-effective sooner. |

In general, limited loyalty programmes will be the better approach for companies:

- trying to reach/reward their top customers
- preferring a more focused approach
- with smaller budgets
- in clearly segmented markets
- in business-to-business markets
- in markets with homogeneous customers.

Open loyalty programmes will be the better approach for companies:

- with very little knowledge about current and potential customers
- following a more general approach
- with long-term larger budgets
- in unsegmented markets
- in business-to-customer markets
- with commodity products.

In order to focus on the main target groups, to limit financial involvement and risk, and to increase efficiency by being able to channel communication more effectively, a limited loyalty programme is to be recommended in most cases. This is supported by the current loyalty programme situation. A survey of customer loyalty programmes in Germany found that only 26 per cent of all loyalty programmes are open loyalty programmes, and 74 per cent are limited and sometimes have very strict conditions for membership (Holz and Tomczak, 1996, p.37). Another survey in 1995 showed that only 21.6 per cent of the loyalty programmes analysed do not charge an annual membership fee (Kirstges, 1995, p.29). Although yearly charges are not the only prerequisite of a limited loyalty programme, it is another indication of the general preference for limited loyalty programmes. This trend has intensified over recent years.

## Business-to-business and distributor loyalty programmes

Apart from this general differentiation between limited and open loyalty programmes, customer loyalty programmes can be further segmented, for example according to their target group. For instance, business-to-business loyalty programmes do not target the end-user, but instead address intermediaries, professional users and businesses that use the product as a component in their own product. The Profi Loyalty Programme ('Professionals Loyalty' programme) sponsored by Spiess Hecker, the market leader in car repair paint in Germany, is an excellent example. Five suppliers control 80 per cent of this market, which mostly consists of 8500 garages and auto body shops. The Spiess Hecker Profi Loyalty Programme now has 1800 members and has managed to improve customer loyalty, market share and company image significantly (Becker, 1996, p.127).

A special form of business-to-business loyalty programme is the distributor loyalty programme. In this case, the businesses at which the loyalty programme is aimed are dealers or other distributors that carry the products of the sponsoring company. A distributor loyalty programme is set up by a manufacturer primarily to support its dealers and to improve the relationship with them. The dealers might receive assistance with window decoration, local advertising, product display or personnel training in exchange for a membership fee, special promotions for the company's products, or giving these products extra shelf space. Chapter 17 will look at business-to-business loyalty programmes in more detail.

## Summary

In general, customer loyalty programmes can be split into two groups: limited and open. Limited loyalty programmes require a joining or membership fee and a completed application form, and try to channel membership towards their primary target group. Certain criteria must often be met before someone can be considered for membership. Open loyalty programmes can be joined by anyone without any entry condition or hurdle. This openness often leads to very high membership numbers, but many members may be of no benefit to the company, as they do not belong to the primary target groups. Loyalty programmes can be further split into end-user loyalty programmes, business-to-business loyalty programmes and distributor loyalty programmes, depending on their primary focus and target groups.

# 9 *The loyalty programme benefits*

The most important part of any customer loyalty programme is the benefit package that the members of the programme are offered. These benefits are the heart and soul of any loyalty programme, and are the main factor which determines whether or not the programme will be a success and fulfil its retention goals. As a customer loyalty programme primarily aims at building up emotional relationships, the task of finding the right benefits becomes even more important. The benefits need to be valuable and capable of establishing this emotional connection between the customer and the company.

## Selecting the right benefits

When thinking about joining a customer loyalty programme, customers will weigh their input (membership fee, data release, membership obligation and so on) against the output they receive from the programme (benefits, special customer status, image and so on), as shown in Figure 9.1. Only if the balance of input and output is in favour of the potential member will they sign up for the programme. A favourable balance is also necessary for the customer loyalty programme to establish a relationship with the customer, use their data in a customer loyalty programme database, and pick the fruits that stem from a long-term customer relationship. To emphasize this again: *everything comes down to selecting the right benefits*.

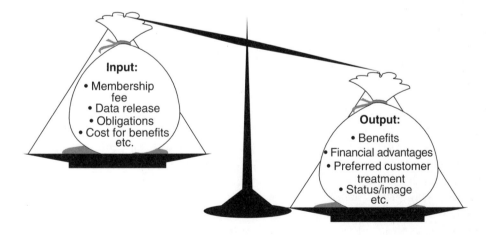

**Figure 9.1**    Importance of loyalty programme benefits

But what are the right benefits? The right benefits are those that have a high perceived value from the customer's point of view. Three key elements are important in this statement:

- The first is 'high value'. Every benefit has a certain value for customers, but only those benefits that have a high value will make membership attractive. In order to have a high value, a benefit must meet the expectations of the target groups, have a certain exclusiveness and/or 'stand out from the crowd'. The value of a benefit must also be high in absolute terms, and not only in comparison to other programmes' benefits. If the overall value level of the benefits is low, then it is probably better not to launch the loyalty programme at all, but invest more time in finding higher-valued benefits or other promotional activities.

- The second important aspect is 'perceived value'. The benefits must not only be good from the sponsoring company's perspective, the customers must also see it that way. It is not enough to think that a benefit offers a high value. If the customers perceive it differently, because it is not the benefit they desire, has not been explained well enough or is too complicated, then the value is certainly reduced.

- Therefore – and this is the third aspect – the selection of the benefits must be made from the customer's point of view. The customer's opinion is what matters, and the only way to find out what they think is to ask them. The programme will only work if it offers benefits that the customers like, rather than those that you want them to like.

In order to manage the selection of benefits correctly, the value of every potential benefit must be measured. This is not possible without a well-planned approach and, of course, without a customer survey. Despite the importance of such a value-oriented approach, our research has shown that the majority of customer loyalty programmes are put together with little or no integration of the customers or other potential members. Very often, these programmes are put together on an ad hoc basis and they end up offering superficial benefits with little or no value. In such cases, the benchmark for the benefits was often what other loyalty programmes in the industry offered, and creativity was reduced to a minimum.

It is also common for companies to develop the loyalty programme concept in conjunction with an outside agency that will later also take care of the programme infrastructure, such as the loyalty programme service centre, call centre or logistics. As many of these agencies look after various loyalty programmes, they often try to include the same or similar benefits in every concept. The advantages for the agencies are obvious: less work, greater synergy and better prices, as the benefits can be bought in larger quantities from outside suppliers. But this leads to a situation in which many programmes offer similar services, such as hotel and rental car discounts, ticket service, flower service and so on, so that their perceived value is reduced because of the lack of exclusivity. In general, it is not a bad thing to offer these kind of benefits, but in most cases they are the only services offered, and no other exclusive or creative benefits are added to increase the value of the programme. How many loyalty programmes really offer benefits that are extraordinary, pleasantly surprise the customers because they had not thought about them before, or are simply one of a kind? Unfortunately there are not many. Historically, the legal situation in Germany, as described in Chapter 3, forced the sponsoring companies to develop loyalty programmes that offered something out of the ordinary with a high value, as their options for building loyalty by other means such as discounting were limited. It remains to be seen whether they will stick to their past experience and stay away from blind discounting now that these laws have been liberalized.

## Value-oriented approach to benefit selection

To create a customer loyalty programme which goes beyond what is currently available, one needs to adopt a value-oriented approach. This is the next main step towards building real, long-term customer relationships. Only benefits that are perceived positively by the customers and have a value for them will have the desired retention effect. How much value, for example, does a £20 discount off the normal room rate at the Ritz Carlton really have for most people? Although the Ritz Carlton is a very good hotel, the value is close to zero for the general public, as they will not be able to afford the room even with the discount. Or how valuable do you think a customer is who has switched to your company because you offered a 10 per cent discount with your customer loyalty programme? Are they not likely to switch to your competitor as soon as they offer a 12 per cent discount? Just look at American telephone companies and their success with discount-based loyalty. Most customers follow the approach of 'who writes the biggest cheque wins'.

The overall goal is to find long-term exclusive advantages for the members and to communicate this loyalty programme offer in a way that it is recognized rationally and emotionally (Vögele, 1991, p.8). If a company wants to start a loyalty programme, it must have good ideas to convince customers of the advantages of a membership. In contrast to a socially oriented loyalty programme that is founded because the members have common interests, such as a fan club for a sports team, or a bridge club, the company, as sponsor of a customer loyalty programme, must create these common interests first, then channel and strengthen them (Anon. 1994c).

## Hard and soft benefits

A good and successful customer loyalty programme concept will offer a value-oriented combination of hard and soft benefits, taking into consideration such factors as cost and competencies, as shown in Figure 9.2. Hard benefits are tangible benefits which are immediately

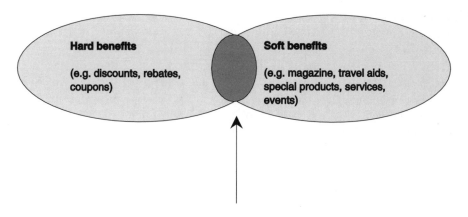

**Figure 9.2**    The right mixture of loyalty programme benefits

recognizable by all members and lead to savings in some form or another. In most cases, hard benefits are financial benefits, for example discounts, rebates or coupons. Although savings are always at the top of your customers' wish list and also have a certain value for them, these financial benefits will not be the retention drivers of your programme. Such benefits are certainly appreciated, but are not the barrier against defection that you are trying to build with the customer loyalty programme. Remember, the customer who joins your loyalty programme simply because of a discount will be the first to leave if the competitor next door offers an even better deal.

What will make your customer loyalty programme successful are *soft benefits*. These soft benefits are the special offers, the value-added services, the special treatment, the recognition and reward that the customer is looking for. The soft benefits are responsible for the major proportion of the loyalty effect. As most of the soft benefits included in a customer loyalty programme are intangible, company- and/or product-related, they are also less likely to be copied by the competition. They ensure that your programme has the unique elements that make it attractive to your customers, and that it offers the high value they are looking for.

## Why hard benefits alone will not work

Looking at customer loyalty programmes in different industries, it is evident that the hard benefits are usually copied first, and that they are often not differentiated among competitors' programmes. Therefore, if no or not enough soft benefits are included, the programmes are so similar that none produces a barrier to defection. The soft benefits are what give successful programmes a winning edge, differentiating them successfully from other programmes and giving them the competitive advantages that attract members and reflect the sponsoring company's superiority. 'Financial advantages are not good enough. Discounts, no matter how we dress them up and try to sell them, are not rewards' (Barlow, 1996, p.3). Too many programmes are founded on discounts or rebates alone. Although every consumer enjoys the prospect of savings, in a world of constant, year-round sales and everyday low prices, the value of further savings alone is limited. Consumers become immune to bargains.

A good example are the frequent traveller programmes in the airline industry. Nearly all the major US carriers give the same air miles for the same routes, form partnerships with the same hotel chains and rental car companies, offer a credit card with which one can collect further air miles and co-operate with the same partners, such as long-distance telephone companies and restaurants. Most frequent flyers are members of several frequent traveller programmes. Ordinarily, they focus their flight activities on one or two airlines until they have reached enough miles for a free flight (the number of miles to be exchanged for free tickets is also nearly identical in all programmes) or for priority membership. But then the game begins again. In order to obtain the next free ticket or priority membership the following year, the customer has to start all over again, and they can do that with any airline. Depending on where their business will tend to take them in that following year and which airlines fly to those destinations, they might stay loyal or shift their flight activities to other carriers.

Another example is provided by the loyalty programmes of different bookstores, such as B. Dalton, Waldenbooks and Books-A-Million. They all offer 10 per cent off nearly everything in their stores for one full year. The membership fee is $10 in most cases, and no soft benefits are included that could make a difference.

Just to make one thing clear: giving discounts is not a bad thing in general. But if you feel that some form of price reductions should be included in your programme, then make customers earn them, instead of just giving them away. There are several intelligent pricing schemes available that specifically aim at customer loyalty. How to use pricing to promote loyalty will be dealt with in detail in Chapter 10.

## Soft benefits are the key to a successful programme

Soft benefits in turn are not without costs, but there are a variety of ways to cover these. For example, a newsletter may be financed by advertisements, external partners may pay commission for products or services sold to members, members may pay a cover charge for special events and so on. We will discuss this aspect in more detail in Chapter 11. As some of these benefits are product-related, they could be provided by other company departments, which lowers their cost through possible synergies. Even if benefits have to be purchased from an outside source at a certain price, quantity discounts will apply and the overall cost will be spread out over the entire member base. But discounts remain discounts and lost contribution for ever.

Do not confuse putting together a *good* list of soft benefits with putting together a *long* list of soft benefits: 'The temptation in developing a program is to include in this category virtually everything that is inexpensive and easy and most department store programs have succumbed to that temptation' (Barlow, 1994, p.5). This is also the case in other industries. Quality is always more important than quantity. Putting together the wrong list of soft benefits that have little or no value for the customers will not only lead to an unsuccessful programme, but could also reflect negatively on the sponsoring company.

As long as you have all the right value-driving core benefits in place, you could, of course, add more benefits as long as their value/cost ratio is positive, meaning that the additional value they create is greater than the additional cost required to offer them.

## Finding the right mix of hard and soft benefits

To reiterate, the main objective is to find the right combination of hard and soft benefits which have the highest possible perceived value for your customers and will build up the retention effect you are seeking. Hard benefits alone will not achieve this goal as they can be copied too easily and have no uniqueness. Soft benefits alone will not always achieve this goal because saving money is what attracts customers to the programme initially:

> Years of soft benefits programs did not generate for the airlines and hotel companies the kind of brand loyalty that caused travelers to rearrange their flight schedules or drive extra miles to use one brand or another. Only free flights and free nights accomplished that end. (Barlow, 1996, p.2)

But in a world where a myriad of airlines and hotel chains offer the possibility of earning free flights and free nights, additional soft benefits could give these programmes a competitive edge and help to build up an anti-defection barrier:

The hard benefits are the trips and prizes, the free stuff, and the hard benefits are actually the bait that brings customers into the program. Research and experience show, however, that it is the soft benefits – the special events, the recognition, the upgrades, the private sales, the advanced information – that really build the relationship with the customer. (Barlow, 1992, p.35)

## The value of the benefits

What determines the value of a specific benefit? There are three main factors:

- the financial value
- the relevance for the individual
- the ease with which a member can use the benefit or accumulate the necessary points to earn rewards.

The financial value to the customer can be measured by comparing the overall savings with the overall money spent. In the case of discounts or rebates, this can easily be calculated. However, in programmes where the currency is air miles, it is much more difficult to extract the exact amount of financial savings.

Relevance for the customer means that an offered benefit must be in some way related to the best interests of the member, so that there is an incentive and interest in using the loyalty programme benefits. Therefore, the benefit must be something that the customer needs or wants, or at least could use. A loyalty programme that only offers irrelevant benefits has no value for the customer.

Finally, ease of use means that loyalty programme benefits are clearly communicated and can be called on without much effort. A simple phone call is always preferred to filling out a form or writing a letter. If the customer loyalty programme includes some sort of reward programme which allows the customer to accumulate points and then exchange these for specific rewards after reaching a certain level, that level must not be set too high. If rewards can only be reached after a very long period and heavy purchases, this is not very encouraging and can often lead to a negative perception. Ease of use also implies that a loyalty programme member does not have to keep track of their status, but is regularly informed by the loyalty programme management of changes in the loyalty programme benefit portfolio, accumulated points and so on (for example, through regular mailings or easy account access via the Internet).

The rewards must not only be adequate, but also relevant. Therefore, it is necessary to consider in depth the needs and value structure of the specific target groups that are approached by the customer loyalty programme. Apart from the value aspects, a loyalty programme benefit must also fulfil other conditions which are more relevant from the loyalty programme sponsor's point of view, such as practicality.

Furthermore, at least some of the benefits should relate to the company's core product or service. In general, the benefits must be directly correlated with the company's image. Before we go into further detail on these aspects and discuss an approach used to filter out the true value drivers that should be included in the loyalty programme concept from the large variety of potential benefits, let us take a look at a few examples of real value benefits.

Again, do not let your members wait too long for their first rewards: 31 per cent of members expect to earn a reward within the first three months of their membership, and another 39 per cent within four to six months (*USA Today*, 1999).

## Some good examples of real value benefits

Porsche, the renowned German sports car manufacturer, offers the 'Porsche Card' exclusively to Porsche owners for about £75 per year. This package includes a Porsche MasterCard and a Lufthansa Air Plus Visa Card. Although the card owners can use more than a dozen different services offered by Porsche and its partner Lufthansa, one service is by far the most attractive: the Avis Park & Wash Service. This service allows any Porsche driver who owns a Porsche Card and possesses a business class ticket to drop off their Porsche at the Avis station of any participating airport in Germany. While they are travelling, their car is parked free of charge on a secure Avis parking lot and, when they return, their Porsche will be ready, waiting for them, freshly washed and detailed, inside and out. Just imagine the exclusiveness and VIP feeling such a benefit offers. It is hard to beat. This is the best benefit I have found in years of research all over the world (see the case study in Chapter 23 for more details).

T-Mobile, Germany's largest mobile phone operator, launched its T-D1 Company Class in 2001 exclusively for its largest company accounts. One of the most important issues for the target group was to devise a platform allowing them to communicate with one another. The Company Class now offers them both several moderated online forums as well as regular personal meetings during regional meetings and the annual member conference. For the first time, they feel part of a group of people with similar interests/problems, with their supplier listening to learn how it can improve its services for them (for details, see the case study in Chapter 22).

Pro 7, part of Germany's second largest private TV station group, started the 7 Club in 1995. For £30 per year, the members get a free subscription to one of the most popular German TV guides and can use over half a dozen other benefits. But one of these benefits stands out. It is called VIP Service, and gives the members a variety of TV-related opportunities, such as tickets for live shows, backstage passes for shows and movie shoots, meetings with their favourite TV stars, trips to movie locations around the world, and last but not least the chance to work as an extra in TV series productions. The VIP Service is one of the most popular benefits offered by the 7 Club loyalty programme, and shows how members can be offered product-related benefits (the members are TV fans) that are unique, as they are related to shows that are only transmitted on Pro 7. Moreover, Pro 7 can even save money: extras that are hired through an agency have to be paid, in contrast to club members who do it for fun. These ideas reinstate the theme of the official loyalty programme slogan: 'Experience TV!'

IKEA, the Swedish furniture maker, started the IKEA Family in the late 1980s, and the loyalty programme is in the middle of its second successful decade. IKEA customers usually collect the furniture they buy, and transport it home themselves. One of the most interesting benefits the 'family' offers is insurance that guarantees immediate replacement of any purchased item that is damaged during transportation. Since many customers spend a considerable amount of money at IKEA, this insurance certainly takes away a number of worries. Nothing is worse than a brand new china cabinet or table with a big scratch, let alone broken. The IKEA Family also used to offer a service that allowed the members of about a dozen different 'families' around the world to use each others' vacation homes.

SWR3 is one of the most popular radio stations in Germany, and has managed to revitalize its business despite increasing competition from new local and cable stations. This revival was achieved by introducing a series of comedy radio characters, with sketches that air at specific times each day. They have become extremely popular. The SWR3 Club sells CDs of the best sketches about each character exclusively to members. Some of these CDs have sold over 50 000 copies. The club also arranges concerts with top local, national and international acts, and invented Germany's most successful comedy show, *SWR3-Gagtory*. Club members receive special prices for all these events, and the chance to meet and talk with the DJs. Meeting the DJs during these events or going on club trips with them is one of the most popular aspects of membership (see the case study in Chapter 20 for details).

Steiff is the world leader in teddy bears, and introduced the Steiff Club in 1992 in Germany and a year later in the USA, where it is based in New York City. Steiff teddy bears have become collectors' items, and some bears are auctioned for £60 000 or more. The Steiff Club offers its members a variety of benefits, the most valuable of which is an annual special edition teddy bear that is available only to club members. As the number of teddy bears in this edition is limited, the value from a collector's point of view is obvious.

These are only a few examples to show how successful programmes can be set up. Instead of depending on discounts, these programmes offer soft benefits with an extremely high value for their target groups. The case studies in Part III of this book will give some more examples from different industries and countries.

## A three-step approach to identifying the real value drivers

To create an effective customer loyalty programme, a value-oriented approach must be taken. The challenge is to find the Porsche Card 'Avis Park & Wash' equivalent for your programme. This value-oriented approach is designed to identify those benefits which have a real value for the customer. These benefits are what the customer really wants and will use regularly, and are what will make the customer join the programme. Make sure you do not underestimate customers' intelligence. They will detect immediately if a benefit is only a hidden sales pitch or insignificant. The effect this would have on the customers' loyalty certainly needs no explanation.

We suggest a three-step approach that has been tested and proven in many projects and which will filter out those benefits with the highest value, resulting in a customer loyalty programme concept that will create real long-term loyal customers. Figure 9.3 shows the general structure of this approach.

## Step 1: Collection of potential benefits

At this point, the goals and target groups of the customer loyalty programme have already been defined and an internal project team consisting of members from different departments and maybe an outside agency has been put together. During this step, all possible benefits for the customer loyalty programme are collected. By using a brainstorming approach, the internal project team should put together a long list of benefits that are potentially interesting for loyalty programme members. Ideally, this is done by means of a brainstorming workshop, in which the team, which should consist of members from different company departments,

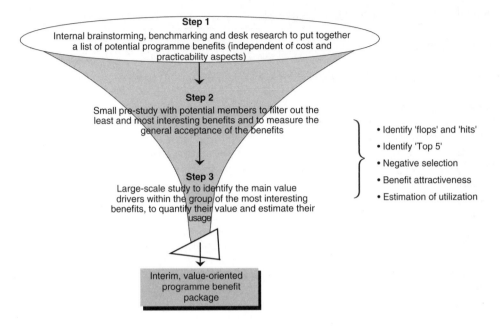

**Figure 9.3** How to identify the most valuable benefits

including sales, is split into separate groups that first collect ideas independently. Then each group presents its ideas to the other group(s). In a final step, the groups re-form again (and may even be re-mixed), now fuelled by the ideas of the other groups, and continue their brainstorming. Aspects such as cost, feasibility, competences and so on should not be considered at this point. These aspects are looked at later, after Step 3 of this value-oriented approach has been completed. The reason for this is that no potential benefit should initially be excluded because of its high cost or impracticality. If an expensive benefit turns out to be the number one value driver, then you should consider how this benefit could be financed before dismissing the benefit. This will be discussed in more detail later in this chapter (see also Figure 9.11).

Basically, there should be no limit to the team's imagination in creating the list of potential benefits. In addition to this brainstorming exercise, thorough desk research and benchmarking should be carried out. Possible sources of ideas and benchmarks are competitors' loyalty programmes, customer loyalty programmes from other industries and/or countries, different types of programmes such as frequent flyer programmes, current services your company offers or that are offered in your industry and, of course, new ideas. The challenge is to come up with new ideas that also move into new territory. The only limit at this point is your imagination. During this process, it is necessary to focus on the selected target groups from the very beginning. Only by doing this can you ensure that benefits that have a potential value for them are identified.

These potential loyalty programme benefits can come from a large variety of areas, such as travel and tourism, entertainment, sports, insurance, products, services, communications and special events. Table 9.1 shows some examples from various areas, but it is not intended to be comprehensive.

**Table 9.1**    Selection of the most interesting benefits

**Travel and tourism:**
- international and national hotel information, reservation and booking service; 20,000 affiliated hotels world-wide; discounts of 10 to 40 per cent; VIP service
- national restaurant information and reservation service
- exclusive trips to major international sports events, like tennis tournaments in Wimbledon, Monte Carlo or New York; VIP package; admission guaranteed
- exclusive educational travel service with experts
- trips to cultural events and events with international flair, like the Opera Ball in Vienna, festival performances in cities like Salzburg and Verona; short trips; admission guaranteed
- cultural and music trips with expert guides
- sports trips: golf, tennis, horse riding, motorcycle trekking, balloon rides
- culinary tours, including cooking classes and wine tastings
- de luxe and medium-class cruising, special conditions, cabin upgrading, VIP service
- arrangement of vacation homes and mansions in Europe and overseas; special conditions
- last-minute travel service; advisory, booking and payment service via telephone
- world-wide yacht charter service; mediation among crew members on request; special tariffs
- summer camp service for children and teenagers; animation and learning programmes
- full service for individual and business travel; obtaining airline, train and ferry tickets; special offers on car rentals
- helicopter and business flight charter service at special rates
- national and international car rental; extra service and special reductions
- camper and recreation vehicle rental service
- motorbike rentals
- adventure flying
- medical information service for overseas destinations and travels abroad
- medical assistance world-wide
- baggage rental
- travel literature rental
- travel video and photo CD service
- airport shuttle service
- VIP lounge access at airports
- visa procurement
- country information packages, including entry formalities and conditions, climate, exchange rate, vaccination and other precautionary measures
- consultation on travel routes and city tours
- traffic reports and travel news
- special discounts on airport parking
- provision of tourist discount packages for cities and communities
- access to talk show and other TV recordings
- holiday exchange market, including vacation homes and apartment exchange opportunities.

**Insurance:**
- guarantee extension
- private third-party insurance
- traffic and general accident insurance
- baggage insurance
- flight delay insurance
- travel cancellation insurance
- health insurance documents for abroad

- third-party insurance for small cars and car rentals abroad
- motorbike offers, including third-party, partial coverage and comprehensive insurance.

**Products/accessories:**
- wine, sparkling wine, champagne, exclusive brands, rarities
- national and international delicatessen; special price arrangements
- gift articles; high-quality accessories; special prices; CD and videotape loyalty programme editions
- sporting goods, including golf, tennis, horse riding, hunting; special prices
- office supplies and equipment; wholesale terms
- supreme gourmet coffee
- fresh oyster delivery service
- marzipan with personal or loyalty programme emblems
- paintings and sculpture
- loyalty programme leather articles; neutral or with seal
- products with limited editions
- watches; loyalty programme seal
- jewellery and accessories
- newspapers and magazines; time-limited, free-of-charge delivery
- baggage bands; loyalty programme imprints.

**Special events:**
- regional loyalty programme round table
- loyalty programme seminars, such as self-awareness, stress handling, speech-making, applications training, time management, customer-oriented telephone behaviour
- loyalty programme internal sports tournaments, concerts, sight-seeing
- security training for car and motorbike users
- international round table
- loyalty programme tent at trade shows, rock concerts, sports events.

**Miscellaneous:**
- pre-paid phone card
- national/international: ticket procurement for theatre, concerts, cultural events, sport events
- national and international office service
- secretarial services, including typing, presentation and graphics service
- document service, including monitoring of expiry dates
- 24-hour information, reception and forwarding service
- congress and seminar organization service
- international present and gift service
- international courier service
- national child care and babysitter service
- international relocation service
- au pair mediation; information exchange
- art objects rental
- ideas for parties
- watch repair
- cinema loyalty programme, including participation at first-night events
- information service on merchandise remainders via tape, voice mail or personal invitation.

*Source:* Adapted from Westphalen & Partner (1993a).

# Step 2: Customer pre-study

In the second phase, the long list of potential benefits put together in Step 1 is reduced through a small-scale customer study. This is ideally done by means of focus groups and exploratory interviews. The goal is to filter out the most and the least attractive benefits, and to outline a rough pre-selection. The value of the different benefits is measured in Step 3. In Step 2, the customer's point of view is included for the first time (although customer focus groups could also be used for idea collection in Step 1) and used to arrive at a rough pre-selection of the existing list and to add new ideas of their own to the list.

At the beginning of the focus group or interview, the respondents should be given a brief and unbiased description of a customer loyalty programme, so that they will have a general idea of what these programmes are aiming at and what the purpose of the interview is. Stress the importance of the customer's perspective during the development of this concept. The interview should begin with several open questions, such as: 'Which benefits should the XYZ Company include?' or 'If you were to set up a customer loyalty programme, which benefits would it offer?' Although open questions do not generally generate detailed and highly significant results, this form of questioning has two advantages at this point:

- It will warm up the interviewees and help them to concentrate on the subject of the interview.
- As the answers are unprompted (without the interviewees having been shown a list or offered help), it can be assumed that they are of above average importance for them.

After the warm-up phase, the interviewees should be shown the long list of potential benefits that was put together during Step 1. Using an uneven (preferably five-point) scale, the interviewees are asked to evaluate each of the benefits. Figure 9.4 shows the details of such a question. This is the only time when importance or attractiveness rating scales should be used. The tendency with such scales is for all factors to be considered very important. But at this point the goal is a rough pre-selection and elimination of some of the less attractive benefits, so identifying trends and measuring the relative importance of one compared to the others are sufficient.

|  | **For me, this benefit is . . .** | | |
|---|---|---|---|
|  | ... not at all attractive | ... somewhat attractive | ... extremely attractive |
| Special product offers | (1) - - - - - - (2) - - - - - (3) - - - - - (4) - - - - - (5) | | |
| Ticket service | (1) - - - - - - (2) - - - - - (3) - - - - - (4) - - - - - (5) | | |
| Flower service | (1) - - - - - - (2) - - - - - (3) - - - - - (4) - - - - - (5) | | |
| Air fare optimization | (1) - - - - - - (2) - - - - - (3) - - - - - (4) - - - - - (5) | | |
| Special seminars for members | (1) - - - - - - (2) - - - - - (3) - - - - - (4) - - - - - (5) | | |
| Travel planning service | (1) - - - - - - (2) - - - - - (3) - - - - - (4) - - - - - (5) | | |

**Figure 9.4**    Benefit evaluation during customer pre-test

As many of the proposed benefits might be new to the interviewees and not necessarily self-explanatory, they should be described in more detail on an explanation sheet. This will ensure that the interviewees understand exactly what each benefit involves and can evaluate them better. Further, it ensures that all interviewees have the same description. Table 9.2 shows how such an explanation sheet should be set up.

**Table 9.2**   Explanation sheet

---

**Special product effects:**
As a loyalty programme member, you will be offered special products on a regular basis. These products are only offered to you and are not available to non-members. They are of the same top quality as you are used to receiving from us, and are priced competitively.

**Ticket service:**
Through our ticket service, you can purchase tickets to any event world-wide simply by calling a designated telephone number and charging them to a credit card.

**Flower service:**
We supply you with a telephone number which allows you to use a credit card to send flowers to anyone, anywhere, anytime through our world-wide flower service.

**Air fare optimization:**
Whenever, wherever you plan to fly, we will make sure you get the best possible price. We will check the competition for you.

**Special seminars for members:**
You will be offered a chance to participate in special seminars on a regular basis. These seminars will be on topics related to the company, and are free of charge for our members. [For example, an automobile manufacturer's loyalty programme may offer seminars such as 'Winterize Your Car', 'Defensive Driving', 'Do-It-Yourself Repairs', and so on.]

**Travel planning service:**
Going somewhere? Let us help you by providing you with inside information on the best routes, hotels and restaurants as well as must-see sights and current events.

---

After this pre-study has been completed, the list of benefits can be split into two groups. The analysis of the evaluations will reveal which benefits are perceived as very or extremely attractive and therefore should be analysed in more detail, and which benefits are not attractive to the potential members. This pre-study serves as a rough pre-selection of the potential benefits, but in most cases already produces clear results showing which benefits to consider further, and which to drop. In general, a list of maybe fifty benefits can be reduced to twenty or so by the pre-study.

In addition, the interviewees should be given the opportunity to add some benefits that they consider interesting and that are not on the list so far. In this way, you can avoid overlooking interesting benefits and ensure that the customers' perception is taken sufficiently into consideration during the loyalty programme's conception phase.

Normally, a sample of 30 to 35 interviewees is ample at this stage. The interviewees should be selected from the different target groups and represent potential members. As the most important results of Step 2 are the individual evaluations of the benefits, the interviews should be conducted in person, as opposed to over the phone. In this way, the interviewer can also encourage and pick up side remarks and so on. Focus groups with larger numbers of participants can also be held, and might produce further interesting results, as the participants can discuss the benefits and the loyalty programme idea in general more thoroughly.

Especially in business-to-business markets with small target groups, Step 2 might be sufficient to determine the final customer view of the potential benefits. In this case, it does not make sense to talk to hundreds of customers (if there are that many). It is much more efficient to conduct a smaller number of in-depth personal interviews. The quality of these results is very good. A third step is not necessary. The right tools and methodologies need to be applied, though (see below). However, in consumer markets, such an approach is not possible. Here, we need this multi-step approach to slowly narrow down the number of options.

## Step 3: In-depth customer study

In the third and final phase, only those benefits which have been identified as 'very or extremely attractive' in Step 2 will be analysed further. In addition, some of the benefits that were suggested by the interviewees during the pre-test can be added. The third phase consists of a large-scale customer study that aims to identify the top value drivers ('Top 5') of very or extremely attractive benefits within the group. This task is certainly not as easy as it might first appear.

To measure the importance or value of specific features, customers have traditionally been asked directly which product factors were important to them or which benefits they wanted to have included in the customer loyalty programme. But such direct questions simply led to the finding that all benefits were important and the interviewees did not differentiate between individual importance levels. Figure 9.5 shows an example for a car manufacturer's customer club. If you asked a new car buyer which features the car should

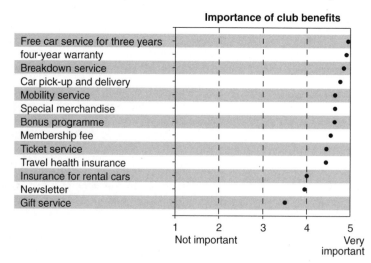

**Example: Customer club of a car manufacturer**

*How important is it to you that the customer club offers the following service benefits?*

**Figure 9.5**    Value measurement – 'traditional method'

have, you would achieve similar results. The buyer probably wants to have a powerful engine, top safety, good economy, plenty of equipment and so on, and all that with top quality at a low price. Or someone buying a dress wants it to be fashionable, from a well-known designer, made from good material, easy to look after, to fit without any extra tailoring and so on, again all for a low price. Unfortunately, such a product has yet to be invented, and in reality the buyer is forced to make a trade-off. For example, the car buyer must accept a higher price for the safety level they want. This trade-off situation is also true for loyalty programmes. For cost, efficiency and organizational reasons, it is not possible to include all benefits in the loyalty programme concept.

## Value-measurement methods

The traditional rating method is good enough to measure approximate trends concerning which benefits seem to be important and which are not, as is done during the pre-study in Step 2. But important decisions such as which benefits to choose should never be based on the results of such an approach alone. Therefore, more sophisticated tools must be used to measure the exact value and the importance of the different options. At this point, a rough estimate of the benefits' value is not good enough. We are now involved in the details of the concept, and the value of the remaining benefits must be measured exactly in order to come up with a valid ranking. Therefore, a larger sample is necessary in Step 3. Our experience shows that a sample of at least 250 interviewees is necessary to obtain reliable results. If the target group is very small, for example in the business-to-business area, then a smaller sample is sufficient. But the more heterogeneous the target groups are, the bigger the regional differences are and so on, the bigger the sample must be in order to achieve good results for each group.

There are three possible ways to measure value: *ranking scales, constant sum scales,* and the more sophisticated and very precise *conjoint measurement.*

### RANKING SCALES

When using ranking scales, interviewees are asked to rank a limited number of benefits according to their preference. In order to achieve better results, the total number of benefits must be split into smaller groups of no more than six. Ranking more than six benefits becomes too complex for many interviewees. One way of splitting the overall list of benefits is by putting benefits from the same area (for example, travel and tourism, entertainment, products) into one group. Figure 9.6 shows an example from the travel and tourism area. Again, the different benefits should be described on an explanation sheet to make sure that the respondents fully understand them.

Using such a split ranking system will result in the identification of the top benefits from each particular group. However, the goal is to identify the most important benefits overall. Therefore, the benefits which the respondent ranked highest in each group should be put together into a new group. This group will now obviously consist of benefits from different areas, for example from travel and tourism as well as entertainment. The benefits in this group must again be ranked. Figure 9.7 shows such a multi-level ranking system structure, and Figure 9.8 gives an example in which the two highest-ranked benefits from each area move to the next level. Depending on the total number of benefits remaining at the begin-

| Benefit | Rank |
|---|:---:|
| Travel planning service | 1 |
| Hotel reservation service | 4 |
| Air fare optimization | 2 |
| Last-minute travel service | 5 |
| Suitcase rental service | 6 |
| Tourism video tapes | 3 |

**Figure 9.6**　Ranking system

ning of this in-depth customer survey, more than two steps or levels might be necessary before the list of benefits has been reduced to the two or three highest-ranking benefits from the customers' point of view. Those benefits are the real value drivers.

A disadvantage of this approach is that by always taking the top two ranked benefits to the next level, third-ranked benefits might drop out that would be ranked higher overall than the top two of another group. This problem can be reduced, for example, by first filtering out benefit groups that do not interest the interviewee in general (for instance, they may have no

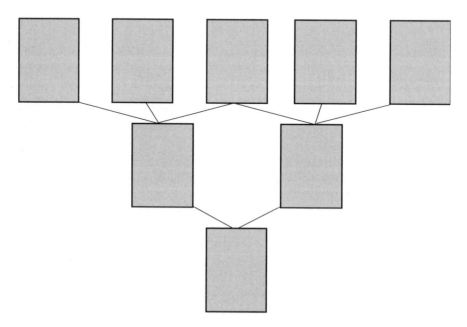

**Figure 9.7**　Multi-level ranking system

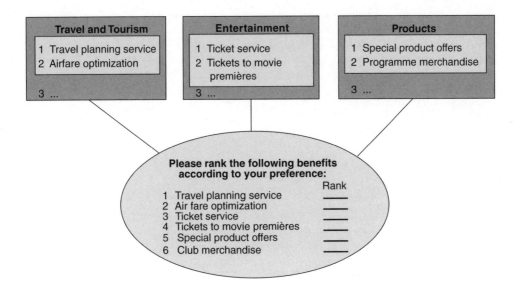

**Figure 9.8**  Two-level ranking system

interest in travel and tourism), and then only ranking the benefits in the remaining groups. Another possibility is to ask additional questions that aim to find out the preferences between second- and third-ranked benefits of different groups. This can be done by again ranking those, by asking directly which areas are more interesting than others, or as a back-up question, asking interviewees to pick a small number of benefits (maybe three to six) from the overall list of benefits that they would include in the programme if they could decide.

## CONSTANT SUM SCALES

Another method is the constant sum scale. With this method, the interviewee is asked to divide 100 points between a limited number of up to six benefits according to their preference (see Figure 9.9). As described for the ranking system, the constant sum scales can also be set up in a multi-step way. Here, those benefits that scored the highest points would move on to the next level, where they would again be given points, but this time compared to the top-scoring benefits from other groups.

The constant sum scale suffers from a similar disadvantage to the ranking system. By choosing those benefits that receive the highest points for the next level, a benefit receiving low points within one group may drop out even though it would have received much higher points in another group when compared to other benefits. Using additional questions, as described in the ranking scales example, can again minimize this problem.

By dividing points among benefits, you not only obtain a ranking (as when using ranking scales), but also the difference in value between two items. Let us take another look at Figure 9.9. The way the points have been distributed means that the benefits are ranked with the travel planning service at number 1, followed by air fare optimization, tourism video-tapes, hotel reservation service and finally the last-minute travel service and suitcase rental service. The difference between the travel planning service and air fare optimization is only five points. They certainly seem to have a similar high value. The gap between the hotel reservation service and the tourism video tapes is also only five points, but at a much lower level.

Please divide 100 points between these benefits from the travel and tourism area according to your preference.

| Benefit | Points |
|---|---|
| Travel planning service | 40 |
| Hotel reservation service | 10 |
| Air fare optimization | 35 |
| Last-minute travel service | 0 |
| Suitcase rental service | 0 |
| Tourism video tapes | 15 |
| Total | $\Sigma$ 100 |

**Figure 9.9**    Constant sum scale

The 25-point difference between those two groups shows that there is a steep decline in value between them.

## CONJOINT MEASUREMENT

The most dependable and most precise tool is conjoint measurement, or conjoint analysis. Conjoint analysis builds on the logical assumption that the value of a product is made up of the value of its different components. For example, a car's overall value is made up of the value of the engine, driving comfort, interior and exterior design, fuel economy, safety and so on. The value of a customer loyalty programme likewise depends on the value of its different components, the most important of which are the benefits. With conjoint measurement, the value of each individual factor entered in the analysis (for example, engine power, driving comfort, safety) and each performance level of those factors (for the factor engine power, for example, the levels could be 100 HP 125 HP and 150 HP) can be calculated. These results can then be used to optimize the overall value and composition of the entire product.

In practice, conjoint measurement is mainly used during the product development and pricing process. With conjoint measurement, the most important factors of a product from the customers' point of view are identified early enough in the development process so that, for example, the R&D budgets can be shifted accordingly and improvements made where it counts. Conjoint measurement is also frequently used for price optimization and to provide the necessary data for market simulation models. For detailed information on the conjoint measurement tool, please refer to Wittink and Cattin (1989), Green and Srinivasan (1990) and Kucher and Hilleke (1993) in the English Bibliography and Mengen (1993) and Bauer, Herrmann and Mengen (1994) in the German Bibliography. The methology is continuously advancing (for example, incorporating direct choice modelling), and has established itself as the leading value-measurement methodology.

In order to be able to calculate the value of the different product attributes, conjoint measurement uses a compensatory approach which reflects a real-life purchasing decision. The respondents are asked to indicate their preference for two products that are described by different performance levels on several attributes. Figure 9.10 shows such a paired comparison for a customer loyalty programme. The reason the approach is called 'compensatory' is that this decision is not made easy. Neither product is obviously better, so that the respondent has to weigh their options. In this example, the respondent has to decide whether they prefer to pay an annual fee of £20 and then receive a 10 per cent discount on all their purchases as well as a quarterly newsletter, or if they prefer to put no money down and obtain no discounts, yet have the opportunity to make individual product consultation appointments. High-valued factors and low-valued factors compensate each other to form an overall value of each alternative, which is then the basis of the respondent's decision. All of these different benefits would again be explained in more detail on an explanation sheet. Each interviewee would not only decide whether they prefer Loyalty Programme A or Loyalty Programme B, but would also indicate how strong their preference for their choice is, indicated by using interim steps on the nine-point scale.

Every interviewee has to answer several of these paired comparisons, each showing different loyalty programme concepts with different benefit combinations. From these responses, the value of each individual attribute, such as the individual consultation appointments, can be derived, both on an individual level for each respondent and on an aggregated level over all respondents. The benefits can then be brought into a sequence according to their importance and value. Thus, the most valuable – meaning the most important – attributes can be isolated.

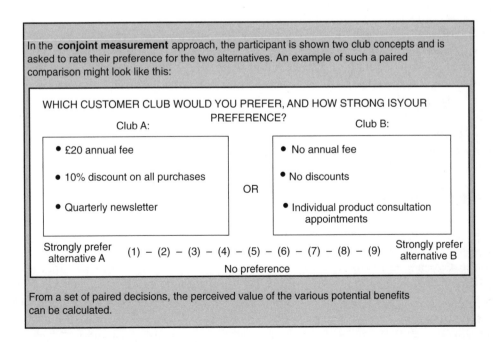

**Figure 9.10** Conjoint measurement methodology

## Cost–value matrix

The value of the different potential benefits can be related to the cost of these benefits in a cost–value matrix (see Figure 9.16 for an example). This matrix divides the benefits into four groups:

- High value –low cost – This is the ideal quadrant.
- Low value–low cost – Benefits from this quadrant should not be offered just because the cost is low, as they are of limited value for the customer.
- Low value–high cost – This is the quadrant from which the benefits should be picked least often, as it combines the worst levels of value and cost.
- High value–high cost – Although the cost of the benefits in this quadrant is high, they should be closely considered for the final benefit package. Their high value is the necessary argument for considering them in more detail and looking into different ways to finance them (the cost aspect will be discussed later in this chapter).

At the end of this chapter, we will look at several practical examples from the retail, telecommunications and car industries in which conjoint measurement was used.

The final result of this three-step filtering process is that the long list of potential benefits from Step 1 has been split into three groups:

1   the top value drivers ('Top 5')
2   benefits with a higher value
3   benefits with little or no value.

The third group should not be analysed further. The final loyalty programme benefits will be composed of benefits from group 1, complemented with benefits from group 2. Now, and only at this point, to make the final decision, factors such as cost or feasibility will have to be taken into account, as indicated in Figure 9.11. These issues were ignored prior to this point because they should not be 'knock-out' criteria for a benefit. If, for example, one of the more costly benefits turns out to be the number one value driver for the loyalty programme, earlier cost analysis would have led to its elimination from the list. As this benefit has such a high value for the customer, it should be analysed in more detail to ascertain whether this investment should be made and what are the options for covering the cost. The idea is to think more in terms of 'What *should* I give the customer?' than 'What *could* I give the customer?'

## Considering cost, feasibility and competence

The cost of an individual benefit does not have to be covered by the benefit itself. Rather, the overall cost of the entire programme should be covered from different sources. Furthermore, not all benefits need to be offered free of charge to the members. A benefit that has an extremely high value often brings with it a certain willingness to pay. In such a case, this benefit can be offered exclusively to members at a low and competitive rate. Also, in the sense of a mixed calculation, revenues generated from some benefits can be used to cover their own cost and at least part of the cost of non-revenue-producing benefits. Do not forget that ultimately, you are designing a customer loyalty programme that, through its retention effect,

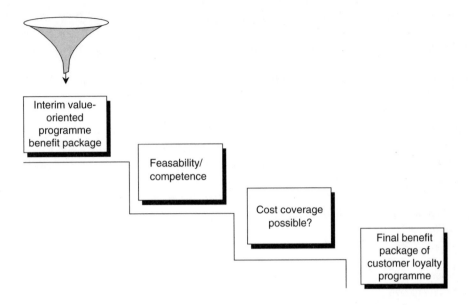

**Figure 9.11**    The next steps towards the final benefit package

will lead to higher revenues from these specially treated and satisfied customers, eventually leading to higher profits for the company (we will discuss these financial aspects in more detail in Chapter 11).

Feasibility and competence are other aspects that need to be considered at this point. Just as a typical customer will critically compare the different product alternatives available, a potential member will analyse every benefit they are offered through a loyalty programme membership. The member will soon realize if a company offers benefits for which it does not necessarily have the competence. For example, why would a publishing house have the competence to offer its members an adventure vacation? Or why would a TV station be competent to offer a credit card? To avoid such a problem and the related loss of credibility, you should offer a certain number of product-related benefits and find external partners to co-operate with on non-product-related benefits.

## Product-related benefits

Obviously, offering product-related benefits should be, in principle, the core of your benefit package, as you are trying to build a relationship between your customers and your product(s). However, there are also other advantages:

- As the customers are familiar with the products, they will better understand product-related benefits.
- The value of such benefits is recognized more quickly than the value of non-product-related and possibly unknown benefits.
- Because these benefits are related to the company's core competences, customers will also see that it has the competence to provide these benefits.

- Because of the closeness to the company's core business, these benefits can be offered at a lower cost due to experience, economies of scale or better use of capacities than benefits that are further away from the company's products and require additional expertise or outside help.
- Finally, these benefits are also easier to offer, as the company has experience in this area, the employees are trained in the product and so forth.

Nevertheless, non-product-related additional benefits have proven ideal to supplement the benefit package of the customer loyalty programme. In order to offer such non-product-related benefits, the best solution is to co-operate with external partners such as hotels, airlines or service companies. Table 9.3 shows a list of potential co-operation partners. In this way, non-product-related benefits can be offered that widen the loyalty programme's portfolio and add to its overall attractiveness, and the competence problem can be overcome.

**Table 9.3**    Selection of the most attractive co-operation partners for customer loyalty programmes

---

- health clubs and other sports facilities
- dancing schools
- discotheques and night-time clubs
- organizers of cultural events such as musicals, rock concerts, open air concerts, theatre performances, classical concerts
- cinemas
- bars and restaurants
- party service and catering companies
- companies providing seminar and training services
- health resorts
- car rental companies
- airlines
- hotel and motel chains
- telephone service providers
- express and other special delivery services
- providers of various business services
- publishers of newspapers, magazines, books and so on
- amusement parks
- insurance companies

---

*Source:* Adapted from Westphalen & Partner (1993).

However, not only the loyalty programme would be interested in such co-operation. As soon as loyalty programmes have been launched successfully, they become attractive not only to the public, but also to the business community. Loyalty programmes are sought-after co-operation partners for all those businesses which want to expand their sales potential by selecting clearly defined customer groups such as the members of a customer loyalty programme. Through one co-operation agreement with a customer loyalty programme, the external partner could gain access to thousands and sometimes hundreds of thousands of potential customers. This must, however, be controlled by the programme management. In no way can the external partner use the programme for active selling. This would quickly be followed by a backlash and alienate the customer.

Two points must be borne in mind, however. One point is that the co-operation partners must fit well with the overall image and quality of the sponsor company and its customer loyalty programme. For example, a manufacturer of luxury cars should not co-operate with a no-frills airline or a motel chain. The risk is too great that such co-operation would negate and detract from the loyalty programme's general image. The second point is that the members should not be bombarded with constant sales pitches from the co-operation partners. These should not be allowed to approach members directly with product offers. All communication and activities must be controlled by the loyalty programme. The partners' products can be offered in the loyalty programme magazine, in the usual loyalty programme mailings, or simply added to the loyalty programme benefit list.

## Loyalty programme benefits need constant updating

You must recognize that a customer loyalty programme, just like any other product, has a life cycle, and thus develops its own dynamics. Basically, this means that a customer loyalty programme concept is never completely finalized, but must be continuously checked and updated. In order to keep meeting the target groups' needs, a customer loyalty programme must grow with the dynamics of those target groups and its chosen segments. Through regular, small-scale customer surveys, changes in demand and value perception can be detected and assessed. This will help the customer loyalty programme to keep abreast of the market. In the mass of loyalty programmes in the market today that offer mediocre benefits with little uniqueness and value, marketers responsible for loyalty schemes in their company should strive not only to develop, but also to maintain a programme that has the winning edge.

If the three-step filtering process described above leads to a group of top value drivers consisting of several benefits, they should not be offered all at once. Instead, some of these benefits should be used at a later point, maybe after a year or so, for a loyalty programme 'facelift'. This ensures an increase in value, and is a demonstration of the loyalty programme's progress. It is important to show the members that the loyalty programme is eager not only to maintain a high level of performance, but also constantly to improve. In turn, if the loyalty programme is continuously developing, it stays alive in the members' minds, further communication opportunities are created, and its long-term attractiveness is guaranteed. Ideally, you include the members very intensively in this process, as they are an excellent source of new ideas for benefits.

Obviously, this need for dynamic development challenges management's imagination, since they have to develop new, valuable benefits all the time. Equally, this shows the similarity of loyalty programme and product management. In product management, you also have to find answers to questions such as: 'What should the next product generation look like?' or 'How can we further develop and diversify the product line?'

The need for regular updating of the customer loyalty programme is also demonstrated by research that shows that the interest in specific loyalty programmes decreases after three to four years (Zorn, 1991, p.15). In order for the loyalty programme to lengthen membership or even reach the ultimate goal of lifetime membership, the members must continually be offered enticing new assets. Despite the need for dynamic development, the loyalty programme's portfolio should include a few benefits which are offered regularly. These benefits should preferably come from the product-related area. Such a group of core benefits will maintain a constant perception of the customer loyalty programme over time, and will strengthen the link between the members and the products that the loyalty programme supports.

Another possible way to secure continual improvement is to offer benefits for a limited period only. In this way, members are moved to action, communication opportunities are created, and the loyalty programme is kept present in the members' minds. Other advantages of offering benefits for a limited period are the possibility of offering seasonal benefits, the chance to offer more costly benefits without being stuck with them for a long time, and the opportunity to offer limited editions, driving up their price, thus increasing cost coverage.

The more homogeneous the target groups are in terms of their interests, and the more potential the core product has to weave an emotional thread around itself, the higher the number of product-related benefits offered should be. Remember that quality is always more important than quantity. A study of customer loyalty programmes in Germany showed that 60 per cent of customer loyalty programmes offer more than a dozen benefits (Holz and Tomczak, 1996, p.39). This large number is not always to be recommended, mostly because of cost and the danger of offering more benefits than people can use. But in many cases this is driven by the fact that customers often look at the number of benefits offered when they judge the quality of a programme, rather than at how many they can realistically use. This is similar to a situation in which people boast about having access to 120 cable channels with their satellite dish, but in reality only watch a handful of them.

In a detailed analysis looking at which kind of benefits customer loyalty programmes offer, results showed that nearly 80 per cent of loyalty programmes offered benefits aimed at giving extra information through telephone consultation and so on. The data further revealed that between 40 and 50 per cent of customer loyalty programmes offered special products or accessories exclusively to loyalty programme members, or discounts and special prices for leisure-oriented benefits. A last group of benefits offered by between 25 and 35 per cent of customer loyalty programmes consisted of more business-oriented benefits and special events, seminars and so on (Kirstges, 1995, p.11).

## Estimation of future purchasing behaviour

Another important aspect that should be included in the customer survey in Step 3 is an estimation of members' future purchasing behaviour. This can be done by first asking the interviewees to indicate their current spending level on specific products or product groups for the sponsor's products, and also for competitors' products. The sum of these expenditures shows what the interviewee is currently 'worth'. Then, after the interviewees have evaluated the benefits, have indicated which benefits are valuable to them and have been informed of the customer loyalty programme concept and what it could offer, they are asked to estimate how much of their current expenditure on competitors' products they would shift to the sponsoring company if the customer loyalty programme offered the most valuable benefits from their point of view. If the interview is computer-programmed, the answers to the current spending questions can be shown on-screen to help the participant to answer the spending transfer questions. From the amount of expenditure shifted and an estimate of possible additional purchases, the monetary effect on the bottom line and estimates of market share changes can be calculated. Of course, these results have to be interpreted with care because the stated change in purchasing behaviour and the actual changes usually differ. Yet the data gives you a rough idea of the sales increase you can expect on an individual and a more cumulative level, and of whether the customer loyalty programme will pay off through the degree of retention it brings about.

Let us now look at two examples to show how this benefit evaluation system works in practice: one example is from the retail industry and one from the automotive industry. The two companies have been given anonymity through the use of pseudonyms.

## EXAMPLE 1: RETAIL INDUSTRY – QUICKSELL

The retail company in this example was a strongly diversified regional player, covering approximately 10 per cent of the UK. We will call it Quicksell. Quicksell's strongest and by far its biggest and best-known division, accounting for 75 per cent of its revenue, consists of its Home Centre stores, which offer quality products at above average prices. One of its strongest competitive advantages comes from its well-trained employees,who provide a competent and well-regarded service to the customers. The second division is a chain of car service stations providing general repairs, brake, exhaust, battery and oil services for all major car brands. The third division has dozens of fully automated car wash facilities across the region. Both car-oriented divisions offer top-quality service at reasonable but not low-end prices. Finally, Quicksell's new environmental division offers various services targeting the residential sector. This division is less than a year old, and is still in its start-up phase. Some of its services include: special waste disposal for oil or paint, alternative energy sources consulting (for example, solar energy) and installation of rainwater collection systems that prepare rainwater for domestic use.

Quicksell was facing increasing competition from several low-price hardware and do-it-yourself chains and from major car service chains with larger nationwide networks and more competitive prices. Although there was a strong customer base that deliberately shopped at Quicksell because of the guaranteed quality of the products and the excellent service, an increasing number of customers seemed to transfer at least part of their business to the competition. Therefore, managers decided to develop a customer loyalty programme that would have two primary goals:

- to increase customer loyalty and keep or win 100 per cent of the sales of their customers in each division
- to increase the volume of crossover sales between the different divisions.

Primary target groups consisted of the current customers, especially from the Home Centre and the car service area. A well-maintained customer database was available in the latter area.

The first step consisted of assembling a project team that was made up of five people, one each from the finance department, the marketing department and the management of the three business areas (the two car divisions are considered one business area). The team started with a detailed analysis of loyalty programmes in the retail industry around Europe, but also looked at other industries in the UK. They consulted their service employees, who have constant contact with the customers, to gain a perspective of what they thought was important from the customers' point of view. The result was a long list of benefits that the team considered worth analysing in more detail. This list included product-related benefits from all four business units of Quicksell in order to increase customer awareness of these divisions and to make sure that all were included in the concept. A selective list is shown in Table 9.4. Note the dominance of product-related benefits, which is very consistent with the loyalty programme goals.

**Table 9.4**   List of potential benefits for Quicksell programme

| Home Centre | Car repair | Car wash | Environmental | Overall |
|---|---|---|---|---|
| • Special product offers | • Special car-related seminars | • Free wash after 10 visits | • Special environmentally friendly products | • Pre-paid telephone card |
| • Individual consultation appointments | • Car pick-up and delivery | • Free upgrade to best wax category | • Environmental seminars | • Customer magazine |
| • Children's corner | • Automatic use of premium oil for oil change | | • Environmental consulting | • Extended warranty |
| • Easier credit approval | | | • Development of waste reduction programmes for small businesses | • Birthday present |
| • Order by telephone | | | | • Payment by debit transaction |
| • Special home improvement seminars | | | | |
| • Rental of travel equipment | | | | |
| • Early entry to special events | | | | |
| • Test purchases | | | | |
| • Home delivery service for purchases over £50 | | | | |

After explaining the reasons for the survey, the idea behind a customer loyalty programme and how the customer would benefit from it, 30 customers were asked to evaluate these benefits on a five-point scale, as described above. The results of this evaluation showed that there were a handful of benefits that clearly seemed to be very interesting for the customers. The top group with average ratings of 4.1 and higher is well separated from the rest, which start at 3.5. It was decided to include the ten highest-rated benefits in the third step of the conception process, the large-scale customer study. The ratings for these benefits from the second step are shown in Figure 9.12.

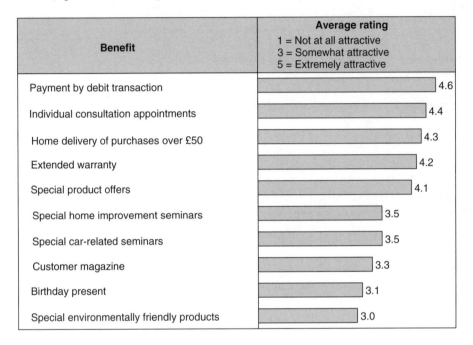

**Figure 9.12** Top ten pre-study benefit ratings – Quicksell

The interviewees were further asked to enter benefits that were not included on the list but that they found interesting or that they knew from other loyalty programmes. From this input an additional two benefits were included in Step 3: early entry on clearance sale opening days, and special ticket prices for local attractions such as visiting circuses or nearby fun parks. Another factor was also added: the membership fee. The different options considered were: no membership fee, £10 joining fee, £20 joining fee or £5 annual fee. It was also decided to put the home improvement and car seminars together into one group, as this would later broaden the spectrum of possible themes and interested members, rather than being too focused. Table 9.4 shows the remaining benefits and their description.

**Table 9.5** Remaining 13 benefits for Step 3 – Quicksell

---

**Customer magazine:** This quarterly magazine is exclusively for our members, and will cover topics related to the Home Centre area, home and car improvement, product information and so on. It will also include several pages for your comments, a section where you can advertise second-hand items for sale, and a children's page.

| | |
|---|---|
| **Birthday present:** | On this special day, we will send you a little surprise. |
| **Special environmentally friendly offers:** | We will present products that have environmental features exclusively to members on a regular basis at very competitive prices. |
| **Early entry:** | Twice a year, on the first day of our summer and winter sales, we will open our doors to our members one hour early. |
| **Special tickets:** | Our members will be able to purchase tickets for all sorts of local events and attractions at a discounted price. |
| **Membership fee:** | No fee/£10 joining fee/£20 joining fee, £5 annual fee. |
| **Payment with debit transaction:** | Purchases can be made with your debit/cashpoint card, and the money will be taken directly from your bank account (no credit approval from Quicksell is necessary). |
| **Individual consultation:** | An appointment can be made with a sales consultant from the relevant department. |
| **Home delivery for purchases over £50:** | If you purchase goods for over £50, if you wish, they will be delivered to your home free of charge within six hours during regular business hours. |
| **Extended warranty:** | On all products with a manufacturer's guarantee, we will give an extra six-month warranty. |
| **Special product offers:** | Every quarter, you will be offered products at competitive prices from various areas of interest that you normally cannot obtain at our stores. |
| **Special home improvement/ car care seminars:** | We will offer seminars to our members on a regular basis covering subjects such as 'electrical wiring', 'window and door insulation', 'winterizing your car' and 'easy do-it-yourself car repairs'. They are free of charge, but places will be limited. |

Finally, in Step 3, 600 people were interviewed, 450 current customers and 150 non-Quicksell customers. Using the conjoint measurement approach, interviewees were asked to evaluate different loyalty programme concepts that included the remaining benefits. From these evaluations, the values of the different benefits were calculated, exposing a very clear picture of what the real value drivers were. The values of the benefits also reflect their relative importance. 'Membership fee' obviously has a negative value, but in order to be able to compare it with the other benefits, the minus symbol ('–') is only indicated in brackets. The importance or value of the factors is shown in Figure 9.13.

The results show that there are two factors that are extremely important for the interviewees: free home delivery for purchases of £50 or more, and the individual consultation appointments. These are the real value drivers. Furthermore, the membership fee is important, which means that the potential members do care about how much the membership is going to cost. We will take a closer look at this factor below. In a second group, four other benefits of higher value come together (payment with debit transaction, extended warranty,

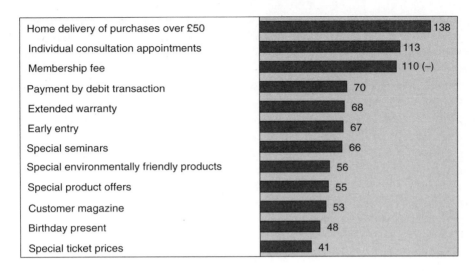

**Figure 9.13**   Importance of remaining benefits – Quicksell

early entry and special seminars), although they are not as important as the top two. The remaining factors are all less valuable compared to the others.

Let us return to the membership fee. Asking for a membership fee has various advantages, and one major and very obvious disadvantage: members would have to pay for their membership, which nobody really likes (we will discuss this aspect further in Chapter 10). Figure 9.14 shows that the members do prefer not to have a membership fee (value of 0), which is obvious. The value is reduced for the various other alternatives. The most important and most interesting result is that the value curve is very flat between a £10 joining fee (value of –55) and an annual fee of £5 (value of –62), indicating that both options are on a similar level for the interviewees. A joining fee of £20 has the lowest value (value of –110), well below the other alternatives.

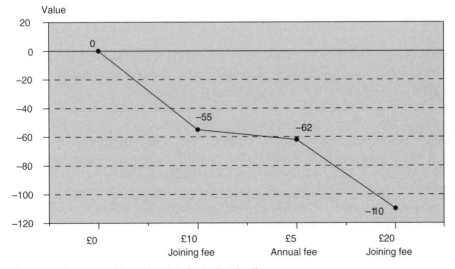

**Figure 9.14**   Value curve of 'membership fee' – Quicksell

The team then took a closer look at what the cost of the different benefits was, and which could be provided with and without outside help. It was finally decided to offer the individual consultation appointments and free delivery for purchases over £50. The staff were already well trained and service-oriented, so these individual consultation appointments were not difficult to implement. Free delivery could be carried out by the current van fleet of the Home Centre division, which had free capacity, especially after 11 a.m. when all the new stock for the day had been picked up and delivered to the different stores. It was further decided to charge a joining fee of £10, which would be communicated as necessary to cover the cost of the application processing, the membership card and so on. Also, a one-time payment such as a joining fee would require much less effort, administrative duties and cost than would be involved in making sure that all members renewed their membership and paid the fee each year, as would have been the case with an annual fee. The extended warranty was also added to the programme, as Quicksell mainly sold quality products and did not expect a large volume of claims from this warranty, so it would cost very little. Also special seminars would be offered once a month, partly in co-operation with other businesses such as road service companies and hardware producers. These seminars would include the Home Centre, the car care and the environmental division. It was also decided to offer payment by debit card at a later time, because Quicksell was already looking into the possibility of accepting credit cards and would need to acquire the necessary technology in any case, and this benefit was an ideal way of giving the loyalty programme a value boost after a year or so. Early entry to sales was dropped, as the management was reluctant to see non-members left waiting because they had arrived too early. Finally, Quicksell decided to publish a quarterly magazine even though its value was not that high from the customers' perspective, mostly to use it for cross-divisional promotions by running features from all areas.

In a section of the interview, the interviewees had also been asked to estimate their current expenditures in each of the four divisions at Quicksell and elsewhere, and how they would change their buying habits if they were a member of the customer loyalty programme. From this data, estimates were made of how the sales of loyalty programme members would go up. The management also gained a better idea of how strong the cross-selling effects were, and how they could be increased.

Following this thorough analysis, the customer loyalty programme was introduced to the public nine months after the project had started. The purchase data was collected on presentation of the membership number at the point of payment, and was fed into a database. The database was used to identify products, product groups or services that specific customers bought more regularly than others in all four divisions. This data was used to optimize the stores' product range and to send special mailings to selected segments. These activities created significant extra store traffic in the Home Centres, and a moderate increase in visits in the two car divisions. Cross-selling effects were increased by more than 10 per cent. One of the main goals of loyalty programme management now is to keep these positive numbers at their current level, or even to increase them in the subsequent years of the loyalty programme's life. A good start does not mean that it will continue the same way. Effects such as getting used to the advantages of membership and competitors' loyalty programmes are a constant challenge for the loyalty programme management. It is difficult but important to improve the concept continually and use the database for even more detailed analysis of purchasing behaviour, changes in these patterns and customized product offers and direct mailings.

## EXAMPLE 2: CAR MANUFACTURER – SMOOTH DRIVE

Smoothdrive is a major player in the international luxury car industry. This segment has been facing increasing competition over the last decade as more and more car manufacturers from the USA, Japan, Germany, the UK and other European countries have introduced models aimed at this relatively small group of customers. Therefore, Smoothdrive decided to develop a customer loyalty programme with two primary goals:

- to increase customer loyalty (including encouraging current Smoothdrive owners to consider a smaller Smoothdrive car as their second or third car)
- to develop a solid database, containing all the necessary personal and purchasing data in enough detail for future database marketing activities.

A customer loyalty programme should be set up in such a way that internationalization is possible without having to reorganize the database or the loyalty programme infrastructure in general. It was clear, however, that the benefits offered could and probably would have to differ from country to country. As a start, it was decided to analyse Smoothdrive's home market (which is also its main market) in order to develop a flexible programme based on the results, and then consider the next steps towards internationalization.

Because one of the main goals was data collection for the database, it was obvious that the loyalty programme had to include a credit card. This would have to be done in co-operation with one of the major credit card companies: American Express, MasterCard, Visa or Diners. All four were contacted, and negotiations on alternative ways to co-operate were conducted. The final decision on which credit card company to co-operate with was not based on the individual conditions offered. Instead, the credit card brand was included in the customer survey to find out which credit card company Smoothdrive drivers preferred. Furthermore, an analysis was carried out to determine which credit card brand best complemented the Smoothdrive brand.

While these contacts were being made, a customer survey was planned. The first step of the project was again an internal brainstorming session to collect a list of potential benefits. This brainstorming session was preceded by a world-wide analysis of current loyalty programmes and co-branded credit cards on the market, not only for luxury car makers, but also for other car manufacturers. The list of potential benefits resulting from this first step was then evaluated in two focus groups consisting of current Smoothdrive customers, in order to eliminate uninteresting benefits and add new benefits from the customers' point of view. The third step consisted of a large-scale customer study of 260 current Smoothdrive owners. The interview concentrated on two different areas:

1 Interviewees' current credit card behaviour was analysed in great detail. This included questions such as number and brand of currently used credit cards, annual revenue with each card, and the financial background of the household. Other aspects covered were the international mobility of the interviewees, their mobile phone usage and the possession of other cards such as telephone, store or gas cards.

2 The remaining benefits were evaluated using the conjoint measurement approach. The list of tested benefits included: potential loyalty programme benefits provided by Smoothdrive, potential loyalty programme benefits provided by the dealers, potential loyalty programme benefits provided by external partners, the credit card brand and the

annual credit card fee. Furthermore, some benefits such as a 24-hour breakdown service were analysed in greater detail by reducing them to smaller categories and measuring the value of their different components in additional questions with constant sum scales. For instance, the 24-hour breakdown service was split into free road service, free towing in case of a breakdown, free hotel accommodation in case of necessary repairs, and a free replacement car if repairs were needed.

This procedure resulted in a clear assessment of the value of every benefit included in Step 3. These values were then fed into a cost–value matrix, which combined the value of the different benefits and their cost. Figure 9.15 shows a simplified version of the results from the Smoothdrive case. The privileged dealership service, the breakdown service, the service delivery and pick-up service (if your car is due for a regular check-up, the dealer picks up the car and delivers it back after the car has been serviced, saving you the trouble of driving to the dealer and finding a way to get back home or to your next destination from there) are the only three benefits in the ideal quadrant I. They have a high value for the customer, and can be provided at a low cost. Quadrant II contains four benefits that could be provided at a low cost but do not have a high value for the customer. Therefore, these benefits should only be offered in addition to the value drivers, but never simply because of their low cost. Benefits from quadrant III are no longer considered. They combine low value with high cost – the worst possible combination. Finally, the benefits from quadrant IV were analysed in more detail in order to find out which possibilities for cost coverage exist. The high value of these benefits makes them very attractive for the loyalty programme.

Further results from this three-step approach included a distinct preference for MasterCard or Visa as the credit card brand, and a willingness to pay an above-average annual fee for the credit card. Different design alternatives and names for the card had also been tested (for example, Smoothdrive Gold Card v. Smoothdrive Preferred Customer Card).

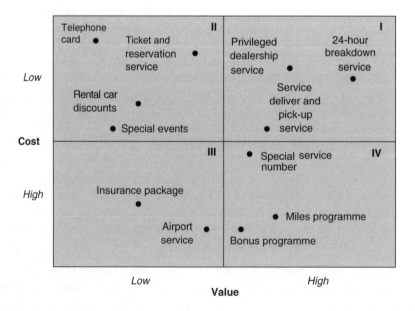

**Figure 9.15**    Cost–value matrix for Smoothdrive

Eventually, it was decided to introduce the loyalty programme as the 'Smoothdrive Gold Programme'. It included a 24-hour breakdown service, the privileged dealership service (such as a free car wash after servicing the car, or a rental service for ski boxes and bike racks), the service delivery and pick-up service, the ticket and reservation service, special rental car discounts and a special bonus programme (for example, bonus points can be accumulated through service expenses and so on that can then be exchanged for special products such as limited-edition products, golf equipment and Smoothdrive extras). The credit card would be offered as a MasterCard or Visa in order to achieve the highest possible world-wide acceptance and thus to be able to gather as much purchasing information as possible for the database while making the internationalization of the programme easier. The annual fee was set at about 50 per cent above the current average fee for MasterCard and Visa in the country analysed. In order to penetrate the target group sufficiently (the current credit card usage was already very high), it was decided to offer special promotions such as 'first year no annual fee' during the introductory phase.

## SUMMARY

Identifying the right benefits is the most important part of the customer loyalty programme concept. If the perceived value of the benefits is not high, loyalty programme membership is not sufficiently interesting and the loyalty programme will fail. To find the right combination of hard and soft benefits, a value-oriented approach is necessary. This approach consists of three steps. In the first step, a list of potential benefits is brainstormed. The only limit to creating interesting benefits is the imagination of the project team. The second step is a small-scale pre-study which aims to filter out the most and the least interesting benefits from this list by asking a small sample to rate the different benefits. In this phase, the interviewees are also asked to add new ideas of their own. Some of these new ideas as well as the best-rated benefits enter Step 3, the large-scale survey. Here, a sample of at least 250 people is interviewed. Using methods such as ranking scales, constant sum scales or the more sophisticated and very precise conjoint measurement, the value of the remaining benefits is measured. In some business-to-business markets, Step 3 can be left out.

The result of this three-step approach is that the long list of benefits from Step 1 is split into three groups: the top value drivers, benefits with a certain value, and benefits with no value from the customers' point of view. The final loyalty programme benefits should be chosen out of the first two groups after taking into consideration factors such as cost, practicality and competence. These aspects should not be considered before this stage, as the value to customer is what counts. If the value of a benefit is extremely high, for example, high cost should not be an early knock-out criterion. There are many ways to cover the cost of such benefits. Competence problems can be overcome by co-operating with external partners, although these have to be chosen with care. Although a customer loyalty programme should offer several product-related benefits, external partners offer the opportunity to expand the loyalty programme benefit portfolio and increase its attractiveness.

A loyalty programme also has a life cycle and must be constantly improved and further developed. Therefore, you should keep some of the top value drivers for future 'facelifts', rather than offering all of them from the beginning. Such 'facelifts' are necessary to keep the loyalty programme dynamic, to constantly improve it, and to make sure it does not lose its attractiveness.

# 10 Pricing for customer loyalty

### With Julia Goldenbaum

As mentioned in the previous chapter, the benefits bundle can be made up of financial (hard) and non-financial (soft) benefits. We showed a process enabling you to identify the most attractive and most valuable benefits from the pool of options. We also argued that the soft benefits are the primary long-term loyalty drivers. The danger is that many companies will focus too much on the hard benefits, as giving discounts is easy to do and always attractive for the customer. However, giving discounts is also one of the biggest profit killers.

## Giving discounts reduces loyalty programmes to price cuts

Giving discounts means giving away contribution. You can only make up for that by increasing sales.

Let us look at the example of a retailer shown in Figure 10.1. The retailer gives a 10 per cent discount to the members of its loyalty programme. Let us assume that the original revenue of member John Doe was £100 and the retailer's margin is 45 per cent, or in this case £45. The discount reduces each by 10 per cent, or in this case £10, so revenue is only £90 and

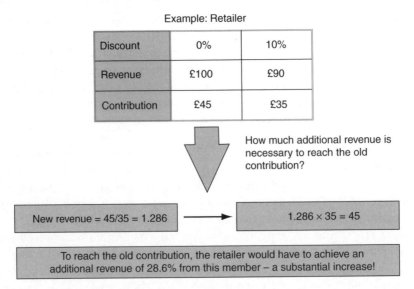

Example: Retailer

| Discount | 0% | 10% |
|---|---|---|
| Revenue | £100 | £90 |
| Contribution | £45 | £35 |

How much additional revenue is necessary to reach the old contribution?

New revenue = 45/35 = 1.286 → 1.286 × 35 = 45

To reach the old contribution, the retailer would have to achieve an additional revenue of 28.6% from this member – a substantial increase!

**Figure 10.1** Additional revenue necessary to compensate for discount

the contribution goes down to £35. In order to reach the same contribution as before, the retailer would have to increase revenue with John Doe by 28.6 per cent. (The new revenue is calculated by dividing the target contribution by the new contribution, in this case £45 divided by £35. The result shows the overall revenue necessary to achieve the old contribution. A figure above 1.0 means that revenue has to be increased, a figure below 1.0 means that revenue may be reduced.) This 28.6 per cent of additional sales are additional sales without the 10 per cent discount. If the 10 per cent discount was given on the new sales too, the 28.6 per cent would go up to around one-third of the original revenue. In addition, with a revenue increase of 28.6 per cent, you have only *made up* for the discount. You have not *increased* contribution or considered the overall cost of running and administrating the programme.

With how many of your customers do you think such a significant increase in sales is achievable? The necessary sales increase changes, of course, if you alter either the margin or the discount in the equation. But the message remains the same: *discounts must be compensated for by a substantial increase in sales*. We encourage you to do this simple calculation for your own company – you will certainly be surprised.

## Sophisticated pricing strategies for loyalty

This calculation is not meant to imply that discounts should not be offered in general. However, it does mean that simple discounting cannot be the solution. It attracts bargain hunters and does anything but build long-term loyalty. If you want to offer better prices to your members, then make use of one of the several sophisticated pricing strategies available that are much better suited for loyalty which we will introduce in this chapter:

- multi-step quantity discounts
- multi-dimensional pricing schemes
- time- and loyalty-based pricing
- multi-product pricing
- multi-person discounts
- price guarantees
- contracts and exclusivity agreements.

These strategies have several aspects in common:

- Customers are not simply given discounts, they have to earn them.
- Customers have to take the first step, and are then rewarded with discounts. These discounts are communicated in advance, however, so that the customers can calculate what discounts they will qualify for.
- A win–win situation is created – both the company and the customers benefit.
- They are easy to understand, and fair.

### MULTI-STEP QUANTITY DISCOUNTS

Multi-step quantity discounts (also called incremental discounts) offer increasing discounts at higher purchase levels. For instance, a manufacturer of industrial light bulbs, which are normally sold at £10 per unit, gives the following discount pricing schedule based on annual sales: the first 100 units are not discounted, units 101 to 200 are discounted at 5 per cent, units 201 to 300 at 10 per cent, and all units over 300 at 20 per cent. As the purchased quantity increases, the discount it also increased progressively. The effect of such a multi-step discount programme is that it encourages increased purchases, as the next discount level is easily attainable. This may lead to a consolidation of the customer's overall purchasing activity, normally divided among several suppliers, to one supplier. The smaller the differences between the non-price characteristics of the alternative products, the more important this effect.

The key advantage is that the average discount given is much lower than the current discount. Consider, for example, the purchase of 250 units. The average discount is only 4 per cent. At the same time, in this particular case a competitor can only break into the market by offering discounts greater than 10 per cent. This discount scheme is a win–win situation for both supplier and customer. The customer receives high discounts (up to 20 per cent), and the supplier is guaranteed a certain purchase level in return.

## MULTI-DIMENSIONAL PRICING SCHEMES

Multi-dimensional pricing schemes use two or more pricing dimensions. One example is the two-part tariff, a mixture of an up-front flat payment and subsequent discounts spread out over a fixed period of time. The best-known example of this is the BahnCard from Deutsche Bahn AG (the German national railroad), which has been a huge success for many years. At the time of introduction, the price for a train ticket was 24 pfennigs per kilometre. Most customers compared this with the approximately 15 pfennigs per kilometre that it would cost to drive by car, and would typically choose the car as their preferred mode of transportation. The BahnCard was introduced for a flat fee of €110, which earns the user the right for a 50 per cent discount on all train tickets for one year. Subsequently, the price per kilometre is reduced to 12 pfennigs. The break-even point (total savings = €110 card fee) is at 1,833 kilometres (see Figure 10.2). However, the more the card is used, the lower the cost per kilometre becomes, as the €110 card fee is distributed over more kilometres. Once spent, the €110 for the card are sunk cost, and there is a strong incentive to maximize its use as this means saving

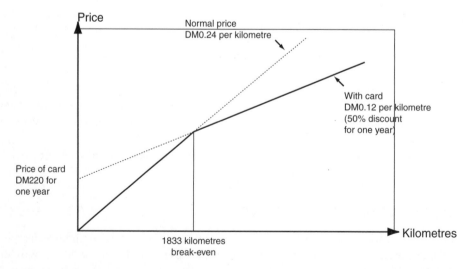

**Figure 10.2**   BahnCard (railcard) – two-part tariff

more money. The BahnCard is still a huge success for Deutsche Bahn AG, and has significantly increased its revenues and profits, as well as dramatically broadening its customer base. Today, airlines and telecom companies are using similar two-part tariff pricing schemes to increase the loyalty of their customers. Two-part tariffs are commonly used with cell phone packages, combining different monthly rates with different peak/off-peak minute rates and free minutes.

From a competitive perspective, the level of competition is shifted from the individual transaction (one trip) to competition between systems (rail, car or airline). Thus, the competition is altered radically, creating an advantage for the company which has a generally superior system even though it may be weaker in individual components.

Another example is the seller of industrial gas, a commodity, that introduced a two-dimensional pricing scheme, replacing the usual scheme in the industry which was purely based on price per kilogram. Price wars were common in this industry, as the price per kilogram was easy to compare and the product itself offered few opportunities for differentiation. The new pricing scheme had a lower price per kilogram, but also charged rent for the cylinders the gas was sold in (see Figure 10.3). The loyalty effect was huge, as heavy users ended up paying much less for the gas than low users, as Table 10.1 shows.

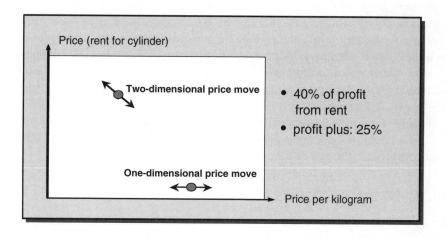

**Figure 10.3**    Industrial gas – from one-dimensional to two-dimensional pricing

**Table 10.1**    Price comparison for different segments with a two-dimensional pricing scheme

| Usage in days | Actual price for 50 litres of gas |
| --- | --- |
| 1 | €10.25 |
| 25 | €16.25 |
| 50 | €22.25 |
| 100 | €35.00 |

*Assumption:* Rent for cylinders €0.25 per day, and price for 50 litres of gas €10.

## TIME- AND LOYALTY-BASED PRICING

Time- and loyalty-based pricing differentiates discounts over time or the length of a contract. A good example is the price difference per edition a magazine subscriber receives for a one-year versus a three-year subscription. Bell South's President's Club allows cellular phone customers to collect points based upon the telephone bill, the services they use (for example, a mailbox), as well as the length of their customer relationship with Bell South. The points may then be redeemed for a variety of goods and services. Again, instead of giving away discounts, these pricing schemes offer incentives for increased and longer usage of existing services or adding new services to an account. The more the services are used, the greater the customer benefit. Similar systems are in place in frequent flyer programmes. Time- and loyalty-based pricing is ideal for relationships between a company and a customer that are based on contracts, as the length of relationship can be measured and discounts be determined. Also regular payments maintain cash flow to amortize discounts.

## MULTI-PRODUCT PRICING

With multi-product pricing, the strongly discounted sale of the main product is linked to a longer-term agreement to purchase complementary products or services exclusively from that supplier, such as buying a copier at a discount and agreeing to purchase toner cartridges, paper and services in return (tie-in sales). In some cases, the main product is even sold as a loss leader. This method ensures a regular stream of income to offset the discounted product, and is an effective tool to ward off potential low-price, unbranded competition because the customer is tied to the long-term agreement. The loyalty effect is very strong, although additional action will be required at the end of the agreement.

Another form of multi-product pricing is price/product bundling, which combines products and services that are generally sold separately. The bundle is sold at a significant discount compared to the prices for the individual products.

## MULTI-PERSON DISCOUNTS

Multi-person discounts offer the benefit not to the main buyer, but to an additional buyer if their purchases are tied together. Good examples are the 'partner flies/rides free programme' from Southwest Airlines and Greyhound and the Friends and Family Program from MCI. Here, the loyalty programmes are aimed at the additional participants as well as the main purchaser. They exploit different price sensitivities between those purchasers, and create a price advantage for the entire group. This scheme is generally used for revenue maximization, and is ideal for companies/industries with low variable costs and high fixed costs. Many conference organizers take advantage of this method, and offer 'if three attendees from one company pay full price, the fourth is free'.

## PRICE GUARANTEES

Price guarantees are another underused pricing mechanism to build loyalty. Stores such as Circuit City or LensCrafters use it as a significant part of their marketing communication. Here, the company will pay the customer the difference if a product bought in their store is found at a lower price elsewhere.

## CONTRACTS AND EXCLUSIVITY AGREEMENTS

Contracts and exclusivity agreements are, of course, another form of loyalty scheme. One example is the exclusivity agreement between airlines and Boeing/Airbus. Such contracts could also include regular price reviews or guarantee a price development that is linked to the development of significant indices like the inflation rate, which assures a constant relative price and a foreseeable price development.

While these pricing strategies are smart techniques to build fences against competitors, they are not trivial to implement. Precise analysis is necessary. A decision support model must be developed which calculates price response functions, the profit and revenue-maximizing price, and simulates alternative discount levels. But rather than cutting into profits by simply discounting, this thorough preparation will be rewarded with higher profit and competitiveness. A win–win situation is created: the customers as well as the company will benefit. For more information on pricing strategies, please refer to Dolan and Simon (1996), Fuerderer, Hermann and Wuebker (1999) and Butscher and Simon (2001).

The ultimate loyalty-enhancing pricing scheme is, of course, pure individual price customization. The Internet is an ideal technology to make price customization logistically possible at a reasonable cost. Visiting customers are identifiable by IP address or login name, and can be exposed to individualized product and price offers or information. Combining the Internet with modern database technology will provide unbelievable opportunities for shrewd pricers in the future.

## Summary

Rather than simply offering discounts, they should be earned by customers, and given to them as a reward. A win–win situation from which both sides benefit must be created. Several sophisticated pricing strategies are available that do this in an intelligent way (multi-step discounts, multi-dimensional pricing schemes and so on). Precise analysis is necessary to install these strategies in the right way, but the benefits are huge.

# 11 *The financial concept*

Customer loyalty programmes are sophisticated marketing tools, and are not only difficult to set up, but can also be costly. In this chapter we will discuss what costs might arise and what possibilities are available to create loyalty programme-generated revenues that can cover at least part, if not all, of these costs. However, we must point out that creating a self-funding loyalty programme is nearly impossible, as these programmes have limited possibilities to create direct revenues at such a high level.

After selecting the right benefits, putting together a sound financial concept for the loyalty programme is the second most important step. Financial problems are one of the main reasons for the failure of customer loyalty programmes, which shows that this problem has so far not been taken seriously enough.

## The cost of a customer loyalty programme

When contemplating establishing a customer loyalty programme, do not be deluded into thinking that a low-budget programme will work and reach its goals. Starting a customer loyalty programme will always mean entering into a long-term financial commitment. It will take time and money to set up, it will take time and money before membership has reached numbers when economies of scale are effective, and it will take time and money to keep the programme running, constantly updating it and keeping the value high.

Of course, the cost will differ from case to case, depending on the industry, the customer structure, the competitive situation, the set-up of the programme and so on. Most companies are very reluctant to give out financial information on their loyalty programmes, or do not even measure the cost. But on average you can estimate a cost per member per year in the range of £10–30 for end-user loyalty programmes and £50–150 for business-to-business loyalty programmes (Wiencke and Tribian, 1996, p.156; Linke, 1996, p.5; *Ancillary Profits*, 1995, p.1; Barlow, 1992, p.37; various Simon & Kucher projects). In addition, there is the initial cost of developing and establishing the programme, which can easily reach six figures. Subsequently, for extremely large-scale and globally oriented operations, reaching even seven figures is not impossible. This does not include the cost of advertising and promotion of the programme during its launch, and larger investments in the infrastructure such as a modern computer system to run the CRM tools and database.

The main cost factors are:

- the technical, organizational and personnel infrastructure
- the loyalty programme service centre
- the development, storage and shipping of the benefits
- the communication measures
- the initial development and constant improvement of the programme concept.

These figures are certainly high, but should not be discouraging: 'When you apply those kinds of numbers to your customer base you might gasp, but it might not be a question of whether you can afford it. It might actually be a question of whether you can afford to wait any longer' (Barlow, 1992, p.37). But you must consider that in most cases you will focus on specific segments and smaller target groups, which reduces the multiplier. In addition, there are several ways a loyalty programme can create direct or indirect revenues.

A recent study of customer loyalty programmes in Germany showed that 45 per cent of the analysed loyalty programmes financed 76–100 per cent of their cost through revenues of their own (Holz and Tomczak, 1996, p.60). This shows that it is possible to run a loyalty programme without excessive support from the general marketing budget. In some (rare) cases, the loyalty programme even produces a profit (for example, the customer club run by the SWR3 radio station, which is described in more detail in Part III). Let us take a closer look at the various ways a customer loyalty programme can create revenues.

## The bottom-line effect of a customer loyalty programme

It is better to call the cost 'investment', as that describes more accurately what a customer loyalty programme is about: an investment in customer relationships to secure/increase future revenues and profits. A customer loyalty programme aims to increase customer loyalty, thus increasing the revenue and profit made from a member (see Figure 11.1). This bottom-line effect is, of course, the main – indirect – revenue effect. The main problem is that it is difficult to link sales increases directly to loyalty programme activities. Too many other aspects could have played a role too, such as competitive activity, price changes, general economic development. This problem is not new, since marketers often have problems in accurately relating the direct effect of a special promotion or a new advertising campaign to a sales increase without any external effects. However, with a good database that is fed with detailed point-of-sale data, changes can be measured on an individual level. But it will be difficult to isolate this effect fully from other influences such as advertising, promotions and discounts at the points of sale, product improvement, competitors' moves (or the lack of them), media coverage and so on (see also Chapter 18 on success measurement).

Nevertheless, various studies have shown how an increased retention rate can positively influence revenue and profit. Reichheld and Sasser's much quoted *Harvard Business Review* article 'Zero Defections: Quality Comes to Service' is only one of the more prominent

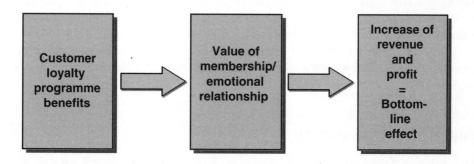

**Figure 11.1**  The bottom-line effect

examples, and shows that a 5 per cent increase in customer loyalty can increase profitability by 28–85 per cent, depending on the industry (Reichheld and Sasser, 1990, pp.55, 110; Reichheld and Shefter, 2000, p.107; see also Dawkins and Reichheld, 1990, p.42). Other sources report an increase in the retention rate of a large newspaper by 5.1 per cent (*Ancillary Profits*, 1995, p.1), 6–9 per cent sales increases for two different major department stores (Barlow, 1992, p.31) and a 15 per cent increase in revenue for users of specific customer cards (Wiencke and Koke, 1994, p.54). It is without doubt that satisfied customers with whom the supplier has a close relationship will stay with the supplier they trust and increase their purchase volume, and will typically be less price-sensitive than others.

Figure 11.2 shows an example of how a loyalty programme can affect the bottom line. By calculating a mathematical example for several customers, the effects that a customer loyalty programme can have become more vivid and understandable.

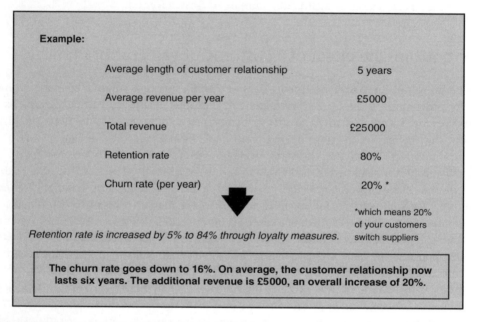

**Example:**

| | |
|---|---|
| Average length of customer relationship | 5 years |
| Average revenue per year | £5000 |
| Total revenue | £25000 |
| Retention rate | 80% |
| Churn rate (per year) | 20% * |

*which means 20% of your customers switch suppliers

*Retention rate is increased by 5% to 84% through loyalty measures.*

The churn rate goes down to 16%. On average, the customer relationship now lasts six years. The additional revenue is £5000, an overall increase of 20%.

**Figure 11.2**    Revenue increase through customer loyalty

A loyalty programme can repay its investment several times over through its indirect bottom-line effect. The time before this effect kicks in depends on the product and the average return of demand. For example, a leather jacket is bought every couple of years, a new paperback book as often as every other week.

Figure 11.3 shows the various possible components of the financial concept of a customer loyalty programme with a focus on the direct revenues which we will now look at in more detail.

## Joining/membership fee

One of the best ways to create guaranteed and measurable revenues is to charge a one-off joining fee and/or an annual membership fee. The joining fee has the advantage of being

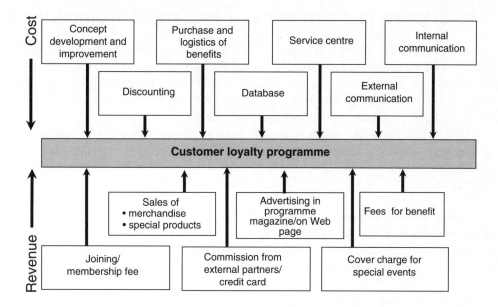

**Figure 11.3**  Financial concept of a customer loyalty programme

justifiable as representing the cost of processing the application, producing the membership card and sending out the welcome package, while keeping to a minimum the financial commitment the interested customers have to make. Also, the loyalty programme will not have to go through the effort of reminding members to renew their membership every year, with the administrative effort that entails. On the other hand, an annual membership fee creates a steadier revenue, and helps to weed out inactive members and keep the database up to date. This issue is closely related to the decision of whether to have an open or limited loyalty programme (see Chapter 8, and especially Table 8.1).

A joining/membership fee gives the customer loyalty programme a certain value, as many customers, although used to 'freebies', perceive things that are for free as being of lesser value than if they come at a cost. The loyalty programme fee should be set according to the financial situation of the target group. The fee to join a kids' loyalty programme would be very low, maybe in the £3–7 range, because children's pocket money is limited (although in most cases the parents cover the fee). The fee for a business-to-business loyalty programme can be £60 or higher. Another factor to consider is the value of the benefit package. The more valuable the benefits are, the more attractive membership becomes, and the higher the membership fee can be.

The majority of consumer-oriented loyalty programmes that have an annual fee charge between £3 and £35 per year, but in the business-to-business area annual membership is traditionally higher, averaging £40–150 per year (the peak being £700) (Kirstges, 1995, p.29, and the author's own research). Which system – free membership, joining fee or annual fee – is best depends on the particular situation, and especially the programme's goals, target groups and value.

When Waldenbooks launched its Preferred Reader programme, over 4.5 million people enrolled during the first year and paid at least $5 (approximately £3) a year to belong. That is at least $20 million (approximately £12 million) worth of customer-volunteered marketing funds (Barlow, 1992, p.33).

## Sales of loyalty programme merchandise/special products

Another possible way to create revenues is to offer exclusively to members a catalogue with special loyalty programme merchandise and special product offers. The merchandise can include everything from traditional baseball caps, T-shirts and coffee mugs to more expensive items such as portable CD players, cellular phones, luggage items and so forth. All these items should display the loyalty programme logo in some form.

In principle, these special products that might be offered exclusively to members could be variations of the sponsoring company's products (for example, a cell phone with a special design, or a tie with a unique look, or a cereal with a special flavour). These special products should:

- fit the general loyalty programme image
- be of good quality, at least as good as your regular products
- be offered at competitive prices, if possible lower than the average retail price
- be marketed exclusively to members.

It does not pay to offer products of lesser quality. If the members are disappointed with a loyalty programme product, this negative perception can easily reflect on the organization's normal products.

## Commission from external partners/credit card

The loyalty programme's members represent an extremely attractive and well-organized target group for many outside companies which may be willing to pay a commission in exchange for being able to offer their products or services to the loyalty programme members. When choosing the external partners for the loyalty programme to co-operate with, the following aspects must be considered:

- The partners must be able to provide the same level of quality as the sponsoring company's products, should help the loyalty programme to achieve its goals, and should complement what the loyalty programme tries to represent. For example, it would be counterproductive for the loyalty programme of an *haute couture* design and fashion company to offer duplicates of similarly positioned brands, such as Dupont or Rolex.

- Contact between the external partner and loyalty programme members must never be direct. The loyalty programme must retain authority over the amount and content of communication between the external partner and members, in order to control excessive and unsuitable offers. Therefore, all offers from external partners should be brought to the members' attention through the loyalty programme media.

- The loyalty programme should not be reduced to a sales frenzy. Careful selection of partners, and when and how often to present the offers (for example, seasonal, or limited for a short period) protects the main product-related benefits from being under-represented: those benefits create the loyalty. Your product – not your partners' offers – should be the centre of attention.

If the loyalty programme offers a credit card, the commission from its use can also create significant revenues. The Porsche Card, for example, has an annual turnover per card of approximately £8000, while the average MasterCard user in Germany has a turnover of only approximately £1500 (Thelen, 1996).

## Advertising in the loyalty programme magazine/on web page

Selling advertising space is another excellent revenue producer. The loyalty programme magazine, the newsletter, the mailings and the loyalty programme's Web page all offer great opportunities to sell advertising space or advertising enclosures. The aspects to consider here are similar to those concerning the selection of external partners. Advertisements have to fit with the loyalty programme's image, and preferably even support it, so their content should be screened to avoid aggressive sales promotions. Furthermore, the advertising space should be limited, to prevent the loyalty programme magazine from turning into a glossy ad collection. Make sure that the ads will not be perceived negatively by the readers (or in the case of a loyalty programme magazine for children, by their parents). Also, the ads should not distract from your own products and related features.

A good example of a well-managed loyalty programme membership list is the Fox Kids loyalty programme. Its list is not officially on the market, but the loyalty programme management is not opposed to working with an advertiser on a mailing, if the offer might add value to the membership (Negus, 1995, p.11).

## Cover charge for special loyalty programme events

If the loyalty programme organizes special events such as loyalty programme tours, loyalty programme meetings, concerts and so on, a cover charge can be requested in most cases. Special prices for tickets to general events (such as Wimbledon) are also perceived as very attractive. In 1991, American Express organized a Frank Sinatra concert in Frankfurt, Germany, exclusively for American Express credit card holders. The price for a ticket was between £20 and £35, and around 7000 tickets were sold in a few weeks. In addition to that, the media coverage of this event was very good, perfectly placing the American Express brand in all major business journals and daily newspapers.

## Fees for loyalty programme benefits

Finally, not all loyalty programme benefits have to be offered free of charge. The higher the perceived value of a benefit, the higher the willingness to pay. Of course, not all benefits with a high value should bear a cost to the member, but certain benefits such as a special breakdown service are not generally expected to be free. Pricing should be competitive compared to comparable offers available in the market.

Covering the cost of the different benefits should be looked at from a loyalty programme perspective, and not a benefit perspective. Revenue-generating benefits can help to cover the cost of non-revenue-generating benefits. The remaining cost is then covered out of the marketing budget Table 11.1 shows a simplified example. The revenue from the loyalty programme merchandise and the loyalty programme trips covers their cost and, in addition, the cost of the birthday presents and part of the cost of the programme service centre. The remainder of the cost has to be covered out of the overall marketing budget.

**Table 11.1**    Cost coverage through mixed calculation

|   |   | Cost | Revenue | Balance |
| --- | --- | --- | --- | --- |
| 1 | Merchandise | 30 000 | 45 000 | 15 000 |
| 2 | Trips | 50 000 | 75 000 | 25 000 |
| 3 | Birthday present | 12 000 | 0 | –12 000 |
| 4 | Service centre | 130 000 | — | –130 000 |
| | **Programme budget** | **222 000** | **120 000** | **–102 000*** |

\* = Sum from overall marketing budget

## Limited number of members

A good way to reduce the cost of a customer loyalty programme is to limit the membership to a specific number of members. Limitations have various advantages:

- With a constant number of members, it is much easier to calculate a fixed budget for a longer period, as costs will only increase slowly and controllably.
- The loyalty programme is forced constantly to control and update its database to eliminate inactive members or members who no longer belong to the target group, in order to make room for new members.
- Such a regularly updated database guarantees that only those customers who are really interested are members. This increases the effectiveness of the loyalty programme's marketing activities and the value of the data in the database.
- A limited number of members increases the attractiveness of the loyalty programme and membership, and enables it to charge higher membership fees (perfect examples of such a mechanism are exclusive golf or country clubs with a waiting list that is years long).
- Highly involved members lead to higher responses to direct marketing activities and increase loyalty programme revenues through higher product sales.

The disadvantages are the following:

- Not all interested members can join, which means that valuable data is excluded from the database.
- Interested customers could be disappointed or even upset by the wait for membership, and might end up boycotting the sponsoring company's products in anger (Butscher, 1995, p.83; Butscher, 1996d, p.40).

## Budget and cost scenarios

All the cost and income information should be collected in a budget spreadsheet, similar to a balance sheet. In order to prevent surprises, it is helpful to go through different cost scenarios and run these through the budget spreadsheet. This process leads to answers to questions such as: 'How would the cost increase if 10 000 instead of the originally planned 5000 members joined during the first year? How high would the necessary investments in the loyalty programme infrastructure be, and how high would the additional revenues be?' or 'What would the effect be if only 2500 members joined? Could the loyalty programme still be successful? What would the cost of the free capacity in the loyalty programme service centre be? Could they be used by other company departments?' The worst-case, most probable-case and best-case scenarios should be included. The answers to these questions will help to set up action plans in the event that one of the scenarios actually occurs. Being prepared for such extreme and unexpected developments will significantly reduce the potential damage.

## Customer loyalty programmes are a strategic necessity

The cost of developing, launching and running a customer loyalty programme should not be seen as a 'cost', but rather as an investment in a marketing tool whose rewards outweigh the cost. The loyalty programme enables better and more targeted communication with customers, feeds the database with detailed and valuable information, and can significantly increase the revenue and profit made for each individual member. It is an investment in a tool that is a strategic necessity in most markets and industries today. In whatever form they appear, there is hardly an industry in which customer loyalty programmes are still unknown. From local take-out delis to global multi-billion corporations, they are simply everywhere.

This implies two things. One is that not having a customer loyalty programme can hurt your business, as more and more of your customers get caught in the nets of competitors' programmes, even if these are not perfectly designed. The other is that this is a great opportunity for your company. Most existing programmes are set up without real planning, without identifying value-driving benefits, without properly integrating the programme into the company, or without utilizing the data that is collected. These poorly planned or unsophisticated programmes only work because they are unchallenged, and even then their performance is weak. Generally, the members joined to take advantage of the discounts, but there is no commitment and no emotional relationship binding them. There is thus an ever-present opportunity for any company that introduces a real value-oriented concept. Suddenly, there would be a programme on the market that really offers value and true benefits which will actually do customers some good. The potential success of such a programme is enormous.

A customer loyalty programme is also a strategic necessity because it can generate the right quality and quantity of data that turns a database into the strategic weapon that it should be. The opportunities that arise with such a well-kept database are immense, and will be discussed in more detail in Chapter 16.

So, overall, there are two reasons not to be discouraged by the possibly higher than expected cost of a customer loyalty programme. One is the various opportunities for revenues through the loyalty programme, and the other is to see the strategic importance and opportunities of a well-planned and executed customer loyalty programme.

## Summary

After selecting the right loyalty programme benefits, putting together a sound financial concept is the second most important step of a customer loyalty programme concept. The quality of this kind of programme has its price, which can be anywhere between £10 and £150 per year per member, depending on the type, size and concept of the loyalty programme. The loyalty programme can cover a large part, if not all, of its cost by using all possible ways to generate revenues, such as a joining/annual membership fee, sales of loyalty programme merchandise and special products, commission from external partners and/or the credit card, advertising in loyalty programme communications, cover charges for loyalty programme events and fees for loyalty programme benefits. Most importantly, it must be understood that a customer loyalty programme will lead to higher revenue and profits, and will thus also have a significant, but difficult to isolate and measure, direct revenue effect.

One possibility for obtaining better cost control is to limit the membership to a certain number of members. It is also worthwhile to run through different cost scenarios concerning the development of the loyalty programme's size, in order to be prepared for changes in the necessary investment caused by extraordinarily high or low membership.

In general, the cost of a loyalty programme should not be seen as a 'cost', but rather as an investment in a marketing tool that is a strategic necessity in today's competitive environment.

# 12 *Communication*

As explained in Chapter 6, one of the main goals of a customer loyalty programme is to create opportunities to communicate. In order to achieve this goal, the customer loyalty programme concept must include communication methods that reach the members with themes that are of interest to them. These themes should be open to all members, and at the same time should enable them to communicate actively with the loyalty programme organization. The communication concept must further bear in mind that the customer loyalty programme has to communicate in three different environments, each with different interests and goals (see Figure 12.1).

In the first group are the loyalty programme members, in the second group are the company's employees and management, and in the third group is the external loyalty programme environment, which includes the media, the industry in which the sponsoring company operates, external partners, and so on. For each of these three groups, different means of communication must be developed to send the appropriate messages. In addition, the loyalty programme members will, in many cases, want the programme to serve as a platform to communicate with one another.

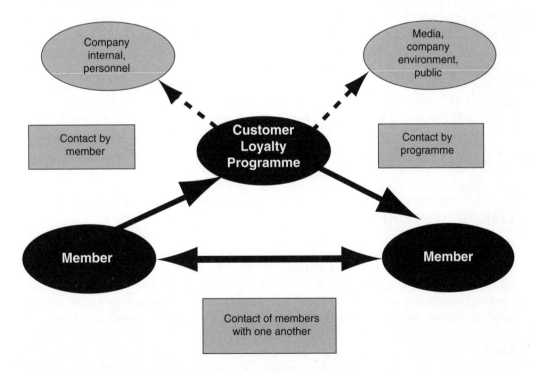

**Figure 12.1**   Communication areas of a customer loyalty programme

## Communication with loyalty programme members

Communication with members must be exclusive, meaning that it is only accessible to members. If everybody were able to log in to the programme's Website or receive the e-mail newsletter, their values would be significantly reduced and the exclusivity of the membership jeopardized. The goals of the loyalty programme's internal communication are:

- to give information about loyalty programme benefits
- to give information about current loyalty programme activities
- to give information about special events and special product offers
- to build a connection with the products the loyalty programme is promoting
- to inform about subjects of general interest to the members
- to encourage members to be proactive in contacting the loyalty programme service centre
- to encourage an increase in purchase and repurchase volume
- to support the other loyalty programme goals.

The communication with the members can be split into different groups: active regular, active irregular, and passive. Active communication means that the programme management contacts the members. This can happen on a regular basis (for example, through a monthly newsletter) or an irregular basis (for example, a report on a current event with photos of the participants and so on). Passive communication means that the members contact the programme management (for example, through a hotline, or letters to the editor of the magazine).

Our experience has shown that too much communication (for example, daily or weekly) can be counterproductive as the members will feel pressured and annoyed, especially if many of these contacts are open or hidden sales pitches. Conversely, too much time between communicative activities, for example annually or semi-annually, will not be effective enough, as the number of annual contacts is too low to build up an emotional connection. Ideally, the members should be contacted between six and twelve times per year using different quantities and types of communication. Some of the alternative communicative tools that a customer loyalty programme can use to communicate with its members are shown in Figure 12.2. While loyalty programme magazines, mailings, newsletters and loyalty programme hotlines have always been popular, the Internet and e-mail are increasingly becoming the most important communication tools.

## Welcome package

As a first contact, every new member should receive a welcome package within a few days of sending in their application. This welcome package should include a recent copy of the loyalty programme magazine and/or newsletter, detailed information about loyalty programme benefits and how to claim them, a welcome gift, perhaps some special offers, and a personal welcome letter. Remember, this is the first official contact the new member has with the customer loyalty programme, so the quality and value of this welcome package must match or exceed the new member's expectations. A welcome letter expressing gratitude for joining the loyalty programme is not enough. The member has joined the loyalty programme with certain expectations, and in most cases has even paid a joining or membership

**Figure 12.2**    Methods for communicating with members

fee. These expectations must be met from the very first contact until the end of the relationship. In the case of a joining fee, members must have the feeling that most of their investment has already paid off. After having received the welcome package and used any special offers or coupons that the package may contain, they should feel compensated for that investment. Loyalty programme marketing is direct marketing, and a major step towards one-on-one marketing. It is therefore unacceptable to start the welcome letter or any other written communication with the member with 'Dear Member' or 'Dear Frequent Flyer'. How personal does that sound? It is crucial to make the member feel like an important individual to the sponsoring company.

Another error that is frequently made is allowing too much time to pass between the membership application and the arrival of the welcome package. The new member has given the matter some thought before joining the loyalty programme, has weighed the pros and cons, and has finally decided to go ahead with it. Now, the member is eager to participate in the loyalty programme life and enjoy its benefits. On average, it takes between four and twelve weeks for many loyalty programmes to send out their welcome package or merely confirmation of receipt of the application. New applications should be dealt with within a few days of their arrival at the company, so that the welcome package is sent out within the first two weeks. The worst way to start this new relationship is to keep the new member waiting.

## Loyalty programme magazine

The loyalty programme magazine is probably the most important communication element, and is standard for nearly all customer loyalty programmes in a business-to-customer environment (business-to-business programmes are slowly moving away from customer magazines and use the Internet, e-mail and even SMS (Short Messaging Service) for communication, as they have realized that their members hardly have the time to read another magazine). Loyalty programme magazines are published between two and twelve times a year, can have anything from four and forty or more pages, and come in a large variety of editorial forms. The contents of these loyalty programme magazines are as diverse as the loyalty programme benefits. Let's have a look at some examples:

- SWR3 is one of the most popular radio stations in Germany. Its loyalty programme magazine, *ON*, carries interviews with SWR3 DJs, information on different bands, concert, CD and film reviews, as well as articles on recent and forthcoming loyalty programme events. It has become so popular that it is not only sent to members for free, but is also sold at news stands across the country.

- Dr Oetker Baking loyalty programme's Guglhupf offers its members a large variety of information from the world of baking, such as seasonal recipes, baking tips and so on.

- The American Burger King kids loyalty programme primarily targets children between the ages of 3 and 8. Its magazine, *Adventures*, includes games and comic strips involving a group of special loyalty programme characters. These characters come from diverse ethnic backgrounds and include one child who has special needs. He is called Wheels because he uses a wheelchair. One of the messages the magazine tries to convey to its young readers is that they should learn about values such as fairness in sports and openness towards people who are different from themselves.

- The Steiff loyalty programme magazine, both in Germany and in the USA, primarily covers the history and origins of various Steiff products. As the main targets are teddy bear collectors, the magazine also includes a valuable exchange market.

- Delta Airlines' *Fantastic Flyer Magazine* for their frequent flyers aged between two and twelve years presents an interesting mixture of regular features such as 'Kids in the Galley' and 'Fantastic Games and Activities', and carries items on current events such as the Olympic Games and subjects related to the world of flying.

Generally, all of these magazines focus on product presentation in the broader sense. However, in most cases the publications also feature general stories and reports that are of interest to the target groups. One of the most important aspects of any loyalty programme magazine is the response elements that enable and encourage the member or the reader to contact the loyalty programme. The approach varies, and can include features where individuals send in a completed questionnaire, call a specific telephone number to receive free product samples, send in tips and tricks on how to use the products, or address letters to the editor. An extreme example of reader involvement is the magazine of 1.FC Märklin, the kids' loyalty programme of Märklin, the world leader in model railways, which is entirely written by children.

There are three categories of loyalty programme magazine. The first category consists of magazines that are solely for loyalty programme members and include only loyalty pro-gramme-related news. The second category includes magazines that are also solely for members, but are set up more like popular magazines with articles on a variety of topics, and include only a few directly loyalty programme-related pages. The third category contains magazines that, although sent to loyalty programme members for free, are also available to the public at a certain cover price and are sold at news stands. The Nintendo magazines loyalty programme *Nintendo* in Germany and *Nintendo Power* in the USA, the SWR3 loyalty programme magazine *ON* and the Herpa Collectors loyalty programme magazine *Der Maßstab* are all examples of this third category, which is a less common means of programme communication.

Other advantages of a loyalty programme magazine are:

- The contents can be aimed specifically at the needs and interests of the loyalty programme members. The identification of the loyalty programme with the lifestyle of the readers increases the bond between them.
- Regular advertising can be carried out at a much lower price, and it can include advertisements or articles that offer more information and have a higher credibility than normal advertising in other magazines or newspapers (Rapp and Collins, 1991, p.187).

The variety of possibilities for designing, putting together and distributing the loyalty programme magazine illustrates the flexibility of this tool.

## Personalized mailings and newsletters

Personalized mailings are also an effective tool for creating loyalty and increasing members' purchase volume. These mailings should be sent out two to four times a year (or more frequently if you do not have a magazine or Web page), and inform the recipient of the loyalty programme's activities, the latest news from the loyalty programme scene and so on. They can also include special offers, descriptions of new or improved products, and/or product information. This tool is primarily to inform the member of new products and developments, but is also intended to create demand for these products. These mailings are one of the best opportunities a loyalty programme and the sponsoring company have for effective one-on-one marketing, as the offers included can be individualized based on analysis of recent purchasing behaviour. If these mailings are set up correctly and contain current information that gives loyalty programme members a head start or personalized product offers, they are the perfect vehicle to make a loyalty programme member feel special and important to the company, thus increasing the probability of loyalty. Birthdays and membership anniversaries are ideal opportunities to contact the member with a gift or special offer. This also reinforces the feeling of personalization.

Unfortunately, so far only very few customer loyalty programmes and customer loyalty programmes exploit the full potential of these personalized mailings. The main reasons for this are that they have not set up professional database marketing and do not use the information available to them efficiently, if at all. But these mailings can include response elements that provide the company with highly valuable and exclusive information for R&D, market research, product marketing, product pricing and other areas, which can be included in their respective strategies. Furthermore, by using personalized mailings, special offers can be communicated more clearly, after-sales contacts can be established more easily, and loyalty programme members can communicate actively with loyalty programme representatives. These mailings should not be downgraded to merely trying to sell loyalty programme merchandise or products, but should also contain information and features that are interesting to the recipient.

Newsletters can be sent out more frequently than a loyalty programme magazine, as they are easier and faster to produce. Thus, they are a perfect way of informing members about new developments or current events at short notice.

## Loyalty programme hotline

Since the telephone is today's most common method of communication, a loyalty programme hotline, preferably with a toll-free phone number, is an essential part of the loyalty programme's communication portfolio. The availability of a loyalty programme hotline encourages spontaneous active contact from the member. It is surprising how many loyalty programmes still do without a hotline, considering that 99 per cent of all communication with a loyalty programme is via the telephone (Wiencke, 1993, p.3).

But simply offering a telephone number to members is not enough. By calling the loyalty programme hotline, the members must be able to order products, obtain other loyalty programme benefits, gain access to qualified help and/or consultations, or have their complaints dealt with. This implies that the loyalty programme service centre (which in some cases will be responsible for the hotline) or the call centre, must be staffed with qualified and trained personnel. It shows poor judgement if the members, your most valuable customers, have to communicate with the general company hotline, an automated answering system or have their calls answered by the company's switchboard. This certainly does not help build up the emotional relationship which the loyalty programme is aiming for. The hotline should be staffed during the times members are most likely to call, which may include evenings and weekends. While a business-to-business loyalty programme with mostly professional members probably does not need a weekend or Sunday service, a video game producer's loyalty programme line must definitely be staffed at the weekends.

The hotline agents must have access to the programme database in order to be able to access and update the contact history, pass orders on to the programme service centre and so on.

### USE LOYALTY PROGRAMMES FOR CUSTOMER COMPLAINT MANAGEMENT

A hotline should also be actively used to support the company's complaint management. While 96 per cent of dissatisfied customers never complain, 36 per cent of these silent dissatisfied customers will not buy from you again, and 90 per cent of those who do complain will also not buy from you again (*Marketing Report*, 1996, p.1). Rather than avoiding customer complaints, you should actively encourage as much feedback as possible. Customer complaints are the best way to identify problems with products and demand for new and different products, and best of all, they are free of charge. Taking care of customer complaints in a quick, honest and professional manner is the best way to turn dissatisfied customers into loyal ones.

A perfect example of such a move is something that happened to the general manager of

Club Med in Cancun, Mexico (Hart, Heskett and Sasser, 1990, p.23 or 233). A charter flight with Club Med guests from New York had left six hours late, two unscheduled stops made them lose even more time, and finally the plane had to circle the Mexican airport for half an hour before getting permission to land. Overall, the passengers had spent ten hours more on the trip than originally planned, and there was no food or drink left on the plane. To make this situation worse, the landing at Cancun was so hard that the oxygen masks fell down from their compartments. By that time the Club Med guests were so enraged that they happily handed their names to a lawyer who had coincidentally been on board, in order to file a joint lawsuit against Club Med.

The general manager of Cancun's Club Med had been informed about this horror flight, and came up with a great plan. He drove to the airport with half his crew and set up tables with snacks and drinks as well as a stereo to play music. All arriving guests were personally greeted by the manager, their luggage was taken care of, and after some refreshments they were driven to their holiday quarters. At the Club Med, a large buffet had been set up, including a Mariachi band and free champagne. Other guests of the club had also been invited, and the party continued until the next morning. Later, many guests said that they had not had that much fun since their college days.

Although the initial experience was very negative, the quick reaction of the general manager certainly turned many of the angry customers into loyal ones that night. As a customer loyalty programme mainly deals with the more important and/or frequent customers, the potential to have a good influence is enormous.

## The Internet and e-mail

The Internet has also opened up opportunities for customer loyalty programmes to use this new medium to communicate with members, either through their own Web page or via e-mail. At the moment, only a few customer loyalty programmes, such as Swatch The Club, SWR3 Radio or the Volkswagen Club in the USA, use the Internet effectively. Frequent flyer programmes are much more advanced in this area, and have shifted the majority of programme activities online (for example, you can check your mileage account online, book tickets and rewards online, receive the newsletter via e-mail and so on). They have realized the huge potential to save cost, and at the same time serve the members more effectively. No glossy magazines have to be printed and mailed if you put the content on your Web page as a PDF file ready to be downloaded. For the members, it probably does not make a difference, especially if you are targeting segments which use the Internet on a regular basis. If your target groups are more mixed, then slowly phase in the Internet and e-mail as communication vehicles by offering information online to members who have access to the Web, and using traditional means for those who don't. Over time, the latter group will shrink and more cost savings can be realized. But even though less expensive, the Internet allows more frequent, more current and more variable communication, which is a strong loyalty driver. Furthermore, it can serve as the vehicle for all communication streams (programme–member and member–programme, company internally and with the external environment, as well as member–member).

The loyalty programme's Web page should not only be used to describe the loyalty programme benefits and activities, but should be targeted to attract new members. An online guest has already shown interest in the company and its products by visiting the Web page, and should be given the opportunity to join the loyalty programme directly via the Internet. The marketing effort involved in a Web page is the same regardless of the number of visitors (Mayer, 1996, p.32). A Web page has many advantages, as it can be used to sell loyalty programme merchandise and products, its high interactivity enables an individual dialogue with members, members' opinions can be solicited, and offering updated information on a daily or at minimum on a weekly basis encourages Web surfers to visit the site repeatedly, thus increasing communication opportunities (Mayer, 1996, p.33). However, members should have a section on the Web page reserved exclusively for them, accessible only with a login name and password.

## Other means of communicating with loyalty programme members

Other means of communication include loyalty programme events and meetings, where the members can meet other members and people from the sponsoring company and the loyalty programme. Events such as loyalty programme trips and loyalty programme booths or lounges at trade shows enable the loyalty programme management to meet its members face to face, and encourage the exchange of information and dialogue not only between loyalty programme members, but also between members and management. But this form of communication has to be planned carefully, and it must be borne in mind that many members may not be interested in meeting other members. This largely depends on the environment of the programme. Collectors of trains or teddy bears might be more interested in meeting one another than other groups. Loyalty programme meetings and events make more sense if the product environment is emotional or professional (for example, cars, movies or business-to-business areas). Loyalty programmes such as HOG (Harley Davidson Owners Group) regularly organize these kind of meetings, which are a big success.

Very few members use loyalty programme outlets where loyalty programme members can get together and meet, but this might be a good idea for companies that already have a network of outlets that are frequently visited by customers, for example in the retail industry. IKEA has a family shop for IKEA family members in every outlet in the participating countries, where the members are offered special products and so on.

## Communication between members

In some cases, members will be very interested in meeting one another and having the opportunity to exchange ideas, discuss common problems and so on. Mostly, this will be the case in business-to-business programmes and in business-to-customer programmes where the members are collectors or share a common hobby (such as model trains), areas in which all members share a strong common interest in a subject or have the same problems and issues in their jobs. When planning the programme benefits, this aspect must also be covered in the market research. The member–member communication can be achieved via moderated online chat rooms, regional meetings, an annual programme conference, a members-only lounge at a trade show and so on.

## Communication within the company

Information about the loyalty programme must also be communicated within the company. A customer loyalty programme will only work if all employees throughout the sponsoring company support the loyalty programme and its concept, as well as playing their part in making customers loyal. It is especially important for those employees who have regular contact with the customers to understand the principles and goals of the loyalty programme, the importance of its members, and to treat loyalty programme members with the appropriate attitude. If a customer is treated unsatisfactorily two or three times, or repeatedly has problems with the company's product, no customer loyalty programme in the world will be able to turn this customer into a loyal, lifetime customer, no matter how good the loyalty programme concept is.

Problems arise when the gap between loyalty programme performance and company or product performance is too broad. To combat this, all employees should be informed about the loyalty programme and its purpose, and should receive special training before the loyalty programme is officially started. Staff should be able to answer customer requests or questions regarding the loyalty programme, and should know how to respond to all comments politely and informatively. A negative example is the business-to-business loyalty programme of a European manufacturer of work safety clothing and equipment which was introduced at a major occupational health and safety trade show in 1996. When we telephoned the company to obtain further information about the loyalty programme, we were put through to three different people in the public relations and marketing departments, but none of them knew about the loyalty programme, let alone who could provide the requested information.

Top management must also set an example for other employees by openly supporting the loyalty programme. Management must be aware of the long-term perspective of the customer loyalty programme and ensure long-term financial and infrastructural support. It is their responsibility to convince possible critics, be they external partners, financial backers or corporate management, that the loyalty programme is working well and producing good results.

## Communication with the external environment

The final area of loyalty programme communication is between the loyalty programme and its external environment. By placing the loyalty programme in the media, either by press coverage of the loyalty programme's activities, loyalty programme advertising, or mentioning the loyalty programme in general reports by the sponsoring company, the loyalty programme can be better positioned in the minds of customers and win new members. Regular press releases containing the latest information on membership growth, loyalty programme activities and the like are interesting to the media.

This area also includes loyalty programme advertising by sending out information leaflets, placing ads in relevant industry publications, TV commercials, including loyalty programme information on the sponsoring company's Web page, or sending information packages to existing customers, provided that a database is available. Especially in the first few months of the loyalty programme's existence, plenty of advertising must be done to ensure that membership grows rapidly. This is important, as some loyalty programme benefits need a critical mass to become affordable or profitable, and also because fast membership growth is an indicator (but not a guarantee) of the success of the loyalty programme, and can motivate loyalty programme management and silence sceptics.

## Summary

A customer loyalty programme communicates in three areas: internally with loyalty programme members, internally with the personnel of the sponsoring company, and externally with the loyalty programme's environment, such as the media. In order to set up the necessary communication system with its members, the loyalty programme can use a variety of communication means, such as a loyalty programme magazine, regular newsletters or mailings, a loyalty programme hotline, a Web page, e-mail, loyalty programme meetings and events, and/or loyalty programme outlets. Member-to-member communication must also be made possible in many cases. Internal communication with the sponsoring company's personnel and management is important, as they have to be informed about the loyalty programme's existence and goals before they can support the loyalty programme idea fully. Internal support is crucial, and includes everybody from top management to employees who have contact with customers. Finally, the loyalty programme should interact with its environment to achieve press coverage, to advertise its activities, and to increase awareness.

# 13 E-loyalty: customer loyalty on the Internet

## With Verena Burger

At a time when loyalty programmes are sprouting up left and right, many companies are trying to define what role the Internet could play in their loyalty strategies. Let us first briefly discuss whether the Internet has a positive or negative effect on customer loyalty in general. This question cannot be answered with complete certainty, and there are several arguments for both sides. On the one hand, the Internet gives the consumers access to a wider range of alternatives and product information, which increases the risk that they might desert. On the other hand, the Internet also allows companies with competitive advantages to communicate these better and increase the loyalty of their customers. Also, competitors have much better access to your information, and you to theirs. This means that competitors' price advantages and so on are detected much more quickly, and can be neutralized. So the Internet increases competition and stabilizes the competitive situation at the same time, but the result of these two effects is probably stronger competition in most markets. However, with the individual communication, customization and data collection possibilities, the Internet also offers many opportunities to enhance your loyalty strategies.

When we talk about customer loyalty on the Internet, we need to differentiate between two alternatives. One is pure Internet sites such as *Ipoints* and *Beenz*, both pure online programmes, that entice visitors to remain logged on for long periods by rewarding them Web money for taking part in certain activities. The longer they remain interactive with the site, the more Web money they earn towards discounted products. Other programmes such as *Webmiles* offer bonus points for online purchases from participating e-commerce sites. In all of these cases, loyalty is primarily achieved through the respective currency, and the focus is on online target groups and activities. The second alternative is a conventional loyalty programme that also uses the Internet for (some of) its benefits and communication. While the former can, of course, be integrated into your loyalty programme, we want to focus primarily on the latter.

The key questions that need to be answered are:

- What basic requirements must we meet before going online with a loyalty programme?
- Should the entire programme be conducted online, or just parts of it?
- Which programme elements should be offered online?
- Do e-programmes generate advantages that traditional loyalty programmes cannot realize?
- What drawbacks do they have?
- What other aspects must be considered when designing an e-loyalty programme?

This chapter will help to answer these and other relevant questions.

The first question companies must ask themselves before starting an e-loyalty programme is whether the group they intend to target is online. Loyalty can be built online only if the target group has access to the Internet and uses it regularly. Whether customer loyalty should be pursued solely through an online programme or whether a combination of a classic and an e-based solution would be more effective depends on the target group's affinity to the Web. The Germany-based company T-Mobil, the mobile network subsidiary of Deutsche Telekom, conducts a significant part of its loyalty programme online – not a bad option, considering its members are IT and telecommunications decision-makers who use the Internet on a daily basis (see Chapter 22 for the case study). For groups such as this, the Internet is an ideal channel for increasing customer loyalty, as they actually *prefer* to communicate via the Internet and e-mail instead of traditional media. Most loyalty programmes are slowly phasing in the Internet, and currently consist of a combination of online and offline components.

## The pros and cons of e-loyalty programmes

E-loyalty programmes have both advantages and disadvantages (see Table 13.1). Traditional offline programmes require enormous amounts of money to support communication activities, as they communicate with members through direct mailings, member magazines and so on. It is considerably less expensive to communicate with members through the Internet. Expensive mailings or publications can be replaced by economical alternatives such as e-mails and electronic newsletters. Not only is online communication cheaper than its printed counterpart, it tends to improve the quality of customer contact as well. Important, up-to-date information can be passed along instantly to loyalty programme members. If a loyalty programme wants to inform its members about a special offer, it can do so simply by sending an e-mail. Another advantage is that, in many cases, loyalty programme members can communicate directly with one another. The most common ways to promote member-to-member dialogue are to set up a chat room where the like-minded can connect, or a bulletin board where members can exchange messages. This interactive element serves to strengthen the identity within the loyalty programme, causing it to evolve over time from a simple group to a genuine community. Members of this community develop a close relationship with one another and the company. Interactive tools can also help reduce R&D costs. Companies can

**Table 13.1**    Pros and cons of using the Internet for a loyalty programme

| Pros | Cons |
|------|------|
| • cheaper than traditional CRM measures | • security risks |
| • increases quality of customer contact by providing current and short-term information | • high level of maintenance required. |
| • provides a forum for like-minded people to exchange ideas | |
| • reduces R&D costs | |
| • membership requirements automatically limit the number of members, thus reducing costs | |
| • database includes only those members with an above-average interest in the product. | |

turn to online focus groups to test and discuss the attractiveness of products or services. Focus groups conducted at very early stages of the development process can even help prevent product flops. The Märklin loyalty programme, an association of model train enthusiasts, always asks its online loyalty programme members their opinions on new models before launching them on the market. This method has proven to be very effective: very few of the many new models have failed.

Most of the negative aspects of e-loyalty programmes are due to the inherent nature of the Internet. Internet activities usually carry a higher level of security risk. Visitors might be more reluctant to disclose personal information. This problem is especially true for new and inexperienced Internet users, who tend to be very suspicious about the virtual world. If companies want to motivate users to participate in e-loyalty activities, not only must they have a strong Internet offer, but they must also be good at building trust. There are three basic principles to winning trust:

- provide information about the company and its Internet security standards
- give customers security guarantees
- become certified by a well-known, independent and accepted authority.

A number of companies and institutions specializing in certification already exist. Loyalty programmes with these credentials have a much greater chance of being accepted by customers and potential customers.

Another downside of e-loyalty programmes is that they require a great deal of maintenance and resources. Providing prompt, up-to-date information requires that there are sufficient resources for collecting, processing and distributing relevant information to members. Nothing is more annoying to members than last month's news. Keeping a Web site up to date is enough work to keep an employee busy full-time – special promotions and activities not included.

## Requirements

In order to implement an e-loyalty programme successfully, a few rules must be followed. The fundamental rules for building loyalty must be applied to Internet programmes as well. This means:

- creating switching barriers by building customer satisfaction
- enhancing loyalty by providing customers with personal, exclusive treatment
- increasing the cost of switching, and immunizing against competitors' offers through monetary incentives
- offering an attractive mixture of monetary and non-monetary benefits.

In addition to these basic guidelines, there are a number of other 'dos' to keep in mind. First, e-loyalty programmes require a strategy. This means having a clear understanding of what goals the programme should help achieve. If the loyalty programme consists of both online and offline components, the relationship between the two parts must be defined. The design of the programme needs to support the overall goals of the integrated strategy. For instance, if the primary goal is to build a close and intense relationship with the programme participants, the overall strategy should focus on online elements. The Internet is more suitable than traditional media (such as magazines or mailings) for fostering two-way interaction.

Second, it is necessary to know what drives e-loyalty among your target group. What technical features, content and other crucial aspects should be included on the Web site? The easiest way to determine these loyalty drivers is to ask your target group (through focus groups or chat rooms). Some companies even ask customers to fill out questionnaires from time to time. They typically cover everything from Web site content to technical features.

Third, you must employ communication tools that enable dialogue not only between the programme management and the members, but among the members themselves. The main purpose of this dialogue is to allow members to share their experiences with one another. The best way to hold onto a participant's loyalty is to have an independent third party reinforce their decision to be loyal. And what better person to do this than another member? There are many communication methods to choose from: chat rooms, bulletin boards, messaging, customer recommendation postings, expert testimonies, just to name a few. Another purpose of the dialogue is to enable a quick exchange between the loyalty programme and its members. Most loyalty programmes use e-mail to ensure easy, rapid communication, or they incorporate so-called 'call me' buttons into their sites. But these features alone don't guarantee a high level of service. It is also necessary to have a strong back office. When someone has a problem, they want the solution right away, not in a week, when the answer might already be obsolete. The success of how dialogue tools are implemented is dependent on the quality of back-office resources.

Fourth, companies need to track and analyse all Internet activities of the programme members in as detailed a manner as possible. There are many CRM software tools, such as *Applix*, *update.com* and *Clarify*, which help measure and analyse online behaviour. Not only do analyses help identify loyalty drivers, but they are also useful in making the programme more customer-oriented.

## Building loyalty programme site traffic

Building loyalty on the Internet generally means getting members to increase their Internet usage. The intensity of usage can be measured as the number of visits, page impressions, hours of connection, session time or number of transactions. There are primarily six factors that determine the intensity of use: content, individualization, trust, complementarity, community and brand. All of these are true for Web pages in general, but in particular for loyalty programme sites.

The factors *content* and *individualization* are closely related. No matter whether you have a virtual loyalty programme or another type of e-loyalty programme, content is paramount when trying to motivate potential members to participate. The main reason many Internet users visit a site is to view the up-to-date and attractive information it showcases. Therefore, it is essential to provide all information that is somehow related to the membership offer. In addition, the perceived value of the site and its content increases if access is restricted to members. For this reason, many companies divide their Web sites into two parts. The first part can be accessed by anyone visiting the site (maybe through a link on the main company Web site). It contains general information about the programme such as how to sign up, rules, benefits, and so on. The second part is a 'members-only' section, and a password is needed to log in.

The Internet serves as an ideal tool for segmenting target groups based on this customization. Some benefits should be granted only to certain visitors These benefits can be separated from unrestricted benefits through password protection. Each time a user logs in using the 'members-only' option, the system identifies which sub-segment they belong to. The member can then be easily routed to a particular set of benefits that has been designed to fit their individual needs. The ball bearing manufacturer FAG Kugelfischer uses the registration data to decide which information users may access and how it is presented. While customers have access to all site information, including the individually agreed prices and detailed product descriptions, students are limited to information about the company and career opportunities. Similarly, journalists can download photos and other press materials, but they do not have access to the same information as customers.

But content alone is not enough to build loyalty. The site must be set up in such a way that users can comfortably and quickly access the content that is relevant to them. This is where tools for easy navigation and data personalization come in. Some companies now offer members the opportunity to create their own home page and customize it according to their needs. Visitors to *Yahoo!* are able to create their own site, 'my.yahoo.com'. The my.yahoo Assistant helps the user personalize the content, layout and even colours of the site according to their personal preference. The virtual assistant recommends content based on a short profile the user provides during the initial registration process. Many companies use these profiles as a basis for individualizing content, but the information contained in them is usually very general. In addition, some users do not provide truthful information. With the help of modern software tools, however, these problems can easily be sidestepped. Passive methods for tracking behaviour on a Web site effectively reveal the target group's *true* preferences and needs. Clickstream analysis, cookies or collaborative filtering are widely used methods for refining data profiles. The user receives only the information that is relevant to them, making the chances that they will return greater. Moreover, the fact that the visitor thinks they are receiving exclusive information makes them feel like a cherished customer and promotes loyalty. There are huge opportunities here for loyalty programmes.

Another aspect that influences loyalty is trust. Gaining the trust of potential members is a basic requirement for any e-loyalty programme. It's very simple: if they don't trust you, they won't participate in the programme. Companies can win the confidence of their customers by offering high-quality products and services, on-time delivery, secure payment and careful handling of personal and confidential data. But they must do this from the very beginning. If users have even the slightest doubt that the programme is trustworthy, it will be almost impossible to build loyalty. As already mentioned, the most common way to promote trust is to openly communicate the high security standards of the site. An increasing number of companies now ask their users for approval before using their personal information for extraneous purposes (which is the law in some countries). Another way to win the customer's trust is to create a loyalty programme that is simple and straightforward. If a member wants to redeem their points (such as *Ipoints*), they should be able to do so easily. If it is difficult to redeem points, for instance if the products are not available or not delivered on time, the user won't make the effort to continue to participate in the programme. Loyalty can be built only if the customer's trust is rewarded from the very beginning.

At first glance, complementarity within the product or service range doesn't seem essential for e-loyalty. In many cases, additional offers help upgrade the value of the core product. The loyalty programme T-D1 Company Class offers its members online information on the company T-Mobil. In order to increase the users' understanding of the telecommunications market, and, in particular the mobile phone market, basic company information is supplemented with background information on the market and its participants. Members consider this mixture of programme-related information and additional germane information to be a true added value.

Loyalty also depends on a company's ability to make the user feel 'at home' on its Web site. Discussion forums are a good tool for promoting this feeling. Members should be given the opportunity to communicate with one another in virtual networks or communities. If a company is successful at creating a spirit of community among its users, loyalty will follow. Members will repeatedly visit the site because they desire contact with 'their' community.

Finally, brand is also a determinant of e-loyalty. A strong brand builds a good basis for customer retention, a rule that applies online as well as off. Being first to the online market is the key to creating a strong brand. The success of Internet activities also depends on how soon a company goes online. One of the main reasons *Amazon.com* or *Yahoo.com* are so successful today is that they were the first to market. There are dozens of online bookstores, but for most people, *Amazon.com* is synonymous with online bookselling. Despite the fact that competitors such as *Barnesandnoble.com* continue to invest huge amounts in advertising, none has been able to win back the time lost to *Amazon*. The name 'Amazon' and the products it offers stand for quality and reliability, so why should customers switch to another supplier? Speed is needed to build a strong brand name. The quality of the products or services, on the other hand, helps create loyalty.

It is very important to achieve the right mixture of rational and emotional added value. Many companies focus on the rational component. They provide benefits that satisfy the members' basic needs in the hope that this will build loyalty. The loyalty programme management sees to it that these hard benefits cannot be copied easily. The emotional component, however, is more decisive for long-term e-loyalty. But how can you appeal to emotions in the cyber-world? The easiest way to do this is by offering exclusivity, which can take the form of restricted access or an elite style, tone and loyalty programme design. BMW's online loyalty programme for drivers of the 7-Series is a good example of emotional added value. After members log in, they enter a site that reflects BMW's core competencies: dynamism, innovation and elegance. The site not only symbolizes the pleasure of driving a 7-Series, but expresses a certain lifestyle. Hard product facts are not presented as mere technical data. Rather, short video clips make it possible to simulate the driving experience online. The contents of the site appeal to both the rational and the emotional. And that is the secret of its success.

## Summary

Online loyalty programmes are generally very effective. But companies should be aware that they demand a great amount of time and resources. The basic rules for creating loyalty in the offline world apply in the online world as well. But some factors, such as relevant content and individualization, trust, complementarity, community and brand, are even more important for online programmes. Communication is cheaper online, and generally better. Online communication also makes it easy to collect customer information which can be used to create new products and services. The success of a loyalty programme depends on the speed at which it is implemented, as well as on the company's ability to realize the right balance of rational and emotional appeal.

# 14 *The loyalty programme organization and service centre*

It will have become clear by now that any sophisticated customer loyalty programme involves several different parties, such as the loyalty programme management, external partners, financial partners and, last but not least, the members. Each party has a demand for different information, tasks, types of communication and so on. To guarantee member satisfaction, which is the main prerequisite for achieving the programme's loyalty goals, and a smooth operation, this complex system must be organized in an efficient way. Not only does this include making available the right quantity and quality of human, financial, technical and time resources, it also encompasses forming the right organizational structure. The best way to achieve this is to set up the organization around a loyalty programme central service centre (CSC). Such a programme cannot be operated efficiently if it is run on a part-time basis by a few associates of the sponsoring company, who take care of the loyalty programme business in addition to their other tasks. In most cases, the CSC is either closely linked to, or even partially identical to, the club management, so that the responsibilities are also of a managerial nature.

## The tasks of the CSC

The CSC co-ordinates, oversees and organizes all aspects of the loyalty programme's business. The CSC is the heart of this organization, and has a wide range of responsibilities:

- All contact with members goes through the CSC. The mail, e-mails, phone calls and so on should all be answered or sent out by the CSC. The CSC is the communications headquarters and nucleus of the customer loyalty programme.
- Not only do current members communicate with the CSC, interested customers also often have their first contact with the loyalty programme via the CSC when they call or write to request further information. The CSC is the main link between the loyalty programme and its environment, and must be equipped and staffed to fulfil this task to a high standard.
- In those cases when the company sponsoring the loyalty programme includes its dealers in the concept, communication with them is also handled by the CSC.
- Members request benefits through the CSC, so delivery and invoicing must be handled flawlessly.
- The CSC is in most cases also responsible for properly maintaining the database and delivering specific analysis to other company departments on request.
- The CSC also takes care of all the loyalty programme administration.
- The CSC is often closely linked to, or even partly identical to, the programme management, so its responsibilities also include further development of the programme concept.

- In those cases in which a call centre handles incoming phone traffic, the CSC must also conduct some quality control to ensure the call centre is operating smoothly.

Figure 14.1 shows the place of a typical CSC in the loyalty programme system, and its relationship to the parties involved. The diagram shows the CSC and the loyalty programme management as two different parties, which might demand some explanation. While the CSC takes care of the everyday business of the loyalty programme, the loyalty programme management is more involved in supervising the overall concept, and is responsible for adjusting and improving it. In most customer loyalty programmes, the loyalty programme management is also actively involved in the daily business of running the loyalty programme, so that it virtually becomes part of the CSC.

Let us take a closer look at one particular process, for example when a member sends in an order for one of the loyalty programme benefits that is provided by an outside partner. The CSC passes the order on to the external partner along with the shipping address and a covering letter. The CSC is responsible for the order, and must make sure that it is correctly executed, either by keeping to the promised delivery time (for example, when a special product is offered) or by having the relevant service available to the member when requested (for example, when the member is eligible for a special hotel rate and is checking in). Then the CSC must keep track of all financial movements by paying the partner or requesting commission from the partner, according to the agreement. On the other hand, if the benefit is not for free, the CSC is also responsible for billing the member and making sure the invoice is paid.

It is the loyalty programme management's responsibility to control the quality of the

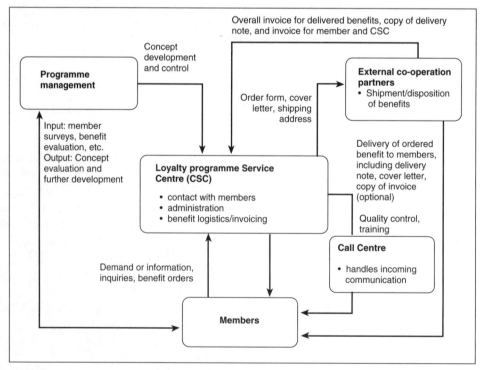

*Source:* Adopted from Wiencke (1992), p.8.

**Figure 14.1**    Structure of the customer loyalty programme organization

CSC's work, and to communicate with it on a regular basis in order to detect problems within the loyalty programme concept and improve it if necessary. But the CSC is the executive organ of the loyalty programme and is responsible for ensuring that the day-by-day operation is faultless.

## The CSC infrastructure

All the CSC's tasks are important. Therefore, the standards for the CSC's infrastructure are high. It does not matter whether the CSC is outsourced to an agency, run as a separate department within the sponsoring company or integrated into, for example, the marketing department. Whatever the case, certain aspects must be considered:

- Everything finally comes down to the people who work for you. If they do not do a good job for any reason, your company will not be able to move on. The same goes for the CSC. The people answering the phones, corresponding with the members and taking care of their orders must be well trained and professional. Remember that they will be dealing with your most important customers. These are not minimum-wage jobs that anybody can do, but require people with good communication skills who have good manners, who love dealing with people, who have a service mentality, who can improvise and are flexible, and who can deal well with problem situations such as complaints. Some of these aspects are part of a person's talent and character, but training is necessary for others. There are too many service centres where the customer service representatives are half asleep, incompetent or even rude to believe that this aspect is taken seriously by all companies.

- The technical equipment must be up to date and able to handle what it is required to do. Automated answering systems, for instance, do make sense, but not if the caller is being kept on hold for ten minutes or longer. Why not have the calling members leave a number at which they can be reached, and make sure they are called back within an appropriate amount of time? Of course, such service standards only make sense if they are maintained. The one customer that has to wait too long does not care if it went well in 99 per cent of other cases.

- The infrastructure must be prepared for the amount of work that is anticipated. For example, if a potential member calls showing interest or directly signing up for the loyalty programme, it must not take weeks or even months before the information package or welcome mailing is sent out. That certainly does not leave a good impression.

- Obviously, the database hardware and software should be able to handle the amount of data that is entered. The software should be customized and flexible enough to enable all necessary analysis. The database is not only there to collect data, but to support other departments, therefore it is not a loyalty programme issue, but a company issue.

- The CSC must be staffed during those times when customers can be expected to call. In most cases, this excludes times between midnight and 6 a.m., and it is certainly better to have enough people handling loyalty programme matters during peak time than to offer a 24-hour service when 15 hours are enough.

- The loyalty programme must possess its own identity, in the sense that it should have its own stationery, its own telephone and fax lines, and its own Web page, or at least a sub-page of its own on the sponsoring company's site. Obviously, a call should be answered by a loyalty programme representative, and not have to be put through by the company's central switchboard.

These high standards are certainly costly, but we have shown in Chapter 11 that a loyalty programme has a variety of possible ways to create revenue. At this point, it should be reiterated that the effort of putting together a customer loyalty programme with all the related financial involvement should not be seen as 'spending money' and 'cost', but as an investment in a modern marketing tool and a strategic weapon. And like any weapon, a customer loyalty programme will only work and can only be trusted to do its job if it was developed perfectly and is maintained adequately.

## Insourcing v. outsourcing of the CSC

One general question that must be answered is whether the CSC should be handled internally or by an outside service provider. A loyalty programme will work well, produce good results and transmit its ideas to customers if it is at least partly run by the company that sponsors it. The company's people are more involved and do not see it as 'another job', and the members are seen and treated more as customers rather than as callers. But outside help also has advantages in certain areas, and can mean reduced cost, special expertise and so on (Wiencke, 1992, p.10). Both alternatives have their advantages, which are summarized in Table 14.1.

**Table 14.1** Advantages of in- and outsourcing the CSC

| Advantages of insourcing | Advantages of outsourcing |
|---|---|
| • The company is closer to the operational club life, and will understand better how the programme in which it has invested considerable amounts of money works. | • There are cost savings through sharing the existing infrastructure of an agency (e.g. telephone system). |
| • Database management and analysis runs more smoothly and quckly, and is more focused on the company's or departments' needs. | • An agency can purchase benefit in larger volumes if they handle several clubs that offer similar benefits (e.g. hotel discounts), and can pass on the lower prices to members. |
| • Performance of the club personnel can be monitored more effectively and improved if they are company employees. | • Storage and logistics of benefits can be handled better and more cheaply because of the higher volume. |
| • Employees' motivitation is higher if they are more closely involved in the club business. | • No costs for unused capacities occur. |
| • Product-related benefits can be handled more efficiently. | • Non-product-related benefits can be handled more efficiently. |
| • There is more independence concerning changes and the future development of the club. | • In some cases, these agencies have substantial experience with service centres, etc. |

The final decision about in- or outsourcing depends a great deal on the company's financial situation or the available human resources. Ideally, everything that happens directly at the member interface, such as the hotline, loyalty programme correspondence and handling the benefits, should be done in-house. External help should be sought for general administrative work, the development of the loyalty programme magazine (in co-operation with loyalty programme management), or in other words, everything that has a more 'back office' nature. The expertise of specialized agencies can also be very valuable during the development of the customer loyalty programme concept or the organization of special events. In general, the selection of any outside help should be made carefully. As with many service companies, what you see and pay for is not always what you get.

A recent study of membership loyalty programmes of various publishers in the USA shows that 88 per cent of all magazines analysed manage their loyalty programme in-house, while only 25 per cent of all newspapers do so (*Ancillary Profits*, 1995, p.4). A study of German customer loyalty programmes shows that only 5.3 per cent of all loyalty programmes analysed rely entirely on outside agencies. The remaining 94.7 per cent at least partly deal with their members through their own employees. Most of them have an internal CSC or a department that is fully devoted to loyalty programme management. In those cases, an average of just under three full-time employees handle the loyalty programme's affairs (Kirstges, 1995, p.22).

Some loyalty programmes have put together substantial loyalty programme departments. For example, the IKEA family has 350 000 members in Germany alone, with a loyalty programme staff of 10 people, and the Volkswagen Club has 1.1 million members with a loyalty programme staff of 20 people. Two other loyalty programmes, which remained anonymous, with 250 000 and 200 000 members, handle their loyalty programmes in-house, with 30 and 18 personnel respectively (Holz and Tomczak, 1996, p.55).

Regardless of whether it is decided to keep the loyalty programme in-house or at least partly to outsource it, the loyalty programme management should always be closely involved in the loyalty programme's daily procedures. This is not only necessary to control the operation – how can a loyalty programme be managed and run the way it is expected if you are not actively involved in it? It is the same at the company level. It is unbelievable but true that there are managers who have not seen a customer in months. How can they know what the customers want? The loyalty programme management has to obtain the necessary input to be able to improve the concept of the programme continuously. Ideally, they should staff the hotline or answer letters from members for a couple of days each month to maintain an understanding of what works well and what does not.

## Summary

A customer loyalty programme is a complex organization, as it involves many different parties, including the sponsoring company, loyalty programme management, external partners, financial partners and members, as well as a variety of processes and tasks such as the benefit logistics, call centre, loyalty programme communication and financial issues. In order to manage the loyalty programme properly and ensure a smooth operation, a loyalty programme central service centre should be set up to serve as the hub for all loyalty programme contacts and activities. This is a very extensive task, and for this reason the personnel, the technology and other infrastructure must be of high quality.

The question of whether to in- or outsource these tasks is difficult to answer, as both alternatives have their advantages. In general, a good solution is to take care of the core loyalty programme tasks that are directly at the member interface within the company, while more routine administrative tasks are outsourced. But the final decision depends on the financial situation of the sponsoring company and its desired degree of independence.

CHAPTER

# 15 *Integrating the loyalty programme into the sponsoring company*

There are two aspects involved in planning how the customer loyalty programme can best be integrated into the sponsoring company's organizational structure and current marketing plan. On the one hand, you have to decide into which department the customer loyalty programme and its management should be integrated, which department it should report, to or whether it should be installed as a new independent division or subsidiary. On the other hand, co-operation between the loyalty programme and other departments of the sponsoring company must be optimized, in order to exploit the full potential of a customer loyalty programme to assist these departments in their work and provide valuable information for them.

## Integrating the loyalty programme into the company's organizational structure

Concerning the integration of the customer loyalty programme into the company's organizational structure, it is difficult to recommend one solution for every company, as they are all structured differently. But, in general, it is the case that the more independently the customer loyalty programme can be managed, the more effective it will be. 'Independent' in this sense does not mean ignoring the other company divisions, since, of course, their goals need to be considered as well. What independence does signify is that the loyalty programme management should have the authority to make decisions on how to run the loyalty programme, how to organize it, or which benefits to offer, without having to confer with outside parties. Again, this illustrates how similar loyalty programme management is to product management. In both areas, the responsible managers have to be able to make rapid and independent decisions concerning the loyalty programme or product for which they are responsible. If situations arise that require a quick decision, such as unanticipated price cuts by a major competitor or the introduction of a new loyalty programme by another major player in the industry, this independence is of particular importance.

In practice, a customer loyalty programme can be integrated into the company structure in a variety of distinct ways. Volkswagen, Audi and SWR3 Radio have formed entirely separate companies to take care of the loyalty programme business. Other companies such as Steiff (world leader in teddy bears) and Märklin (world leader in model railways) or Fischertechnik (producer of toy construction sets, one of, if not the, most innovative companies in the world using patents per employee as a measure, with 234 patents per 100 employees – Simon, 1996, p.105 or 129) have internal departments that manage their loyalty programmes. In this case, the group that is responsible for loyalty programme management is typically part of marketing or sales. If the loyalty programme is set up internationally, with members in different countries or even loyalty programme subsidiaries in other countries, it can also be integrated into international marketing (Butscher, 1995, p.530). Another group of companies have outsourced most of the loyalty programme-related functions to a specialized outside agency.

The decision of how and where to integrate the customer loyalty programme into the sponsoring company cannot be avoided. Regardless of what form is chosen, the loyalty programme should be able to make independent decisions, and thus be entirely member- and value-driven. For example, customers come first (or at least should come first) in product management, so the members, and the value the loyalty programme offers to them, must be the first priority for the loyalty programme management.

## How to exploit the loyalty programme's support potential

A more important aspect that has to be carefully planned is ensuring that the loyalty programme's potential as a provider of information and data is fully exploited by the sponsoring company's other departments. R&D, product management, market research, advertising, customer service, after-sales service and sales representatives are only a few examples of departments and groups that can benefit from the opportunity to have immediate access to a group of customers or members:

- who are accessible in a well-structured way through the loyalty programme organization
- on whom individual data is available through the database
- who have a particular interest in the product, company or brand, expressed by becoming a member
- who are more willing to share opinions and data than the average customer
- who in many cases are even thankful for the opportunity to share their ideas and thoughts with the sponsoring company.

Table 15.1 shows some examples of how the loyalty programme and its members can be used to assist various departments in their decision processes. These examples all represent opportunities for significant cost reductions, as the alternatives of market studies or focus groups would cost much more to set up. Of course, a customer loyalty programme does not make other market research redundant, but it can reduce the amount of resources that flow into it. A customer loyalty programme will not always be representative of the entire population that you want to analyse. The more open a loyalty programme is (see Chapter 8 for the definition of open and limited loyalty programmes), the closer it will get to representativeness, as the number of members is typically much higher than in a limited loyalty programme. However, a limited loyalty programme mostly attracts only genuinely interested customers, which increases their willingness to share information and to participate in special studies, and improves the value of their input.

Consider, for example, a situation in which several software developers of a major software company are discussing whether or not to invest in a possible new feature for the next software update. Within a matter of hours, they can retrieve phone numbers from the member database via the programme service centre that controls access to the database, call a few dozen members – in this case, perhaps some information technology managers from various customer firms – and discuss the idea with them. The questions which could be asked might include: 'Would this feature make your everyday work with this programme easier?' This not only provides them with at least a rough idea of how the market feels about this feature and whether it is worth investigating in more detail, at the same time it makes these members feel special, as the call indicates how important they are to the company and how much their opinion is valued.

**Table 15.1**    Examples of how to exploit the loyalty programme's support potential

**Use the loyalty programme and its members:**

- to encourage comments, criticism and perceptions on today's products
- to identify areas of improvement for current products
- to obtain new product and service ideas
- to test new products and product ideas
- to test other marketing tools, e.g. planned advertising campaigns
- as your ear to the market which helps to detect new trends and developments
- for market research
- for collection of hard data on usage, willingness to pay etc.
- to support your entire company.

The Internet is an ideal platform from which to interact directly with the members and gather their opinions on a wide range of issues, such as new product ideas, new advertising campaigns, tips and improvement ideas for the current product. Members can visit the loyalty programme's home page, see what current issues are being discussed, enter their comments, and leave. To encourage them to come back soon, it should be indicated that the results of these surveys or discussions will be displayed on the Web page. When they return to read these results, they may be attracted by the current issues discussed through this forum (see also Chapter 13 on how to use the Internet for customer loyalty programmes).

Despite the opportunities which a loyalty programme and its members represent, there are limits to how often they should be contacted for help or participation. They have joined the loyalty programme in order to benefit from it, and not to be asked for their opinion or to test a new product every week or month. By choosing different participants for each test or interview and by feeding the database with information regarding which member participated in which study, and how often they were contacted, an overdose of contact can be avoided. Another possibility is to let the members be proactive in contacting you when they feel like participating, by posting information on current issues in the loyalty programme media (loyalty programme magazine, Web site) and including response elements that the members can use if they want. However, the return rate is much lower through this more passive approach than through a more personal approach.

Currently, the support potential of customer loyalty programmes is not even partially used by most loyalty programmes. Typically, a loyalty programme takes care of its own business and does not co-operate in any way with other departments. One exception is the Microsoft Advantage loyalty programme in Germany and the UK. Microsoft Advantage regularly co-operates with market research, marketing communications, public relations, fairs and events, seminar marketing, product marketing, finance, product support and customer service and fulfilment These departments are provided with information from the loyalty programme database, booths for fairs are jointly planned, new software and demos are tested by the loyalty programme members, and so on. Customer loyalty programmes are seen as a marketing instrument with a bright future, especially because of the positive effects which the integration of the loyalty programme into general marketing activities can have (Thieme, 1996).

Customer loyalty programmes can also be used to support the dealers and distribution partners of the sponsoring companies through launching special activities that encourage members to increase the frequency of store visits. Examples of how to achieve this include having members pick up the latest loyalty programme magazine at a dealership, installing special loyalty programme displays with current and frequently updated loyalty programme information, or initiating special activities at dealers' premises, such as product presentations, for which the members are sent a personal invitation. These activities primarily aim to increase store traffic. Other ways of supporting dealers include providing them with information and material to support their local advertising. Members of the Steiff loyalty programme are assigned to a particular dealer with whom they are in regular contact from the very beginning of their membership.

## Summary

One of the questions that must be addressed is how to integrate the customer loyalty programme into the sponsoring company's organizational structure. There are a variety of alternatives, from founding a totally independent company that manages the loyalty programme, to integrating the loyalty programme into one of the existing departments, to outsourcing the entire loyalty programme management to an outside agency. There is no best solution, so this decision has to be made according to the individual situation of the sponsoring company.

In addition, customer loyalty programmes have enormous support potential. Departments of the sponsoring company, such as market research, product marketing or R&D, can profit from the loyalty programme by using the information in the loyalty programme database and the members themselves to test new products, to discuss existing products to identify problems and areas of improvement, to test new advertising campaigns, and in many other ways. Loyalty programme members show more willingness to participate in such surveys than do ordinary customers, as they have a stronger affinity to the products, expressed by their membership. When the right procedures are implemented, dealers can also profit from the loyalty programme, because it can increase store traffic and improve the relationship between the dealers and their customers.

# **16** *The loyalty programme database*

Without building and fully utilizing the potential of a customer database, companies will not be able to compete successfully in today's competitive environment, let alone tomorrow's. With the increasing popularity of Customer Relationship Management (CRM), whose main component is a data warehouse, the importance of systematically collecting, analysing and using customer data has gained additional momentum. The database is a corporate memory that helps to capture, analyse and group individual transaction needs and behavioural information, and to use this information to execute the tactics and strategies demanded by your business in a very specific context and environment (Poulos, 1996, p.34). With the advent of CRM, the database has also taken on a growing strategic role, increasing its importance as a central element of corporate marketing.

Database marketing today is still far from perfect. Positive examples do exist, such as American Express, but overall, databases are primarily used for direct mail and telemarketing. These are more tactically oriented applications (Rosenfield, 1996, p.40). This will not be enough in the future. A database must be seen and used from a more strategic viewpoint. Databases are strategic weapons. Whether they applied in the right or wrong way may decide the winners or losers of tomorrow's struggle for market share and profits. Table 16.1 shows an example for database marketing in the retail industry.

## Customer loyalty programmes and databases

Data mining, the modern term for data analysis, is also becoming more and more important in the context of relationship marketing and customer loyalty programmes, for two reasons. First, customer loyalty programmes are an ideal source for detailed customer data. Second, customer loyalty programmes are the perfect channel to launch customized marketing activities, such as communication or product offers.

Loyalty Partner, the largest bonus programme in Germany, combining participants from several dozen industries, asks its members to provide personal data on the sign-up form such as number of children, income and so on. Over 50 per cent of the customers provide this information, which is shared with the participating companies. Additional data on purchasing behaviour and so forth is also provided (Bunk, 2001, p.32). The more programmes use the Internet for their activities, the more access they will have to customers' online data, which is easier to collect as nearly all activities leave electronic 'fingerprints'. Now, while one should not collect and use this data without the customers' consent, the members of your loyalty programme will be much more willing to share such information with you than your average customer:

**Table 16.1** Example for database marketing – retail

| Basic description | 1 Classic retail | 2 Local researched/ grouped | 3 Basic database | 4 Full relationship |
|---|---|---|---|---|
| Main characteristics | Management of customers focused almost entirely on what happens on site. | Management of customers still focused mainly on what happens on site and on national and regional understanding of merchandise sales and competitive patterns, but also on what kinds of customers live/pass by the site and what their needs are. | Most customers – particularly most frequent customers – have been identified by name/address, and simple questionnaire completed indicating journeys to/on work, spouse/partner patterns, usual times of buying fuel, and types of purchase do/would make at site. | As basic database, but with clear focus on defined market segments known – through analysis of purchasing history – to have high value. |
| | Site management forms judgement about local requirements (e.g. in terms of merchandising) and overall sales potentially by talking with customers and by analysing own sales patterns. | Site potential estimated not only by past performance and performance of similar sites (size, traffic, location – including relative to competition/catchment areas), but also by market research of customers who visit individual sites, by geo-demographic/postcode techniques, and possibly by sourcing data from credit card companies. | Purchasing history being accumulated but not used in detail apart from at a summary level e.g. total purchase by category. | Merchandising and promotions strongly focused on target segments, possibly at different times of day/week. |
| | General (national, regional and local) product range requirements identified by national merchandising using data from sales performance, suppliers of merchandise, and market research. | | On-site merchandising focus now balanced by database focus, particularly focus on what most regular customers buy – or want to buy, as indicated, by intermittent database questionnaire, and on results of promotions targeted at particular areas and customer types (especially journey types). | Mailings segmented. |
| | Strengths and weaknesses of individual site performance identified by trends and comparisons with sites of similar size/traffic/location – including relative to competition (latter using data from retail audits and market research). | Site management still forms judgement about local requirements by talking with customers, by analysing own sales patterns, but also through market research and by testing additional merchandise both in store and by local promotions (e.g. through free newspapers, leafleting). | Identifier almost certainly a plastic card, but not necessarily a loyalty card (could be own credit card). If loyalty scheme, points allocated strictly on purchasing – not skewed to favour 'best' customer patterns. Scheme may include partnership deals. | Some customer service differentiation in favour of best customers e.g. reserved newspapers/magazines, special bakery and other food items, loyalty scheme skewed to their patterns – including types of partnership deals. |
| | Traffic stimulated by blanket local promotions (i.e. not selected by postcode, but targeted through local media – press, radio, TV if local available) and by national and regional media-based promotions. | May include local marketing aimed at specific targetable groups such as 'retired' or 'mums with kids'. | Strengths and weaknesses identified not only by trends and comparisons with sites of similar size/traffic and of sites with similar catchment areas, but also by growth and value of database and purchasing patterns of different types of customer. | Customer data may be available at point of sale. |
| | | Strengths and weaknesses identified by trends and comparisons with sites of similar size/traffic and of sites with similar catchment areas, supplemented by national and regional data. | | |

*Source: Stone (1997), p.15*

- The members are more willing to share information about themselves, as they have greater affinity for and trust in the sponsoring company, the product and the loyalty programme. This affinity has already been expressed by the fact that they joined the loyalty programme.

- By joining the loyalty programme, the member is implicitly allowing – and even expecting – you to maintain this type of database, thereby by-passing many privacy concerns.

- Members are generally product users, so that not only personal data can be collected, but also information on product usage, product choice or frequency of purchases.

- Data collection is easier and more complete through a loyalty programme than, for example, by using TV commercials promoting a toll-free phone number and then matching the callers' telephone numbers with addresses and inputting this information into the database. If members give data voluntarily, they tend not to be angry if their name appears on such a list.

- For all contacts in a database, the chance of having a wrong name or address is between 10 and 15 per cent, meaning that about one in ten names or addresses in a database is misspelt or wrong. This number can be reduced to close to zero in a customer loyalty programme, as the initial data such as name and address is taken from the application form, which is normally filled out more carefully than a coupon or promotional card. As the addresses are regularly used to send out the loyalty programme magazine, returned mail can indicate wrong or misspelt names or addresses. Members have the opportunity to have misspellings corrected or to notify changes by using the loyalty programme hotline or sending in a special form for this purpose.

Consequently, a customer loyalty programme database contains the data of the sponsoring company's most important customers in extreme detail. Or, as *The Economist* put it: 'Smart companies are trying to … gather information first-hand from the customer', rather than relying on purchased mailing lists and so on (*The Economist*, 1999). Let us take a look at the Fox Kids loyalty programme of the Fox Children's Network in the USA. Detailed analysis of loyalty programme members by the American Computer Group and by Simmons Market Research Bureau, initiated by the Fox Children's Network, resulted in very detailed information:

- 63.6 per cent of all members are between 5 and 11 years old, and the average age is 9.7 years
- gender distribution is nearly 50/50 between boys and girls
- 47 per cent of all members live in households with an annual income of $40 000+, 22 per cent in households with an annual income of $60 000+
- 63 per cent of the children have at least one parent with a college and/or postgraduate degree
- further information is available on their TV viewing habits, hobbies and so on.

This background results in (from a manufacturer's or advertiser's point of view) an extremely attractive target group with a high buying power. Compared to the average US child, Fox Kids loyalty programme members are:

- 74 per cent more likely to own electronic games
- 50 per cent more likely to play with video games for six hours or more per week
- 15 per cent more likely to have gone to the cinema in the last 90 days
- 23–64 per cent more likely to go to a fast food restaurant, depending on the meal
- 44 per cent more likely to participate in team sports.

Furthermore, the database revealed that 90 per cent of readers of the Totally Kids' loyalty programme magazine have their own spending money, and 22 per cent have more than $5 per week (American Computer Group, 1995; Negus, 1995; Simmons Market Research Bureau, 1993).

It is not difficult to see the value of such detailed information, even though it does not represent the entire customer base. The Fox loyalty programme has about 5.5 million members, and around 10000 join every week (Negus, 1995), so that the data is probably reasonably representative.

These advantages do not necessarily hold true for all loyalty programmes. Consider frequent flyer programmes. Anybody can join these programmes by simply filling out a form. You do not even need to have flown with the airline concerned. The consequence is that many frequent flyers are members of several frequent flyer programmes, just to make sure that they do not lose any miles should they end up on one of their less preferred airlines. This multi-membership is encouraged by those programmes where the miles do not expire after two or three years. Yet, effectively, these travellers do try to use only one or two airlines in order to focus their mileage collection. Their value to the other airlines, and even to their preferred airlines, is relatively small, as none will be able to collect sufficient data to reflect the frequent flyers' complete or at least partial flying behaviour. Sometimes, one airline might only receive data on a passenger's flying habits on one specific route. Furthermore, these frequent flyers do not develop an emotional relationship that would attach them to any one of the carriers.

## Customer loyalty programme database management

Figure 16.1 shows the cycle of customer loyalty programme database management. While we do not want to go too much into detail on the technical side of steps 1 to 3, step 4 needs to be looked at more closely. If the data is analysed correctly, it will reveal ideas for personalized approaches to the customer. This could be customized product offers, communicative elements or the like. One aspect must be managed carefully here: you must prioritize between the different alternatives, and limit the number of contacts with each member. Too much contact, even though customized, can backfire. Although it is called 'customer relationship', many customers perceive it as extremely annoying if they constantly receive material marketers think would be of interest to them. Permission marketing is the key, meaning that you use your close contact with your programme members to optimize the contact frequency and closely monitor their reaction to current activities (step 5).

A well-organized database is critical to a loyalty programme's success, not only because the loyalty programme itself can be managed more efficiently, but also because the entire company can benefit more from the customer loyalty programme if it has a database. Here are some factors to consider when planning the implementation of the database:

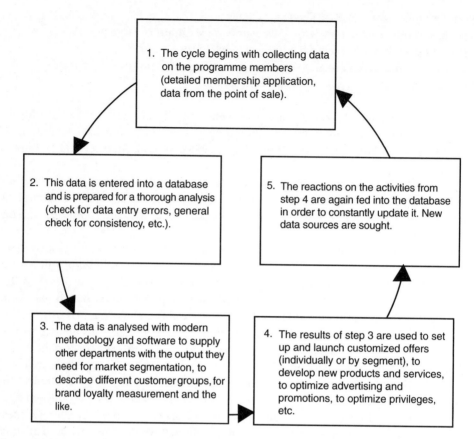

**Figure 16.1**    The cycle of customer loyalty programme database management

- The database technology must be capable of handling large amounts of data in a fast, reliable and efficient way. Always plan on at least 50 per cent more capacity than you originally estimated, as the database should be able to handle additional information that will be collected in the future.
- The technology should be expandable and compatible with other systems and programmes (such as analytical software or dealer network support systems).
- The database should be created so that data analyses can be extracted and presented in a highly customized and flexible way, depending on which department requests the information.
- The operational systems of the customer service department should interface with the database, so that customer service representatives can extract or add data while they are on the phone with a member or in a similar situation.
- The people who set up and maintain the database must be well trained. Nothing is more frustrating than a database whose full potential is not exploited due to lack of knowledge.

Another important decision is which data to collect. The information fed into a customer database should include, but not be limited to:

- demographic data on the individual

- demographic data on the household
- financial information
- currently used products
- purchasing data, such as place, time, frequency of purchases and the products and brands bought
- purchase motivation
- reasons for non-usage of specific products and brands
- availability of telephone, TV, computer, Internet access, e-mail and other technologies in the household
- time, place and frequency of usage of specific products.

For business-to-business databases, additional information should include:

- delivery and billing addresses
- structural company data, such as size, revenues, growth, product range, industries served
- partnerships, shares and holdings of other organizations
- members of the buying centre, with individual data on each of them
- purchase history, including specifics on products, volume, time and place of purchases and orders
- customer care information, such as number of contacts with customer service, contacts by telephone, with sales representatives or during trade shows.

For the loyalty programme itself, the following data should be added:

- contact history
- how often which benefits were used by the member
- a detailed overview of how often the member received and reacted to special offers and other customized contacts.

This list is by no means exhaustive and will differ depending on the company, the industry, the structure and type of customers. The list can serve to indicate how detailed the data could, and ideally should, be.

## Customer loyalty programme cards as data collectors

By offering a customer loyalty programme card and encouraging members to use it for payment (if it includes a credit function), or at least for identification at the point of sale, it is easier to collect data on the purchasing behaviour of members. The picture becomes more complete the more points of sale accept the customer loyalty programme card as a form of payment (for example, when it includes a credit card of a major credit card brand) or as a form of identification (for example, through partnerships with retail chains).

Currently, most customer loyalty programmes issue their members with a membership card, but in many cases this card serves no other purpose than to indicate membership. There often isn't even anyone to whom this card should be shown, as there is no location where the members would have to identity themselves as such. In essence, these cards serve no real purpose.

In order for a loyalty programme card to make sense, at least one of the following conditions should be fulfilled:

- The loyalty programme organizes events or co-operates with external partners, where the members are forced to prove their membership status before being allowed to enter or before qualifying for special offers or treatment.
- The loyalty programme card has a payment function, so that it can be used at points of sale.

In other words, the customer loyalty programme card must have a value. One can imagine, however, that certain loyalty programmes, such as those for children, have to offer a paper or plastic card to members, as they perceive a card as valuable and do not realize or care that it has no real function.

Table 16.2 summarizes the most important areas in which a customer loyalty programme database can be used.

**Table 16.2**    How the loyalty programme database can be used

---

**Use the loyalty programme database:**

- to learn more about who your customers are
- to analyse their purchasing behaviour and changes in it
- to identify and describe different segments
- to identify the hidden demands of your customers
- to send out individualized product offers, mailings etc.
- for after-sale services
- to identify the need for new products
- to identify new markets and niches
- to provide other company departments with information or data and assist in their projects

**Your database is a strategic weapon if used wisely.**

---

# Summary

A database that contains detailed and correct information on your customers is a strategic weapon that will largely influence the success of your company in the future. Databases must be seen from a strategic rather than a tactical viewpoint. A customer loyalty programme is the ideal instrument for data collection on your most important customers in the right quality and quantity. The increased willingness of members to share information and provide data in volume and detail comes from their higher affinity with the loyalty programme and the sponsoring company. Not only can this data then be used for loyalty programme activities, but also to support other company departments with information they need for their business. Potentially, this could move your company one step closer to one-on-one marketing. But careful use of the available data is necessary in order to prevent your members from being overloaded with communication and offers, which could easily alienate them.

In order to reach maximum effectiveness, the database must be well planned and executed, by deciding what information it should contain, how this data should be collected, what technical and human resources are necessary, how the data should be analysed, and for which purposes the data can be used.

# 17 *Business-to-business loyalty programmes*

Creating and maintaining good relationships in the business-to-business (B2B) environment is at least as important as a good relationship between manufacturer and end-user. In addition to the different end-user segments, the manufacturer may also have to deal with business customers, as well as with other business partners such as dealers, distributors and intermediaries. It is not easy to handle such a network of relationships in a professional and efficient way. Sophisticated and flexible tools are necessary to achieve this. That is why customer loyalty programmes work very well in the B2B area (we will take the liberty of interpreting the term 'B2B' more widely than usual, to include other partner businesses, such as distributors). A customer loyalty programme provides a platform for bundling different forms of relationship marketing in a way that serves the different business partners as well as possible and puts these tools to use in the most effective way.

## Mutual dependency in B2B relationships

In the B2B area, manufacturers and their customers depend on each other. The relationship with professional customers is important to the manufacturer, who depends on them to use its products. But the business customer also largely depends on the manufacturer. The user, the installer and the constructor all have to be able to rely on the quality and performance of the product. They are in contact with the end-user, and need to be able to offer them products of the right quality, quantity, style, price, design, grade of customization, time, place and so on. They depend on the manufacturer to offer and deliver exactly what they require to do their job properly, while the manufacturer needs professionals to sell what it has to offer and also to convince end-users to choose its products.

The manufacturer also needs to have a close relationship with the distributor and dealer network, to make sure that its products are placed as close to the customer as possible and to provide the customer with special product consultation. In order to support dealers, and thus indirectly its products, most effectively, the manufacturer needs to know about the sales partners' requirements and problems. Dealers, on the other hand, want to have the best brands on their shelves, offer a good quality–price ratio, and co-operate with suppliers that support their needs. Depending on their relative situations, the power is more on the manufacturer's or the dealer's side, deciding who has more influence on pricing, delivery sequence and so on. But neither could do without the other.

A customer loyalty programme is an ideal platform to bring company and customers together and enable an intensive exchange and co-operation.

# Dealer and professional loyalty programmes

B2B loyalty programmes are the ideal marketing tool to cope with this complicated mesh of relationships, dependencies and connections. B2B loyalty programmes can come in different forms, depending on whom they are primarily targeting:

- A professional loyalty programme targets the professional user of a product, such as a builder, the printer or architect. Professional users are trained in the use of the product, their consultation capabilities are improved, special seminars are given on how to improve their business in a particular market, or special services for small businesses may be offered by the loyalty programme. The professionals in turn then promote the product more effectively, try to convince the end-user and final decision-maker of the product's quality and performance, or send their people on special technical training sessions.

- A dealer loyalty programme primarily aims to assist the dealers (mostly smaller speciality dealers) in their struggle to survive in an environment more and more dominated by large regional and national chains. The dealers might receive assistance in display design, local advertising, training of staff or marketing in general. The dealer then displays the manufacturer's products more prominently, promotes its sales more aggressively, or positions the manufacturer's products more effectively in the different advertising media, such as flyers.

# Differences between end-user and B2B loyalty programmes

B2B loyalty programmes and end-user (B2C) loyalty programmes are similar in their core mechanisms and in the approach that has to be taken to put together a good programme. The different steps of a customer loyalty programme concept described in this book are just as valid for B2B loyalty programmes as they are for end-user loyalty programmes. Goals, target groups, benefits, communication means, loyalty programme organization and the financial concept have to be planned in the same way, and just as carefully. The most important aspect is to approach a B2B concept from the same value- and customer-oriented perspective described in the previous chapters mainly for end-user loyalty programmes.

However, although both loyalty programme types are similar in the way they work and are developed, there are some differences that must be considered:

- B2B loyalty programmes typically deal with smaller and more clearly defined target groups. In order to reach most of this small group, the benefit package must exactly meet the demand of the target group. Therefore the value-oriented three-step approach described in Chapter 9 must be executed with high concentration, particularly because the sample sizes will be smaller.

- In many cases, the relationship with members of these more manageable target groups is driven by personal contacts between the sales representatives and the purchasers, or between customer service and professional users. These personal relationships should not be replaced by the loyalty programme, but rather the existing contacts should be integrated into the loyalty programme concept and be supported by the loyalty programme. One of the strongest factors that influences the purchasing decision and can help to reduce the probability of defection is the personal relationship and trust which are formed between the members of the selling and the buying centre. This, combined with the services and benefits the loyalty programme can offer, results in a very strong relationship-building tool.

- B2B loyalty programmes are more partnership-oriented. Both loyalty programme sponsor and member know that they depend on each other and that they must each contribute to the relationship in some way. Therefore, the loyalty programme not only offers services for free, but in many cases a loyalty programme member has to contribute in some way first (for example, by sending its employees to special product training) in order to be able to receive and benefit from the loyalty programme benefit package.

- Membership fees in the B2B area are much higher than in the end-user area. The reason for this is that B2B loyalty programmes are set up in a more partnership-oriented way, and members join the loyalty programme for professional reasons. They know that their company can benefit strongly from the membership. Their membership might enable them to carry out marketing activities and offer their customers products and services in a way which was not possible before. They see the membership as an investment in the improvement of their business by forming a partnership with a strong manufacturer.

- B2B members are more rational than emotional in their evaluation of the value of loyalty programme benefits, because they mainly seek professional rather than personal advantages.

- Nevertheless, although members are primarily looking for professional advantages, they should also be offered specific benefits that are more targeted at giving them personal value. Such benefits could include tickets to sports events, special vacation offers, or products.

- In a B2B environment it is important to involve members in the everyday loyalty programme life, and possibly in its management as well. Many B2B loyalty programmes have therefore installed a special committee which consists of the loyalty programme management and elected or selected members. This ensures greater identification with the loyalty programme, dynamic development (as the committee can decide which benefits should be added or discontinued), and can even lead to a form of self-management (Wiencke and Tribian, 1996, p.154).

- Because of its professional nature, most of the loyalty programme benefits must be product-related and concern the loyalty programme sponsor's basic fields of competence.

- A B2B loyalty programme should always assist rather than replace classic marketing activities such as advertising, promotions or point-of-sale displays. They can be integrated and bundled through the loyalty programme, giving them a more strategic framework and more focus on the main target groups.

In the B2B area, a more focused approach is necessary to identify the right benefits. The members of a B2B loyalty programme want to obtain solutions to specific problems from the loyalty programme. In order to select the right value drivers, the three-step approach presented in Chapter 9 can be used. To find out in which areas additional services and benefits are most required, a portfolio technique can be used that relates the importance of different success factors for the professional or dealer to how much each of these factors can be influenced by the manufacturer. Figure 17.1 shows an example for a kitchen furniture speciality dealer.

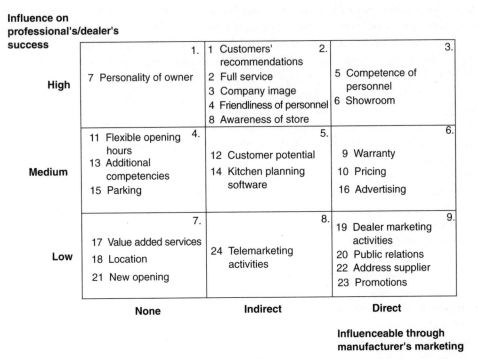

Influence on professional's/dealer's success

| | None | Indirect | Direct |
|---|---|---|---|
| **High** | 1.<br>7 Personality of owner | 2.<br>1 Customers' recommendations<br>2 Full service<br>3 Company image<br>4 Friendliness of personnel<br>8 Awareness of store | 3.<br>5 Competence of personnel<br>6 Showroom |
| **Medium** | 4.<br>11 Flexible opening hours<br>13 Additional competencies<br>15 Parking | 5.<br>12 Customer potential<br>14 Kitchen planning software | 6.<br>9 Warranty<br>10 Pricing<br>16 Advertising |
| **Low** | 7.<br>17 Value added services<br>18 Location<br>21 New opening | 8.<br>24 Telemarketing activities | 9.<br>19 Dealer marketing activities<br>20 Public relations<br>22 Address supplier<br>23 Promotions |

**Influenceable through manufacturer's marketing**

*Source:* Schmadalla (1996), p. 75.

**Figure 17.1**    Portfolio technique for professional/dealer assistance – kitchen furniture dealer example

The matrix divides 24 possible success factors for a dealership into nine sectors. Sector 3 contains the most ideal factors, as they have a high influence on the dealer's success and are also directly able to be influenced by the manufacturer. In this example the competence of staff can be improved by offering special product training, while the showroom could be improved with free samples and displays. The manufacturer should primarily aim at improving the factors in sectors 2, 3 and 6, where improvements could have the greatest effects. Other sectors are of secondary importance, because effects or accessibility are limited (sectors 5 and 9), because they are not accessible to the manufacturer (sectors 1, 4 and 7) or because they are not worth any major effort (sectors 7 and 8).

## Examples of successful B2B loyalty programmes

Let us look at some examples of B2B loyalty programmes that have been very successful over the last few years, and in some cases have become an integral part of the sponsoring company's marketing.

Märklin, the world leader in model railways, has the Märklin Dealer Initiative. Speciality dealers supply 90 per cent of Märklin's revenue in Germany, so the company largely depends on their performance against major competitors such as Toys R Us. Especially in a period when children are turning away from traditional toys such as railways and adults' time for hobbies is becoming more and more limited, it is important for dealers to make every effort to attract new customers to the world of model railways. At the same time, they must keep existing customers – old and young – fascinated by the hobby. The member dealers are assisted with their shop window display design, advertising, technical training for their personnel, local activities for the two Märklin end-user loyalty programmes (1.FC Märklin for children, and Märklin Insider for adults), and Märklin sells certain models exclusively through speciality dealers. These speciality dealers have to carry the complete Märklin product line, prominently position Märklin in their showrooms, employ trained staff, and participate in local advertising and loyalty programme activities. The Märklin Dealer Initiative currently has around 1500 members and is a huge success, stabilizing Märklin's position in a shrinking market.

Spies Hecker is the market leader in car repair paint in Germany, and founded the Spies Hecker Professional Club in 1990. More than 1800 auto body paint shops have joined the loyalty programme, nearly a third of all companies in this market. The club offers a large variety of services to its members, mostly smaller businesses and body shops. Members pay £30 per year for the entire package, which includes services in the areas of:

- marketing (body shop design, business strategy workshops for small businesses)
- communication (club-info magazine, club hotline, club service centre)
- environment (workshops, environmental certification of the business indicated by an official seal)
- training and consultation (workshops on legal issues, market strategy, advertising, tax issues, problem of successorship in family businesses)
- club meetings, general members' meetings, regional activities, club trips)
- leisure (club trips, club shop, ticket service).

An advisory board of experts, consisting of representatives from the most important suppliers in the industry, supports the Spies Hecker Professional Club management, offering expertise on legal, technical, market and business issues and giving the loyalty programme greater integrity.

One of the most successful B2B loyalty programmes in Germany is the Professional Club of Friedrich Grohe, the market leader in bathroom and kitchen fittings. A case study on this loyalty programme can be found in Chapter 24. This case study will also give further insight into the specific features of B2B loyalty programmes and B2B marketing. Another very successful programme is T-Mobil's T-D1 Company Class, for which a case study can be found in Chapter 22.

## Summary

Customer loyalty programmes are not only successful in the end-user area, but also in B2B environments. The procedure for setting up a B2B loyalty programme is the same as for an end-user customer loyalty programme. It is most important to offer benefits that have value for the members.

But B2B loyalty programmes have certain specific characteristics that need to be considered, such as the relatively small target group, consisting mainly of professionals or businesses, the clear demand structure of this target group, and the necessity of meeting this demand precisely with loyalty programme benefits. Further special characteristics of B2B loyalty programmes are the partnership character of the loyalty programme as loyalty programme sponsor and loyalty programme member join forces to reach mutual goals in the market, and the higher involvement of members in loyalty programme management and development.

# 18 *Measuring the loyalty programme's success*

One of the most important questions the loyalty programme's management will have to address is: 'Is the customer loyalty programme successful?' With any marketing effort, such as an advertising campaign, a special promotion, a product launch or sponsoring of an event, the managers responsible are under pressure to show the success of their project and to ensure future support for it within the company. The customer loyalty programme management will also be obliged to provide answers to this kind of question. Therefore, the customer loyalty programme concept must include different qualitative and quantitative means and indices that will indicate whether the loyalty programme is successful.

## Clear definition of success

Naturally, success is often a very subjective term, and largely depends on what goals were set and what level of achievement is considered a success. Should a customer loyalty programme that primarily aims at customer retention but steadily attracts new customers to the company be considered a success or a failure, as it has not met its primary goal? Or what about a customer loyalty programme that managed to increase customer loyalty from 80 to 81 per cent: is that a success, or could that have been achieved without the loyalty programme? The problem in defining success is not unique to loyalty programmes, but is rather common in many business areas and beyond.

These areas also share one other problem: how can you totally isolate the effect of one stimulus from all other factors that could have influenced the target factor? For example, how can you be sure that a 15 per cent sales increase can be accredited entirely to the new advertising campaign? Is it not possible that dozens of other factors, such as local promotions, competitors' advertising and pricing moves, or the more prominently displayed product at dealerships during a promotion that ran at the same time as the advertising campaign, accounted for at least part of that sales increase?

Customer loyalty programmes in particular have to live with this problem, as the loyalty effect for which they strive is built up over the medium to long term, and members may stay with the loyalty programme for many years. Over this period, members are exposed not only to various loyalty programme activities, but to a host of advertisements, promotions, special offers, new competitors and products, as well as changes and shifts in their personal preferences and interests. All these variables will influence members' behaviour on loyalty programme-relevant factors such as product loyalty or purchase volume. Therefore, it is hard to pinpoint a single variable that is responsible for an increase in sales, profit or market share. However, through empirical observation and research, an understanding of the loyalty programme's achievements can be reached.

Consequently, the programme management, together with the upper management they report to, must define which goals the programme has and which scales have to be used to measure these goals. In addition, the levels for success and failure on each scale have to be defined. This must be done before the programme goes live, and must be recorded in written form in order to avoid unnecessary disputes later on. Differentiation between primary and secondary goals is possible. Figure 18.1 shows how such a goal list might look for a B2B Internet Service Provider (ISP).

As you can see, some goals are easy to quantify (such as 'increase customer loyalty', which is measured using the churn rate), while others are more qualitative (such as 'create communication opportunities', especially one-to-one communication). This has consequences for the actual measurement.

## Quantitative goals

After defining the quantitative scales, you need to measure the status quo (such as the current churn rate overall), as not only the absolute figures are important, but also the relative development over time (and compared to the control group – see below). Regular measurement, typically once a year, will then produce the current levels, which need to be analysed in absolute terms (Is my churn rate high or low?) as well as in relative terms (Is the member churn rate lower than the non-member churn rate?). In order for this to run smoothly, the following questions must be answered:

- Where will the necessary data be generated? With which departments do we need to co-operate?

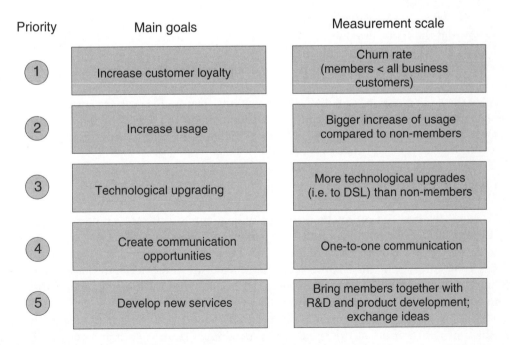

**Figure 18.1**   Prioritization of main goals with measurement scales

- Is a split between members and non-members possible?
- Who is responsible for the actual measurement?
- How often do we need to measure?
- How is the reporting organized (format, addresses, and so on)?

## Qualitative goals

The measurement of the qualitative goals is a little more tricky. The following steps need to be taken:

1 Break down the qualitative goals into several more detailed questions that can either be answered with 'yes' or ' no' or that can be measured with quantitative scales.
2 Answer/measure these questions objectively.
3 Reach conclusions regarding success or failure.

Let us look at an example taken from Figure 18.1. The goal 'create communication opportunities' with its scale 'one-to-one communication' is very qualitative, soft and hard to measure in this form. However, the success measure could be broken down into the following questions, which make it much easier to measure objectively:

- How often did the programme initiate contact with the members last year?
- How many of these contacts were individual, and how many were part of standard activities?
- How often did the members contact the programme via the call centre, e-mail or directly through the CSC?
- Did a dialogue begin with these members?
- How did the traffic develop on the customer loyalty programme Web site (hits, one-off visits, total time of visit, and so on)?
- Were the communication platforms offered online used (such as discussion forums)?

All of these sub-questions can now be measured with quantitative scales or answered with an objective 'yes' or 'no'. Again, as with the measurement of the direct quantitative goals, the levels of success and failure must be defined for the scales, in order to avoid disputes later on.

## Using a control group

To tackle the problem of isolating the loyalty programme's effects, you must measure the relevant factors not only for loyalty programme members, but also for a group of non-members (control group). Both groups will have been exposed to the same marketing activities, competitors' activities and market environment. Any difference in the measured factors must be identified, and can be interpreted as the result of the loyalty programme's activities. In order to achieve optimal results, two issues must be borne in mind.

Ideally, the factors analysed must be measured for both groups from the very beginning, which means from the day of the loyalty programme's launch. Both groups have to start from exactly the same situation. The non-member group should be defined as part of the loyalty programme's planning process. If a test group can only be installed at a later time, it should consist of non-members from the same target groups as the loyalty programme members. The changes from that moment on can be measured and the two groups can be compared, but the results will not be absolutely free of any previous influences.

In order to compare the two groups, you should measure changes rather than absolute figures. For example, the statement 'Loyalty programme members have a higher purchase volume than non-members' could be misinterpreted. Loyalty programme members in general already have a higher affinity to the product, and most probably also a higher-than-average usage than non-members. Statements such as 'The increase of the purchase volume of members was 10 per cent higher than that of non-members during the same period' or 'The satisfaction index of the members increased by 5 per cent compared to a 2 per cent decrease for the non-members' are of much more use, and reflect the true picture more closely (Holz and Tomczak, 1996, p.69).

The most important aspect of measuring the loyalty programme's success is to define clearly what factors should be measured, which scales will be used, and what levels on those scales are considered a success, average or failure. This is necessary to avoid any misunderstanding and conflict when the results are discussed. For example, you could define the loyalty programme as being successful in terms similar to the following:

- an increase in loyalty programme membership by 20 per cent this year
- the total revenue from the loyalty programme's activities should exceed £150 000
- the satisfaction index from the company's annual customer satisfaction survey must have increased more for the loyalty programme members than for non-members
- the number of product improvement and new product ideas from loyalty programme members that are passed on to the relevant departments must increase by 15 per cent.

## Further aspects of success measurement

Some other aspects need to be considered when trying to measure the loyalty programme's success.

The success of your customer loyalty programme can be measured on two levels: company level, and loyalty programme level. In the final analysis, only the company results count, so even if your loyalty programme meets all its goals but company sales continually decrease, it is the latter that means more to company management. Therefore, the loyalty programme success measurement system should include loyalty programme and company-related indices.

The indices you select to use to measure the loyalty programme's success depend on the loyalty programme's goals and their hierarchy. The more important a goal, the more important it is to measure its achievement.

Defining appropriate indices to measure cannot be done on a general level. This largely depends on the loyalty programme's situation. Some indices are easy to measure, such as number of members, increase in expenditure on loyalty programme products, and response to special offers. Indices that are more difficult to measure include a member's repeat purchase behaviour or increase in brand loyalty. If the loyalty programme offers a credit card or has another way of linking purchasing information to an individual member, it will be easier to measure such factors, although even then a complete picture of the member's purchasing behaviour will be difficult to establish. The right combination of automatically measured factors and factors measured through additional efforts such as surveys must be found.

In order to meet the condition of measurability, all loyalty programme activities, such as special product offers or mailings, should be set up in a way that enables measurement of response rates. The number of products ordered after a special mailing or the number of calls received after a special feature in the loyalty programme magazine can easily be measured by having loyalty programme service centre personnel enter special codes into their computers for each call or order. These codes can then be analysed later.

In addition to this continual measurement of loyalty programme activities, the loyalty programme should carry out regular surveys measuring satisfaction with the loyalty programme and its benefits. This will help to identify areas that must be improved, but aspects should also be considered that are more difficult to measure, such as brand loyalty, changes in purchasing behaviour or word-of-mouth advertising. The Kawasaki Riders loyalty programme, for example, asks its members the make of their previous motorcycle. It found that the percentage of repeat Kawasaki buyers increased from 30 to 54 per cent through the loyalty programme. To summarize: 'There is no substitute for sitting across the table from a selected cross section of the loyalty programme members and asking them how they really feel about your products, your company, and of course your loyalty programme' (Ashton, 1996). This benefit satisfaction measurement should be carried out on two levels: first, for standard benefits in an annual member survey, and second, for one-time benefits directly at the end of the event.

The success of a loyalty programme does not only come from organizing its own activities. It can also support other company departments by making information and data from the loyalty programme database available to them. If, for example, the loyalty programme passes on the information to a product manager that some loyalty programme members have voiced ways of improving the products for which the manager is responsible, there should be a way to trace how many of these ideas were followed up and how they improved the overall satisfaction ratings of that product. Although the latter effect might be difficult to analyse, indices such as 'number of product improvement ideas from the customer loyalty programme' or 'number of new product ideas suggested by loyalty programme members' are easy to compile. They show how successfully the loyalty programme has supported other departments in improving their performance.

Another area that can be measured is cost savings. Through the loyalty programme's potential to assist in market research, R&D, product testing, or by using loyalty programme members for tasks that otherwise would have to be paid for, such as letting them participate as extras in movie productions, it can substantially decrease cost in other company areas. These savings should be quantified.

The loyalty programme database is also frequently used by other company departments to extract information needed for their work. As the loyalty programme is responsible for setting up and maintaining the database, the intensity of its usage is also an indication of the loyalty programme's success.

Other ways to measure the loyalty programme's success include comparing loyalty programme members with the general development of the industry's customers. Another way is to compare and contrast the sponsoring company's development with the average development of competitors or the general industry. Other possibilities are to compare cost-per-sale for members and non-members, or the fluctuation of customers with and without loyalty programme membership.

How successful do customer loyalty programmes and other value-oriented programmes tend to be? Unfortunately, for most companies their success, if it is measured, is a well-kept secret. Loyalty programme sponsors' high level of satisfaction with their loyalty programme is a strong indication of success. And again, whether a loyalty programme can be seen as successful or not largely depends on the definition of success in each individual case and the indicators used to measure it. However, some examples will indicate what powerful marketing tools customer loyalty programmes and other value-oriented loyalty programmes can be.

Tests from two large department stores showed 6–9 per cent sales increases in test groups compared to control groups. Furthermore, the attrition rate dropped by 5 per cent (Barlow, 1992, p.31). A large newspaper reported a 5.1 per cent increase in its retention rate through a loyalty programme, and *Los Angeles Magazine* improved its direct-mail response by 12.7 per cent, with a simultaneous 25 per cent price hike (*Ancillary Profits*, 1995, p.1). Other programmes report sales growth of between 15 and 25 per cent compared to controls (Wiencke and Koke, 1994, p.54; *Colloquy*, 1994, p.7). Biotherm, a L'Oréal company, reports that while the average Biotherm customer buys 1.5 cosmetics per year, Biotherm loyalty programme members buy 12 products per year (Stelzer, 1997, p.146). In addition, the trend to launch customer loyalty programmes or larger CRM initiatives is unbroken, and seems to be more popular than ever early in the 21st century.

Another (unpublished) study shows more interesting results, which are summarized in Table 18.1.

**Table 18.1**  Examples of quantitative loyalty programme effects

| Industry | Gains in key attitude (%) | Gains in sales volume (%) | Gains in usage (%) |
| --- | --- | --- | --- |
| Household Product | +20 | +41 | +47 |
| Non-food | +23 | +40 | +27 |
| Scotch Whisky | +55 | +12 | +22 |
| Food | +31 | +8 | +11 |
| Dog food | +12 | +17 | +10 |
| Average | +24 | +25 | +35 |

Deliotte Consulting published figures which show that industrial companies which have a particular focus on customer loyalty are on average 60 per cent more profitable than those that don't (Anon., 1999a, p.35).

## What if things go wrong?

Even if a loyalty programme is well planned and executed, it might not live up to its expectations. Or, after many successful years, a programme might slowly lose its edge and need to be replaced by something new. In this case, the question is how best to phase out the programme. There is no ideal solution, as it largely depends on the type of programme, but getting out is never as easy as getting in. Here are a few points to consider:

- If the programme includes a bonus point system, a fair deadline must be set to allow the points to be redeemed. Do not erase what customers have earned, sometimes over many years. Also, think about adding some smaller items to the list of what the points can be used for, in order to help those who do not have enough points for the key benefits to at least get something for their efforts. You could offer them products for a better price, or similar offers, in order to keep your cost low.

- Phasing out your programme obviously means that no new members should be admitted.
- If the members have paid an annual membership fee, end the programme after the period they have paid for.
- Inform the members as early as possible. Remember, these are your best customers, and they deserve your respect and consideration. Communicate openly; more communication and explanation is always better than less.
- Plan the end just as carefully as the beginning. There are many questions to be addressed. How much cost will you really save? Who will own the customer database, the infrastructure and so on in the future? What will happen to the programme personnel? Are there any assets that can be sold to cover some of the cancellation costs?

It is impossible to say with certainty whether a 'big bang' (simply stopping the programme on day x) is better than a slower phase-out. This depends on the specific situation of the programme. A 'big bang' is better if you have no obligations towards your members (such as points) and you know there will not be a major PR backlash. A slow phase-out is better if you fear the customers will develop strong feelings about the programme's end or if you still 'owe them something'.

A good example of how to do it right is the Cracker Barrel Neighborhood loyalty programme. In a newsletter, the members were informed that they would no longer receive programme mailings or points. Instead, the programme would consist of information and interaction available at the programme Web site. That is a smart way to phase out a programme – quietly withdraw communication and benefits until the members just forget the programme exists (Barlow, 2001, p.2).

Here are some additional ways to terminate a programme without offending its members (Barlow, 1999, pp.8f):

- Establish a definite time limit for the programme. Write it into the rules, but do not emphasize it, since you can always extend it year by year.
- Define the lifetime of points, so that you can limit your liability.
- Eliminate marginal members by establishing activity thresholds for maintaining memberships.
- In general, be reasonable without being extravagant.
- Maintain sufficient reserves to support 'aggressive' redemption in the event of programme cancellation.
- Be generous. It is not the customer's fault that the programme is ending. Instead, turn the negative challenge into a positive opportunity to reinforce your relationship with members by giving them a gift, a small token of appreciation.

## Summary

The success of a customer loyalty programme must be measured, just as with any other marketing instrument. Therefore, indices and scales must be clearly identified for all programme goals, and must be used to measure the loyalty programme's success. Furthermore, the levels of success, average performance and failure on these scales must be defined. These indices must include clearly quantifiable factors that can be measured automatically, such as response rates to loyalty programme activities, but also more qualitative factors such as brand loyalty, which then need to be broken down into more quantitative sub-questions or sub-scales. The indices chosen depend largely on the importance of the different loyalty programme goals. The more important the goals are, the more important it is to measure them. Comparing the results for loyalty programme members with a non-member control group can help isolate the effects of the loyalty programme marketing from other influences. Other indicators of the loyalty programme's success are the level of utilization of its database, savings in other departments due to the loyalty programme activities, and the loyalty programme's support of other departments in the sponsoring company.

Just as the programme launch must be planned, the possible exit strategy needs to be put together with great care. The two main options are a sudden 'big bang' ending, or a slow phase-out.

# 19 *A view of the future of customer loyalty programmes*

Customer loyalty programmes have a bright future. They have been used as loyalty-building instruments for many decades, and in today's competitive environment, being close to the customer is one of the most important prerequisites for success. Recent 'buzzwords' such as 'CRM', 'one-to-one marketing', or 'mass customization', and the huge number of new loyalty initiatives that are launched every year are proof of the fact that customer loyalty marketing is nearer its beginning than its end.

Loyalty programmes focus on very specific target groups rather than trying to reach a wide range of heterogeneous groups at the same time. They have proven to be very successful marketing tools, so it is no surprise that loyalty programmes are becoming more and more popular around the world. Loyalty programme concepts have been launched in France, Italy, the Netherlands, the UK, Australia, the USA and many other countries.

Customer loyalty programmes have shown themselves to be more effective than many other marketing alternatives. They can enable a company to communicate with thousands, hundreds of thousands or even millions of its (best!) customers on a personal level, taking the company's marketing a step closer to the ultimate of one-on-one marketing. Value-oriented customer loyalty programmes are among the most powerful marketing tools available to marketers. However, they are also among the most complicated and most difficult tools to develop and run.

But, in the end, only those companies that understand the basic principles of customer loyalty programmes will be successful loyalty marketers:

- *Offer real value.* This is the fundamental idea of customer loyalty programmes. Offer the members benefits that have a high perceived value. This means intensive planning, preparation and measurement of value. If the loyalty programme cannot offer something tangible, then it will not be viable. Ask yourself whether you would join a loyalty programme that fails to offer you anything of high value: certainly not, so why should your customers be different? Remember, quality is more important than quantity.

- *Develop a solid, long-term financial concept.* Use the scenario technique to prepare for unexpectedly high or low financial requirements, secure budgets for the loyalty programme from the company's overall budget, and use all available sources of revenue. Exploding cost is the number one reason for loyalty programme failure, therefore make sure that you are not unprepared.

- *Draw on internal support.* Everybody from top management to entry-level employees must be involved in the customer loyalty programme concept. If the loyalty programme does not have internal support, it will not be able to live up to its expectations. A customer loyalty programme is a long-term-oriented marketing tool, so top management should be willing to support it for several years at least. Employees at the customer interface need to convey the loyalty programme spirit to the customer. When they meet the loyalty programme member in the store or at the counter, they should give them special treatment. These employees need to understand the idea behind the loyalty programme: to create loyal customers through value benefits and special treatment. It is they who are responsible for that special treatment.

- *Create a professional loyalty programme infrastructure.* The call centre, the database and general administrative tasks must be professional. When dealing with your best customers, nothing but the best is good enough. Train your people, buy state-of-the-art hardware, and make sure that Mr Rutgers is not listed as 'Mr Rugers' in your database.

- *Exploit the loyalty programme's full potential.* A customer loyalty programme has huge potential for supporting other departments within your company. Use the customer loyalty programme and its members to provide data and information needed by these departments to improve their performance. This also means that the loyalty programme must be integrated into the company's general marketing plan, in order to maximize its value for other departments.

- *Carefully plan and build up a member database.* A customer loyalty programme is an ideal tool to collect data on your customers and understand them better. But a customer loyalty programme is not a sales tool. Do not use the data for constant selling. Loyalty programmes increase sales indirectly through the customer loyalty they build.

- *Use the Internet and the possibilities it brings with it for your loyalty programme.* Individual communication, member-to-member communication, current information and lower cost are only a few of the benefits the Internet offers for loyalty programmes.

These are the very basic conditions that need to be fulfilled before you decide that a customer loyalty programme is right for your company. If you cannot meet these standards, then other activities might be more suitable. Remember that loyalty programme management is like product management: in both, it is vital to develop a marketing plan, carefully prepare the product launch, and monitor its development in order to make any necessary adjustments.

## Avoid the pitfalls

The most common reasons for closing a loyalty programme are cost explosion and non-acceptance within the target group, mostly because the loyalty programme does not offer sufficient value. The financial and organizational effort necessary to develop, launch and maintain a customer loyalty programme is often underestimated, leading to the failure of initially good loyalty programme ideas. The new generation of customer loyalty programmes is now built on more sophisticated approaches and has learnt from past mistakes. Loyalty programme managers have realized that it is not the loyalty programme that is the loyalty vehicle, but what it stands for: benefits and value for the member.

We detail below several other mistakes frequently made in loyalty programme management, along with strategies for avoiding them (Lürken, 1997, p.24; Butscher, 1996d, p.41; Butscher, 1995, p.87):

- *Wrong definition of target groups* – Target your better customers, and offer what has value to them.

- *No communication* – One of the key elements of loyalty programme marketing is dialogue-oriented communication. Encourage members to communicate with you, and make sure that your means of communication deliver the right message and contain interesting information, but are not reduced to sales pitches.

- *Expecting the loyalty programme to attract all your customers* – A customer loyalty programme will never be able to turn 100 per cent of your customers into members. You should rather aim to attract as many of your top customers as possible. Setting a membership fee or a similar membership hurdle will keep out freeloaders.

- *Lack of activity* – The loyalty programme benefits only make sense if they are used. Members must be encouraged to use the benefits the loyalty programme has to offer, and the best way to do this is to provide constant reminders. The more the members use the benefits, the more they feel that loyalty programme membership is useful, and the more affinity to your products will be built.

- *No loyalty programme promotion* – Even the most attractive loyalty programme will not sell itself without help. The loyalty programme must be advertised, loyalty programme information must be available at your products' points of sale and wherever your customers can be reached. Your sales force and employees at the customer interface, as well as your distribution partners' employees, must be informed about the loyalty programme, and must be able to promote it.

Customer loyalty programmes can work for companies of all sizes. However, in general, medium to large companies will feel most comfortable with the customer loyalty programme concept, as they often have greater marketing knowledge and experience, a stronger financial background, and a better infrastructure to create and support a customer loyalty programme. The smaller the company, the more important a thorough financial concept becomes, and the more loyalty programme functions will have to be outsourced.

The lesson for everyone planning to develop a value-oriented customer loyalty programme is to find the right mixture between financial and non-financial (or hard and soft) benefits. The biggest mistake would be to focus entirely on discounts and rebates, which would lead to a situation similar to that in the USA, where competition in many industries is purely price-based. The only way to create uniqueness, to build real emotional relationships that last and to prevent the competition from copying your marketing moves is to include non-financial benefits. Customer loyalty can only be created in your customers' minds, not in their wallets. Therefore, there need to be benefits on the emotional level, complemented by benefits on the financial level.

Customer loyalty programmes are not easy to develop and manage, but their effectiveness is difficult to match. Setting up a customer loyalty programme in the right way can provide you with a marketing tool that will play a dominant role in your marketing mix.

How long will it be before you will be able to say: 'Welcome to the club!'?

# **20** *SWR3 Radio – The Club*

## Thomas Brinckwirth

*Thomas Brinckwirth is Managing Director of SWR3 CLUB in Baden-Baden, Germany. He was previously a radio editor. He has also worked as a linguist at the opera in São Paulo, Brazil, and for the German Goethe Institut in São Paulo, Brazil. He studied at Freiburg University, Germany, and Harvard University.*

SWR3 is Germany's most popular radio station. But it is more than a radio station – it represents a lifestyle. The station's outstanding feature is the never-ending production of its radio comedy slots. For over twenty-five years, SWR3 (formerly known as SWF3) has created characters and slogans that have become part of everyday conversation. These comedies plus investigative journalism and trend-setting in music are the three essentials of the station's philosophy and success. In terms of music, SWR3 follows an international rock and pop format. Despite hundreds of stations which try to copy its successful mix of music, journalism and comedy, SWR3 has succeeded in remaining the market leader for over twenty-five years.

Over two decades ago, a moose was chosen to serve as the trademark for SWR3. Because the station's headquarters are located in Baden-Baden, a small town in the famous Black Forest, it was soon dubbed the 'Black Forest Moose', which has become almost an official title. Its picture and voice are identification marks for the station. It has become a part of the station's lifestyle, to the extent that quality is referred to as 'mooseproof'.

Every day 2.7 million Germans, Swiss, Austrians and French between 14 and 39 years of age tune in to SWR3. The station broadcasts all over western and south-western Germany, including major cities such as Cologne, Frankfurt, Stuttgart and Heidelberg. SWR3 can also be heard through the cable networks of most German cities. It is distributed Europe-wide via the satellites ASTRA lB (11.494 GHz, subcarriers 7.38 and 7.56 MHz), ASTRA 1C (11.186 GHz, subcarrier 6.84 MHz) and world-wide via short-wave (7265 KHz/41m or 6030 KHz/49m). It can be listened to via online streaming at <http://www.swr3.de>.

## The club

SWR3 established its audience club to create a commercial platform for off-radio activities and as a marketing tool to compete more effectively after deregulation of the German radio broadcasting market. The club provides information about the radio station, its programmes, staff, stars and people in print as well as via its home page, <http://www.swr3club.de>. It also offers a variety of events and services to its members. Membership indirectly originates from subscription to the club's magazine, *SWR3 DAS MAGAZIN*, in order to keep administration simple. The annual fee is approximately £10. The club now has 70 000 members, and grows by 10 per cent per year.

The economic goal of SWR3 CLUB is to be self-financing. Sources of income are the annual membership fee and revenues from events, licensing, ticketing and merchandising. All profits must be completely reinvested in the club, and they can only be spent on additional club projects, marketing for the station or the club, and additional benefits for members. The club was started in 1991 with an initial capital of £400 000. Three years later, self-financing was reached. The various activities by means of print, multimedia or event-related marketing equal £10 million marketing power each year without costing the station a penny. This means that in order to create the same station awareness, press coverage and events as the club creates, the station would have to invest £10 million per year. Total club revenue is £4 million.

In collaboration with the station, an analysis of the radio's marketing needs and audience expectations is carried out every year. Pooling the brainpower of club management and the station's top personnel plays an important part in this process. These efforts result in specific activities and measures that are decided using the club's efficient media network and production pool. With in-house units for the overnight production of print and online communications plus units for event management, ticketing and merchandising, the club provides an almost complete set of marketing tools for the station, and therefore also functions as an in-house agency.

## The benefits

### INFORMATION

SWR3 CLUB publishes its own magazine, *SWR3 DAS MAGAZIN*, which is issued ten times a year and has a circulation of 100 000 copies. Club members receive their copies for free, and the magazine is also available for a cover price of approximately £2.

*SWR3 DAS MAGAZIN* is written entirely by station and club staff. The station's DJs, editors, reporters, correspondents and anchorpersons all contribute to the magazine. The editorial concepts of the magazine and the radio programme are identical. Over 64 pages, the magazine offers the same mix of journalism, music, sketches and services as the station: current affairs, stories, reports, interviews, backgrounds, reviews, CD tips, movie tips and classified ads. *SWR3 DAS MAGAZIN* carries details of more than 500 events per year, 120 of them club events. It keeps club members up to date on current ticket and merchandising offers, news from the station, its programmes and its people.

*SWR3 DAS MAGAZIN* enjoys an extraordinary acceptance from club members: 90 per cent judge it to be good or excellent in content and design (copy tests 1993/1994/1995/1998/1999).

### EVENTS

SWR3 CLUB produces or co-produces some 150 events each year, with approximately 650 000 visitors. The events range from open-air concerts and festivals with over 100 000 visitors to small shows from newcomer bands for a few hundred. Press coverage of these events alone generates over 50 million contacts throughout the year.

SWR3 is the only radio station world-wide with its own professional comedy shows.

*SWR3 Gagtory* and *SWR3 Knallinger* are two five-hour shows packed with gags comic, and sketches. Exclusively written, produced and performed on stage by the station's own DJs and editors, each year a new programme is presented. *SWR3 Gagtory* has become one of Germany's most successful comedy shows. Every year, up to 90 shows are broadcast, with location capacities ranging between 1500 and 3000 people, meaning that the programme is performed in front of some 150 000 visitors each year. For five consecutive years, all shows have been sold out. Members buy preference tickets, and save an average of £2 per ticket.

Once a year, approximately 10 000 members and friends come to celebrate with their favourite radio station. They spend the annual club meeting with the station's staff, participate in workshops and demos, attend concerts and shows, dance and party for an entire weekend.

## TICKETS

Members of SWR3 CLUB receive preference tickets for all important pop and rock concerts in SWR3's broadcasting territory. The service covers concerts by both national and international artists, including Sting, Eric Clapton, Mariah Carey, Bon Jovi, AC/DC, The Rolling Stones, Simple Minds, REM, U2, Madonna, Michael Jackson and Tina Turner. Together with tickets for the club's own productions, the club offers preference tickets to members for over 500 events each year.

The ticket service offers unique conditions never before seen in Germany. On one ticket, the member receives a discount of approximately £2. Tickets for club events are discounted even further. Members can also purchase further tickets at the normal price, but saving the booking fee.

Regular updates on the ticket service are provided through *SWR3 DAS MAGAZIN*. Every month, members receive new information, reviews and tour plans. The ticket hotline, 300 300, was first established as an exclusive service for members. Penetration outside the station's broadcasting territory has now increased dramatically, and the hotline is about to be recognized on a national level. International concert promoters hire the club's hotline as a marketing tool for national sales.

## MERCHANDISING

In the nine years since the club's foundation, it has released over twenty CDs of radio comedy shows. This underlines the station's status as Germany's premier producer of radio comedy. CDs are one of the most popular merchandising products. In 1999, over 100 000 copies of the then top comedy CD were sold. As a consequence, a considerable section of standard merchandising (caps, T-shirts and so on) is dedicated to the comedy characters.

The incarnation of the moose, the station's trademark, in merchandising is a 40 cm plush puppet. After two decades, the moose has densely populated south-western Germany. Overall, around twenty merchandising products are offered.

Club members are eligible for discounts on all merchandising products. Mail or phone orders are processed through the club's own service centre. In addition, the club has points of sales at its 150 public events.

## Service centre

To serve the millions of listeners who want to obtain information on the station, the club and the numerous activities of both, and the thousands of members who want to use the club's services, SWR3 CLUB has the SWR3 Service Centre. It is a modern data-processing centre with 20 online workstations, operated on a 24-hour basis. The centre registers an average of 1500 contacts by phone, fax and e-mail from listeners and members every week. Ticket and merchandising orders generate another 1500 contacts by phone, fax and e-mail.

Insourcing of the SWR3 Service Centre has proven to be a real cost saver. After the club's own call centre was established, £300 000 was saved the following year because of the higher quality of communication. The most important cost-saving factors were greater competence (as a result of training, continuous coaching and supervising, and 'living in the company'), faster processing and enhanced credibility. As a consequence, the number of complaints decreased, identification with the club and the station increased, as did the number of contacts, and merchandising and ticket purchases went up.

The club employs 12 full-time employees and 20 freelancers.

## Summary

SWR3 CLUB is an established institution in SWR3's broadcasting territory, and people would find it hard to imagine being without it. It has dramatically increased affinity with the station, has created a high level of awareness throughout Germany, has managed to develop a strong relationship with its members through the high degree of interactivity and events, and has helped to increase SWR3's ratings. In other words, the club has proven to be absolutely mooseproof.

# 21 *Kawasaki Riders Club*

## Paul Farmer

*Paul Farmer works for Roger Burnett Promotions (RBP), a marketing agency specializing in all aspects of the motorcycle industry which developed, launched and currently manages the Kawasaki Riders Club on behalf of Kawasaki Motors (UK) Ltd. Paul holds a BA (Hons) degree in marketing from the University of Stirling in Scotland.*

Kawasaki Motors (UK) Ltd (KMUK) has been very successful in the UK market since its entry in 1974. This has been achieved with a variety of different motorcycles, but also other products, such as all-terrain and utility vehicles, jet ski personal water craft and power products. As part of KMUK's marketing mix, the decision was made to compete in the domestic road racing championships with a team run under direct control from the company's headquarters. During the late 1980s and early 1990s, various levels of success were achieved, and the pinnacle of Kawasaki's racing endeavours was its complete domination of the domestic road racing championships in 1992.

It was then that KMUK faced a dilemma that it had never confronted before: where did it go from here? The motorcycle market was contracting, and customer profiles were changing. Results from regular tracking studies showed quite clearly that the use of motorcycles had changed dramatically, from a means of transport to a leisure pursuit. Also, its competitors were not dragging their heels when it came to product development. The product life cycles of individual models had grown shorter. All of the Japanese brands were, and to a certain degree still are, producing machines that are extremely similar in terms of style, performance and price.

From those early days, Kawasaki was determined to achieve, pursue and maintain a unique position in the hearts and minds of both dealers and end-users. The word 'differentiation' was new to the industry, but subsequently proved to be the cornerstone of its marketing activities. After studying all viable options, KMUK finally decided to withdraw from racing and invest the same amount of money in a customer club. It firmly believed that as well as improving brand loyalty, a strong Kawasaki Riders Club (KRC) would act as a sales promotion tool for Kawasaki in the largely multi-franchised dealer network. This decision was finally reached after Kawasaki's annual quantitative research, which highlighted the following key areas of concern:

- customer replacement cycles lengthening from two years to four
- average mileage reduced from 12 000 to 6000 per year
- little brand loyalty
- homogeneous product
- declining market.

Faced with a homogeneous product and changing customer profiles, it was decided that a customer club would give Kawasaki the competitive edge it sought. As the club was to be a significant part of its marketing communications mix, KMUK needed to establish whether the club concept was indeed correct, or whether both financial and human resources were best employed in other areas. In order to achieve this, some basic questions needed to be asked, and if the answers to these were favourable, the project would proceed:

- Would the strategy contribute towards the company's short- and long-term financial objectives?
- Was the strategy consistent with KMUK's social responsibilities?
- Did the strategy blend with KMUK's other activities, or was it a new direction?
- Was the risk element of the strategy too high compared to the potential rewards?
- Would it succeed in spite of likely competitor reaction?
- Would the strategy comprise control mechanisms, and how would they be used for future decision-making?
- Would this strategy be preferable to others, or should the funds be used for short-term sales promotion, direct mail or merchandising campaigns?
- Was the new strategy flexible and capable of change?

Having established that the proposed club met these criteria, KMUK was keen to pursue the concept.

## Green light for the Kawasaki Riders Club

Kawasaki's aims and objectives for the new club were as follows:

- Provide a point of difference by adding value to the Kawasaki brand.
- Give customers a reason to ride their machines, increasing mileages and shortening replacement cycles.
- Open a direct communication channel with customers via a club magazine.
- Increase awareness of non-motorcycle products and services such as moto-cross, jet skis, finance and insurance.
- Promote the ability to create regional groups for activities and foster camaraderie among Kawasaki riders.
- Develop a stronger link between the dealer network and the regional groups in order to build loyal customers, thereby increasing the dealers' turnover on the sale of clothing, parts, accessories and service.

With the above objectives, KMUK set about the formation of the KRC. Customers purchasing a new Kawasaki street motorcycle from an authorized dealer would receive their first year's membership free of charge. Existing customers could enroll for a subscription of £80.
   The initial membership benefits were as follows:

- a comprehensive European-wide breakdown and recovery service
- a regular club magazine, *Good Times*
- an information hotline for club activities and general Kawasaki enquiries

- track days, where members could improve their riding skills
- club gatherings at major motorcycle events and road race meetings
- ride-away trips at home and abroad
- regional meetings and activities arranged by local KRC groups nationwide
- discounts on accessories, merchandise, tickets for events and insurance
- a membership card with the Countdown discount scheme included
- a national rally
- a travel service, with the emphasis on cross-Channel ferries
- affiliated membership to the British Motorcyclists Federation.

It was also decided that the KRC would be too much to handle internally, so it would be managed by former British motorcycle racing champion and BBC sports personality Roger Burnett and his energetic team of staff. With the high level of financial investment, accurate evaluation of the benefits was essential. At the dealer conference in March 1993, KMUK announced the new KRC to an enthusiastic dealer network.

## Continual evaluation of the club's performance

Plan–implement–review is the driving force behind KMUK's corporate philosophy. With the club in place, the continuation of the measurement system became an integral element of the strategy. Every event and activity needed to be monitored and properly evaluated so that KMUK could be sure that the benefits were tailored exactly to the needs and wants of the membership base. Further, this would enable corrective action to be taken for future activities, saving both time and wasted investment.

An example of this was the KRC Assistance programme. Although this was a significant benefit to club members, it was also a considerable cost to KMUK at £45 per member. Kawasaki had to be sure that this was an effective use of precious resources. Before the club was established, part of the external audit was to carry out qualitative and quantitative market research. From this it was identified that there was a need for cover in the event of a flat tyre, running out of fuel or a mechanical breakdown. Dealers were polled, and clearly indicated that breakdown cover would give Kawasaki's brand a unique selling proposition when a potential customer was wavering towards competing brands.

When sourcing a service provider for this benefit, part of the specification was to include a systematic approach to monitor and evaluate every incident covered. Every member who contacted the emergency number was sent a post-incident questionnaire, accompanied by a Freepost envelope and covering letter (offering sympathy) to evaluate all aspects of the service they received. The circumstances surrounding negative feedback were thoroughly investigated to ensure complete customer satisfaction. This information could also be used as a measure of product reliability when cross-referenced against warranty claim history. A target response rate of 25 per cent of all incidents was set for these questionnaires and 35 per cent was actually achieved. The most common complaint in the early stages was that an inappropriate vehicle was used for motorcycle recovery. The KRC was able to report this to the provider, which then improved the service by appointing all Kawasaki dealers as recovery agents and supplying purpose-built motorcycle-handling equipment for the remaining agents. Subsequent measurement of this particular benefit also highlighted the fact that only a small percentage of members took their motorcycles abroad, so cover was restricted to the

UK. This saved costs, reduced membership fees and increased renewal rates and the number of new members as a result.

For each and every customer benefit offered by the club, a control method was firmly established, including:

- complaint analysis
- analysis of letters written to the magazine
- member surveys
- telephone surveys
- face-to-face discussions at events, exhibitions and focus groups.

## Overcoming barriers

What problems, if any, did KMUK face with the implementation of its evaluation strategies in a dynamic business environment such as the British motorcycle industry? Evaluation techniques have been and always will be part and parcel of the KRC. Therefore, they weren't considered a problem, rather a benefit from which the club could learn, adjust and forward-plan. Evaluation strategies are streamlined by systematic approaches, for example the review of each survey and resultant recommendations for future projects. These are constantly assessed to increase efficiency and negate any perceived problems. KMUK's research is carried out on a regular basis, usually monthly or annually, so that it can be planned into the company's schedules, minimizing problems.

In simple terms, the KRC assesses areas that could cause possible concern. These are particularly prevalent in terms of the administration problems that may occur – for example, in the way the club was set up. As previously mentioned, membership of the KRC is free to every purchaser of a new Kawasaki street motorcycle. Initially, when the dealer sold the machine, staff were asked to complete a membership request form, giving machine and complete customer details. The completed form was sent to the KRC's administration office, and membership packs were forwarded to the customer. Comparisons of new KRC members were made on a monthly basis against KMUK's warranty database. It was found that there was a disparity between the two databases. Subsequent investigation revealed that some dealers were not completing the KRC membership forms. They stated that at the time of purchase they were swamped with paperwork – invoices, registration documents, finance and insurance agreements and even KMUK's own warranty registration form. By this time, it had also been noticed that while the KRC was an excellent tool for retaining customers, it was not closing sales to undecided customers (membership surveys by post and phone proved this). Finance and insurance considerations came first.

The solution was simple. The dealers were instructed to dispose of the KRC membership forms, and told not to worry about customer registration, which would be taken care of automatically. When KMUK received the warranty registration form and entered it on the system, the details were immediately sent to the club. Customer complaints fell considerably, as did an unnecessary burden on dealers, which increased their support of the KRC as a result. The moral of this story is: keep it simple when involving third parties and end-users.

KMUK also needed to evaluate why people left the club when their complementary membership expired. This could be a significant problem affecting the long-term success of the project if left to the 'second-guess' principle. Again, the solution was simple and systematic. Once a month, all members who were three months past their renewal date were contacted to establish the reason. This was initially done by letter, and then, if there was still no response, by phone. In many cases, it was simply that the members had been too busy or had forgotten. The importance placed on this task and the regularity of the technique has resulted in much-improved subscription rates (proving that it was cost-effective) and established why people do not renew, thus allowing the KRC to change the activities and benefits of the club to suit.

## Obtaining feedback

Obtaining quality and representative feedback from customers depends on the research objectives, and more importantly, what one does with the results. KMUK refuses to carry out research just for the sake of it, or because it has to, only to file away the results and take no action. The company is also careful not to carry out research that is flawed and gives incorrect information on which to base strategic decisions.

Primary research data is more appropriate to KMUK than secondary information, and the company uses a variety of methods to obtain feedback from customers, both quantitative and qualitative. There are two annual surveys, and between five and ten annual focus groups.

The first tracking studies are street surveys carried out nationally across a range of motorcycle owners, both new and secondhand, to monitor Kawasaki and its competitors on the following key measures: awareness, attitudes and perceptions.

The second survey is directed at KRC members, to provide a profile of the Kawasaki customer as well as general information concerning purchase decisions, lifestyles and demographics. The results can be compared with tracking studies carried out among a wider range of customers, who ride other brands of motorcycles as well as Kawasaki. By doing this, KMUK can establish the profile of the typical Kawasaki customer, while checking to see if there are any apparent trends.

A rather ambitious survey was distributed to the entire membership base of around 10 000. The anticipated response rate was 20 per cent, but the actual figure was 40 per cent! Even better was the analysis of the data, which showed that the machine ownership profile fitted exactly with KMUK's sales pattern. For example, 19 per cent of sales were ZX-6R sports bikes, and 18 per cent of respondents were ZX-6R owners. This meant that the marketing department was confident that it could extrapolate this data, as it truly reflected the customer base.

The survey enabled KMUK to break down its customer base accurately in many ways to reveal some vital information, which was then used to tailor the club's magazine, activities and other benefits. The demographic data was also useful in negotiations with KMUK's insurance company to reduce rates for Kawasaki owners – another important benefit that the KRC gave to the organization as a whole.

The qualitative research is also split into two areas: general motorcyclists, and KRC members. These groups are essential to give an in-depth understanding of customers' needs and wants. The groups are kept relatively small: ten is the maximum number catered for. They are always well attended, as motorcyclists enjoy talking about their passion: it is difficult to stop them!

One of the early decisions taken was to split the KRC into regions, drawing on enthusiastic local volunteers to organize local meetings and activities. There are now 35 regions, and these also provide invaluable feedback. The regional representatives are contacted monthly, and invited to two meetings during the year to obtain their views and ideas. During the summer, both KRC and KMUK staff will also informally meet the reps at race meetings and events.

By using the techniques described above, KMUK also monitors the effectiveness of the club. All activities are measured, and satisfaction levels are monitored on a regular basis. For example, a survey after a KRC Track Day indicated poor satisfaction levels from groups for beginners. When this was investigated, it transpired that the groups were too big and faster riders in the group made novices and slower riders feel inferior. The beginners also required more tuition. The action taken involved monitoring the first riding session of the day and upgrading riders who obviously had track and machine confidence to the intermediate or advanced groups. The instructors then debriefed and advised the novice riders after every session and, during the lunch break, took these riders around the track in a car to show them the correct techniques. The satisfaction level went from indifferent to excellent in a short period.

Another example is the survey. One of the first questions asked is, 'What was your previous motorcycle?', followed by, 'Was it new or secondhand?' In the early days, the response to the first question was 30 per cent Kawasaki, but in the last survey it was 54 per cent, indicating an increase in brand loyalty. The proportion of new versus secondhand machines also increased from 40 per cent new to 52 per cent.

## Evaluating success

The concerns highlighted by KMUK's initial quantitative research have been assessed continually following the launch and development of the KRC:

- The desire to increase motorcycle usage has been demonstrated through the KRC's track days, regional events and ride-aways.
- Brand loyalty has increased, as the membership survey has shown that 54 per cent of customers remain loyal, compared to 30 per cent at the start of the project.
- Generally, replacement cycles are reducing again, although this is a product issue not altogether affected by the KRC.

Triumph already had in place the traditional Triumph Owners Club. However, it has developed a new owners' club based along the same lines as the KRC. In addition, Honda has launched its own customer club, Honda UK Riders Club, with a benefits package which mirrors the tried-and-tested Kawasaki structure and format. Imitation is the sincerest form of flattery!

Of course, the most reliable measurement of success is still the number of customers who subscribe to the KRC. This figure is almost 30 per cent (and rising) of the total 15 000-strong customer base.

Finally, it was intended to differentiate the Kawasaki brand from its competitors. Maybe the best way to describe the success in this area is the following statement which was made by one of the respondents in a focus group when asked to summarize his feelings on Kawasaki: 'If Kawasaki was a bloke, I'd buy him a pint!'

# **22** *T-D1 Company Class*

## Horst Leonhard Reufsteck and Silke Hausrath

*Horst Leonhard Reufsteck holds a degree in telecommunication engineering. He is the Head of Sales – Key Accounts. Silke Hausrath holds a degree in business. She is Project Manager in the Sales – Key Accounts division.*

The German company T-Mobil, a 100 per cent subsidiary of T-Mobile International AG, operates in the dynamic mobile phone market, where it is one of Europe's biggest mobile network operators. More than 22 million people (as of June 2001) make their calls through the T-D1 network. The company, which had more than €6.4 billion in revenues in the year 2000, employs more than 9000 people.

## Why a customer loyalty programme?

The reason for establishing a customer loyalty programme can be found in the market situation. Growing competition in the mobile phone market and the fact that considerable growth in an increasingly saturated market is only possible by ousting competitors has increased the necessity to bind customers to the company. This is especially true for the general agreement customers, which are responsible for a large percentage of the company's revenues. Therefore, T-Mobil decided to develop a customer club, called the T-D1 Company Class, for its 'Top 200' accounts, with the two main objectives of reducing churn and increasing usage within these accounts.

In addition to the general agreement customers, the club also targets a second smaller group of customers: 'avant-garde customers'. These are companies that are of strategic importance for T-Mobil, such as software houses for future product development.

The official member of T-D1 Company Class is the company itself, which names up to three employees who represent the company through a 'personalized company membership' and become the primary beneficiaries of the club benefits. The representative should either be the person who prepares decisions concerning general agreements, or the person who actually makes the decisions. It is important that the representative is in a key position within the company when it comes to voting for or against T-Mobil. To ensure this, the T-Mobil sales force, which is in daily contact with these decision-makers, can suggest companies and representatives for membership. The final decision about who is accepted for membership lies with the T-D1 Company Class management. There is an annual membership fee of €250 per representative.

The T-D1 Company Class management is responsible for planning, developing and controlling the benefits, as well as measuring and controlling the achievement of the club objectives. They are supported by three teams: club office, call centre and steering committee. Last but not least, a central database supports the organizational institutions and captures data on representatives as well as their contact history.

T-D1 Company Class was officially founded on 15 March 2001 with a large opening event and about one hundred members.

## The benefits

When designing the benefit programme, the IT and mobile phone background of the club members served as the benchmark for which benefits to offer. Personal interviews with potential members and detailed research led to a package of six benefits, each with a very high perceived value. Most of these benefits focus on business- and mobile phone-related topics. Leisure activities are of minor importance. In addition, the club established various tools to enhance communication with its members and among the members themselves.

The most popular benefit is the pre-launch of mobile phones, whereby the member has the opportunity to test new mobile phones for two months. The mobile phone can be ordered easily via the Internet or the call centre, and is delivered directly to the member. After the testing phase, the member has the option to buy the mobile phone at a reduced rate, or to simply return it to Company Class by courier service. Except for the usual rates (airtime/monthly fee), there is no additional cost for this service, and the member not only stays up to date in terms of technological developments, but ahead of the broad market.

The intention of the global roaming service is to enable club members to make and receive calls using their own mobile number all over the world during business or leisure trips. T-D1 Company Class delivers a mobile phone that operates with the specific local standards for every roaming country. The member calls the club call centre, specifies the destination, and within four days the appropriate mobile phone is delivered. The member also has the option to borrow up to three additional phones for colleagues joining the trip.

One main goal of the club is to enhance communication not just between T-Mobil and club members, but also among club members themselves. Because of this, T-D1 Company Class established two communication forums, one which is conducted electronically, and another consisting of face-to-face events. The electronic forum comprises topic-specific chat rooms on the club Web site. Each forum is moderated by a T-Mobil expert, who is available to answer questions and makes sure that the discussion is fed with any necessary technical input. In each forum, members can state their personal views, comment on postings from others, or pose questions to people with the same interests and background regarding a specific topic. The primary goal is to build a club identity and to allow like-minded people to share their experience.

Workshops, presentations and an annual Company Class congress are the main elements of the personal face-to-face events. In the workshops, the club members have the opportunity to discuss current topics in the mobile phone market with T-Mobil experts, and moreover to influence new product developments. The first workshops were on GPRS and UMTS. The presentations aim to strengthen knowledge and understanding of the mobile phone market, and the annual congress provides an exclusive framework for getting together in a relaxed atmosphere.

Closely related to the face-to-face forums are the 'view behind the scenes' events. These encompass all kinds of events that enhance general understanding of the telecommunications markets. For instance, members are invited to visit the test lab of a mobile phone manufacturer. Many partners of T-Mobile and of its parent, Deutsche Telekom, are involved, to allow access to aspects that are normally closed to the outside world.

The last core benefit is providing club members with relevant information about countries they are travelling to. The information, which is available on the Company Class Web site, ranges from phone tariffs to information about customs in doing business or being a guest in the foreign country. Not only major destinations like the USA or Japan, but also exotic countries like the Ivory Coast or Mauritania are covered in this section. In total, there is information for approximately 100 countries. Members travelling to one of these countries simply go the Web site and download the information. Providing the information on the Web site has two advantages for the club: keeping the information up to date is quite simple, and it avoids the need to print booklets with a very limited number of copies, which reduces costs. Because travel information is not part of T-Mobil's core business, the company co-operates with an online travel specialist. The specialist provides the initial information, and is responsible for all updates.

In terms of leisure activities, T-D1 Company Class offers two benefits: a golf tournament, and VIP tickets for Formula One races. The golf tournament is organized for all company clients of T-Mobil, but club members have access to better services, such as last-minute enrolment and special beginners' courses. The first rounds of the tournament takes place in the different sales regions of T-Mobil. The winners of the regional tournaments are then invited to the final round, which usually takes place on one of the most famous golf courses within Europe. The Formula One VIP programme is exclusively for T-D1 Company Class members. Participating members have the opportunity to enjoy the Formula One world live and on-site for an entire weekend. However, as mentioned earlier, leisure activities are of minor importance within the T-D1 Company Class concept. Research had shown that potential club members had a clear preference for a business-oriented club. From their perspective, leisure activities would be a pleasant diversion, but should never be the sole purpose of the club.

The two main communication platforms are the club Web site and the club call centre. Because of the technological affinity of club members – all of them are IT or telecom decision-makers within their companies – a club Web site was seen as an absolute must. The Web site is exclusively for T-D1 Company Class members – every club member has their own user name and password. On the site, members can find all information about the current club benefits and activities as well as an archive of past events. The site also includes mobile phone-related information, but only information that the member will not find on the regular company Web site. In addition, members have access to a membership list of all member companies and their representatives. Members have the opportunity to send e-mail requests to the club management as well as ordering a call back from the call centre at their preferred time via a 'call-me' button. As mentioned above, they can also participate in online discussions with other members in the electronic forum section.

The T-D1 Company Class call centre was also established exclusively for the club, and can be reached via a special toll-free phone number. It is staffed with specially trained agents from BusinessLine, T-Mobil's hotline for all company clients. Using agents from the regular hotline has a one major advantage: the club call centre can answer all questions from members, no matter whether they are club-related or normal BusinessLine calls, such as requests for product information or billing complaints.

## Outlook

So far, the members are extremely happy to finally have this platform and link to T-Mobil, and many have sent letters of appreciation to the T-D1 Company Class management. The main challenge over the next few years is to ensure that T-D1 Company Class continues to stay attractive to its members. This means analysing the existing benefits regarding their usage, and adapting the programme according to the changing needs of the members. This is a task the club management is well prepared for, and the enthusiastic feedback of the members is an excellent source of new ideas and necessary improvements.

# 23 *The Porsche Card*

## Albert Moser

*Albert Moser, Director of Porsche Financial Services GmbH – a wholly owned subsidiary company of the Dr. Ing. h.c.F. Porsche AG – since 1992, has developed the Porsche Card, which was issued for the first time in 1995.*

Porsche not only stands for prestige and exclusivity, but above all for quality, technical innovation and design. But even within the community of Porsche fans, customer loyalty is an important topic. That is why Porsche introduced the Porsche Card in 1995. The Porsche Card is offered exclusively to the currently approximately 120 000 Porsche drivers in Germany. It combines many attractive services which are tailor-made for the target group of Porsche drivers. These are mainly business people and self-employed persons. On the one hand, they spend a lot of time on business trips, never have enough time, and have a high need for services. On the other hand, they are all addicted to exclusivity.

Like the car itself, the Porsche Card also stands for exclusivity and is completely orientated to the Porsche standard: 'No compromises'. For an annual fee of €125 the member receives a Eurocard and a Lufthansa Visa Gold Card. In addition, the member can obtain a partner card for the special price of €45 (Eurocard Partner Card) or €62·5 (Lufthansa Visa Gold Partner Card). With the card, members have access to the following benefits organized and managed by Porsche Financial Services GmbH.

## Porsche Traveller Service

The Porsche Card Service Centre makes special recommendations, such as restaurants and hotels, to its world-wide members. In addition, shopping recommendations and vacation tips such as tropical vaccination regulations are provided. The service centre also makes reservations for flights, hotel rooms and train tickets. It co-operates with 60 hotel chains, including more than 5000 hotels, and is therefore able to arrange special rates. Lufthansa Frequent Travellers and Senators are given special preferential treatment for Lufthansa flights, such as waiting list priority and the preferred check-in. Further advantages for all Lufthansa Visa Card owners are access to Lufthansa Partner Lounges and the participation in the Lufthansa frequent flyer programme, Miles & More.

## Miles & More Premium Miles

Each time the member makes use of the Lufthansa Visa Card, one premium mile for each

Euro (or the corresponding amount in DM) is credited to their Miles & More account. Porsche plan to add a mile-collecting programme to the Porsche Card, too, in light of the lifting of the restrictive laws in Germany.

## Porsche Emergency Service

Should a member lose their card, Porsche will arrange its replacement. In case of problems, help is available 24 hours per day. In case of medical emergencies or legal problems abroad, an interpreter providing translations via telephone is offered. Furthermore, in emergencies the Porsche Card Service will send cash up to €5000 to its members world-wide.

## Porsche Business Service

The service includes information about fairs, conventions and trade shows. The Porsche Business Service Centre also takes care of a variety of reservations, such as rental cars, hotel rooms and well-equipped conference rooms. Members who are on a business trip have the opportunity to use a world-wide network of business centres, such as fully equipped office rooms or secretary service.

## Porsche Ticket Service

The ticket service organizes tickets for very popular cultural events, from classic to pop, from theatre to open-air festivals, and arranges the trip plus a suitable supporting programme. The service can also be used for sports events.

## Porsche Gift Service

This is a practical service for sending flowers as well as for ordering accessories from the Porsche Selection. Members simply call, and the gift service will assist them.

## Porsche Gourmet Service

Porsche Card members do not need to worry about food preparation for social events. The Porsche Gourmet Service organizes catering services to accommodate members' needs.

## AVIS Car Rental

Members are able to rent a car from the Porsche Card partner Avis at a special rate – for example, in Germany comprehensive insurance is already included.

# AVIS Park & Wash

This service is by far the most popular, and underlines the exclusivity of the target group. The members have the opportunity to hand over their Porsche at nearly all airports in Germany during the business hours of the Avis counters. The car is parked free of charge for up to seven days per stay in a secure parking lot. During this time, the Porsche will be cleaned inside and out, and will be ready for the member at the agreed time. This service is limited to the member and their Porsche and is completely free of charge.

# Insurance Cover

When members rent a car with the Lufthansa Visa Card, comprehensive insurance, with a deductible of only €225 that the member has to cover himself, is automatically included. The purchase protection insurance is only valid for items purchased with the Lufthansa Visa Card. This insurance covers purchased items that have a minimum price of €70 for up to 30 days, beginning at the date of purchase, and includes cover against theft or damage. With both cards (Eurocard and the Lufthansa Visa Gold Card), transportation accident insurance offers security and financial protection world-wide. The total sum insured is €375 000.

# Interest on funds

Higher-than-usual interest rates on funds deposited in the Porsche Eurocard or Lufthansa Visa Card account make them especially attractive. Members have immediate access to their money.

# Financial Airbag

With both cards, members can broaden their financial independence, because on request, the bill can be paid in instalments.

# Porsche Card Service Phone

All the Porsche Card services are available 24 hours a day. These services are accessed by dialing a telephone number provided exclusively to Porsche Card members.

There is no question that the Porsche Card is a popular means of payment among Porsche drivers.

# 24 *Grohe Professional Club*

## Raimund Petersen

*Raimund Petersen was a marketing executive with Friedrich Grohe AG, the European market leader in high-quality kitchen and bathroom fittings. He was responsible for developing and launching the Grohe Professional Club in Germany, one of the most successful business-to-business customer loyalty programmes. He holds a business degree from the University of Cologne, Germany.*

Business-to-business markets in Germany have recently been showing some movement and development:

- There has been a new emphasis on the optimization of processes and electronic communication between companies, while interpersonal relationships are no longer a high priority for development.
- The general pressure for cost reductions has led to a decrease in field service, which is being used in more focused ways, mainly targeting key accounts.
- Today's business customers want to be taken more seriously than ever. They are free to decide where and when to buy, and use this situation to demand a high level of service and attention. They want to be treated on an individual basis.
- The use of short-term marketing instruments such as promotions, coupons, sweepstakes or loyalty bonuses is isolated, rather than part of a long-term strategic concept.
- Relationship marketing instruments are rarely used. If they are, they are mostly focused on individual customers or smaller customer groups. They are seldom combined under the umbrella of a strategic concept that targets a broader group of customers.
- Relationships between businesses are usually established on an individual level, as is the case between field service representative and buyer. Relationships rarely exist on an overall company level.
- Dialogue and direct marketing instruments, originally applied in an end-user environment, are increasingly being used for business-to-business applications.

Good interpersonal relationships, currently typical in business-to-business transactions, are no longer sufficient. Sporadic and unsystematic attempts at relationship marketing also prove ineffective in such a demanding environment. In the context of most business-to-business markets today, the goal must be to establish more intensive relationships at a company level and develop more complete relationship marketing tools. The increasing use of dialogue and direct marketing instruments for business-to-business communication is an innovative part of the solution. However, it is only a small component. To achieve a holistic solution, a concept must be developed that integrates the current marketing instruments and activities into an overall concept. Furthermore, by adding modern relationship marketing tools and fitting the entire concept into a more strategic framework, current activities and relationships can be brought to the next level: relationship marketing.

Despite the holistic structure of such a concept, individuality is not neglected. After all, relationships are cultivated between human beings. In addition, with integrative models of relationship marketing, customers always have the feeling that they are receiving special attention and treatment. This is precisely how the necessary trust and loyalty for a long-term relationship can be created, especially with important or regular customers.

## Relationships in the business-to-business area

In end-user mass marketing, the strength, value and promise of a product largely come from the brand. In the business-to-business area, the brand is an important prerequisite, but it is not the only upholder of the relationship. Here, human beings are primarily responsible for a relationship. Whether they are salespeople, distributors or buyers, these human beings create the trust necessary for business transactions. Relationship marketing is therefore also trust marketing. Trust then leads to sympathy and competence.

## Relationship marketing and its impact on business-to-business relationships

Relationships in business-to-business areas are mainly built on rational business decisions. Figure 24.1 shows how the intensity of a business relationship develops over time. The intensity is lowest during the initial search phase, when a company is looking for a supplier of a specific product or service. The relationship slowly intensifies through the first contact phase, the negotiation phase and the development phase, eventually reaching its peak in the matu-

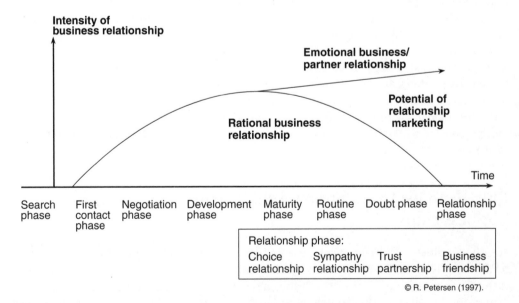

**Figure 24.1**   Impact of relationship marketing on business relationships

rity phase. However, the loyalty, even of regular customers, is not secured at that point. A certain routine within the relationship (routine phase), or even the possibility of feeling bored or neglected in the relationship, can lead customers into a phase of doubt. If this occurs, rational argument will only have limited success. Only relationship marketing can move the relationship from a rational to an emotional level, which prolongs and develops a long-standing business partnership.

## From mass marketing to club marketing

Customer clubs are an ideal way to create such emotional partnerships. Experience shows that new relationship marketing instruments and concepts such as customer clubs can be developed quickly within most companies. This acceleration occurs because typically there are already a vast number of isolated activities in a company. These established customer-contact efforts provide an excellent foundation for a customer club. The existing and traditional services the company offers can be successfully integrated into the club marketing efforts. A customer club can provide the appropriate organizational framework for these separate and unbundled measures, and can combine them into a systematic programme, together with newly developed measures. However, a prerequisite for the success of new relationship marketing instruments such as customer clubs is that they offer concrete additional benefits to the customer: that is, they must be highly value-oriented.

## Business-to-business clubs: The ideal relationship marketing instrument

Numerous experiences of German companies that operate clubs illustrate how business-to-business clubs represent a new quality in marketing and customer treatment if applied correctly. Clubs as relationship marketing tools are highly effective instruments for customer dialogue. They lead to a strong intensification of customer contacts, and therefore inevitably to a stronger relationship. Business-to-business clubs are strategic and oriented towards long-term customer partnerships, and not towards medium-term sales promotion. The relationship between the sponsoring company and club members first has to be created and incorporate a vested interest before the club can be expected to acquire loyal customers. Thus, the dialogue with club members must be personal, permanent, honest and trustworthy. Implementing these elements is the best way to ensure that the club activities lead to trust and to a long-lasting 'real' partnership.

## Club benefits: Foundation for the success of business-to-business clubs

To secure business customers, a customer club needs to offer real value. This value can only be delivered if the right club benefits are defined, which again makes it necessary to know customers' needs. Figure 24.2 shows the business customer's hierarchy of needs. Classic marketing aims mostly at the basic needs of business customers, such as revenue, profit, product range or brand. According to Maslow's hierarchy of needs, a particular needs level must be

Self-
fulfilment

Is not true for the business area.
Market/Customer/Supplier have different
rules

Prestige need
➤ recognition

Development

- Emotion
- Partnership
- Honesty
- Relationship

Social need ➤ Community

Basic need ➤ Revenue/profit/
product range/brand

(Based on Maslow)

© R. Petersen (1997).

**Figure 24.2**    The business customer's needs pyramid

satisfied before the next level can be attained. This is an important concept to take into consideration when designing a customer club: first, the basic needs of the customers have to be fulfilled by the sponsoring company, before a customer club can be developed in order to reach – together with the customer – the next level of the hierarchy. The idea of club marketing or relationship marketing principally starts at the second level: social needs. Through joint club activities, members are integrated into a new community. They can exchange experiences with other members who share the same professional interests. In the same vein, this fosters the relationship between the sponsoring company and its members, since the club acts as an intermediary. However, a prerequisite is that club members are not direct competitors.

Remaining at the second level of the hierarchy is not sufficient in the long run to turn club members into loyal customers. Prestige has to be attached to membership, which is mostly achieved via a limited club. The club's relationship structure and benefits must be oriented to the prestige needs of members. At this point, the club's creativity must be convincing. To meet customer needs, club activities should deliver first and foremost the emotional events and experiences which are the impetus for all relationship marketing instruments.

In order to fashion a real value-oriented benefit package that meets the demand for emotion and prestige, maximum creativity from the sponsoring company is necessary. It is vital, primarily, to ensure that club benefits represent real added value in addition to the basic services the sponsoring company offers with its products. Before a company can establish a customer club and offer special benefits through the club, it must guarantee that its core business (the products or services the customer club is supposed to support) is competitive and will remain so (see Figure 24.3). A customer club can only add value to the existing basic performance of the core products. It can never make up for lack of quality or unacceptable delivery time. How can a club member trust the club idea if the company cannot perform well on its fundamental competences?

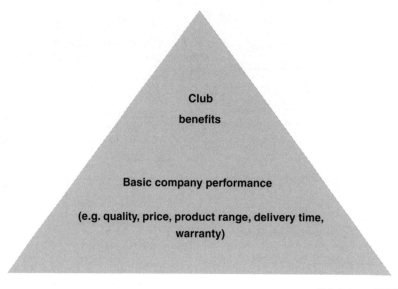

© R. Petersen (1997).

**Figure 24.3**    Club benefit pyramid

A special characteristic of a business-to-business club is that its primary goal must be to support its members' businesses. In order for the benefits to be convincing, they need to be relevant to both the industry and the member company. Benefits that have little or no relation to the members' industries are of lower value to the business customer. The more the club benefits become diluted, the less profile and character the club has. Furthermore, the benefits of the club should bring about the promised and expected value. Only then are they real club benefits, perceived as true added-value benefits from the members' viewpoint.

## Grohe Professional Club

The Grohe Professional Club was founded in 1992, with the mission to 'strengthen the trade for the future'. In order for the trade to be able to cope with more and more demanding and complex markets and local business environments, it needs future-oriented, intelligent ideas, as well as the support of the brand suppliers. The Professional Club was founded in order to take the necessary steps to create a dynamic loyalty programme in which all members are actively integrated. The club has been growing ever since. Now, after nine years, it is considered the largest organization of its kind. More than 1700 master craftsmen have joined the club so far.

The central principle of the club is to foster joint business, meaning to improve business both for Grohe and the member firms. All club activities are underpinned by the goal of achieving real value for the respective member firms. Therefore, the club is focused on joint action, which is reflected in the club's partnership philosophy – mutual giving and receiving for the sake of a common objective. This principle of mutuality creates a unique identity and emotional relationship that cannot be matched by other similar programmes. The intensity of this relationship is one of the key loyalty drivers.

## The principle of 'give and receive'

Members of the Professional Club must work hard, because only active collaboration leads to active partnership. The idea is simple: without giving, there is no receiving. At first sight, one might assume that additional work does not encourage a prospective member to become actively involved in the programme. However, a convincing, value-oriented benefit and contribution programme (redesigned annually in co-operation with the members) has been the key to the club's attractiveness, while satisfying new and old members. Another principle of the Grohe Professional Club is that benefits are limited to market- and company-related benefits. These are most relevant to the goal of improving joint business. One characteristic of the Grohe Professional Club is that the principle of 'give and receive' is handled in an extremely open manner between the club and the members. This openness on both sides fosters understanding and healthy interdependence.

## Contributions mean more benefits in return

In practice, this works as follows. There are two levels of benefits available to members. First, there are the basic benefits that are granted to all members. Some examples of these benefits include: consulting services for marketing, advertising or technical questions, with a 48-hour response time; the club magazine; the service hotline, and VIP service during the main industry trade show. These benefits become available immediately after the member has joined the club for an annual fee of €120 (about £85).

The second level of benefits are the special benefits that are only available in exchange for a certain number of points. Members can collect these points by participating in different programmes (members' contribution), such as technical or sales training, presentation of Grohe products in their shops, use of particular displays and participating in special promotions. For each contributing performance, club members acquire a certain number of points credited to their account at the club service centre. These points can then be redeemed by the member at any time in exchange for benefits offered by the club. Table 24.1 shows the structure of the club benefit and member contribution system

Every year, the catalogue that lists the point structure for the members' contribution and the club benefits is updated in close co-operation with the members. Constant refurbishing of the catalogue is vital in a fast-paced industry like plumbing. Every member can choose benefits from the catalogue according to what they think is most suitable and profitable to their particular business. Notably, member contributions are designed not only to reward the member with points, but to result in immediate improvement of their business in the form of additional store traffic, promoting sales of certain products or strengthening the competence of specialist suppliers.

## Ideas from the members

The driving force in the Professional Club is the member 'senate'. The senators are representatives elected by club members. Together with the senators and other industry partners, Grohe works on new ideas coming from the market, converting them either into new benefits for the benefit/contribution programme or into new products/ideas designed to help

**Table 24.1**   Club benefit and member contribution system – Grohe Professional Club

| Members' contribution | Points earned | Club benefits | Points used |
|---|---|---|---|
| Technical training with Grohe products | •• per employee<br>••• per company | Creation of a radio advertisement | •• per ad |
| Training for key account business | •• per participant | Driver safety training on a well-known racetrace | •••• |
| Workshop training in company | •• up to 5 fitters<br>•••• over 5 fitters | PC software: | |
| | | *The Electronic Colour and Design Advisor* | •••• |
| Product and Sales training | up to 2 participants ••<br>over 2 participants •••• | *Working Hours Calculation, including optimal Shop Size* | ••• |
| | | Hardware exhibitions service | •• to •••• |
| Expert forums | •• | Tickets for | |
| | | Premier league football matches | •• to ••• per ticket |
| | | National football team games | ••• per ticket |
| Spare parts experience | | World-class tennis matches | ••• per ticket |
| Tour of a Grohe spare parts depot | •• to •••• | German touring car championship | ••• per ticket |
| Use of the Grohe Service Case | •• | Dancing world championship | ••• per ticket |
| | | Cultural events for all tastes | ••• per ticket |
| Presentation of Grohe merchandise in a display centre or store | •• | | |
| Presentation of modules in the Grohe Gallery | •• | | |
| Display and shop window decoration | • to •• | | |
| Grohe promotions | •• to •••• | | |

members in their everyday business. In special committees, club senators discuss such delicate topics as how best to support speciality retailers and how to enter new markets. The senate, at the head of the club, works with great efficiency and success.

One example from recent club work is the development of price recommendations for spare parts. Up to this point, the market had lacked the necessary visibility and guidelines for spare part pricing. The different distributors and partners were uncertain how to price, and thus a wide range of different prices for the same spare parts existed in the market, confusing customer and dealer alike. This led to some extremely high prices and annoyance in the market. This problem was voiced by several members and, in collaboration with the club senate, a price table was developed and published that contained end-user price recommendations for all spare parts. This tool not only helped club members, but is now being used throughout the market.

The annual club convention is considered the highlight of each year. The agenda consists of practical issues, such as the club's activities during the previous year and pertinent club situations. Members capitalize on the unique opportunity to network with companies that are not their direct competitors (most tradespeople operate locally). This event is special because members develop a distinct rapport at this conference.

## Everything is perfectly organized

A customer club such as the Grohe Professional Club is a company in its own right within the sponsoring company. It has all managerial functions, and therefore, in order to work smoothly, it requires professional management. In light of this fact, Grohe has set up a special external club service centre in co-operation with an outside agency. This agency handles all organizational and administrative aspects for members. Perfect organization is an arduous task that requires dedication and hard work, but it is undoubtedly worthwhile.

To maintain and guarantee a high level of personal contact, Grohe's field service has taken a special role within the club concept. The field service representatives are the link between the club and its members, and are responsible for both qualitative and quantitative care of club members. They are the club managers, because they know what their customers expect from the club, and because they can assist and consult members in all business- and club-related issues.

## What the Professional Club means to Grohe

Through the closeness with its customers, distributors and dealers, Grohe stays in direct contact with the market and receives first-hand feedback about changes and trends. The information obtained through this direct contact allows Grohe to react quickly to the rapidly changing demands of the market and stay one step ahead of the competition. The intensive dialogue with the craft partners that exists throughout the company allows the processes and performance of specific departments to be optimized in line with market requirements. The successful partnership idea of the Grohe Professional Club has a long-term nature, because only long-term and active partnership programmes can develop common interests and inevitably bring mutual success.

# 25 *The Volkswagen Club*

## Klaus Chojnacki

*Klaus Chojnacki is the General Manager of the Volkswagen Club.*

In an increasingly competitive market, direct contact with the customer is vital. Therefore, the relationship management of Volkswagen – as a strategic customer-binding instrument – has been continually developed and extended.

Increasing competition in a continually developing service-oriented society means that a company has to find a source of greater differentiation in the market. Moreover, consumer behaviour has changed dramatically since the beginning of the 1990s. Customers' knowledge is increasing steadily, and with this, their expectations. Product quality alone is insufficient to meet the comprehensive demands of today's customers, as product quality along with increasing interchangeability of products are taken for granted. Attractive and individual services are required that offer customers a valuable, complete package and provide immunity to the poaching attempts of competitors.

The recipe for success is relationship management. But cultivating the relationship with customers is only possible through a dialogue between company and customer. Customer retention programmes in the form of customer clubs make such a dialogue possible at acceptable costs. Every company that does not develop customer retention instruments, whatever form they might take, is not close enough to the customer, and runs the risk of falling behind its competitors.

## A pioneer in customer satisfaction

Volkswagen is the first German car manufacturer to break new ground in the customer service field and to address the developments described above. The Customer Club GmbH, located in Braunschweig, Germany, is a 100 per cent subsidiary established solely for the management of the dialogue-oriented customer relation programmes, Volkswagen Club and Audi A plus. The key approaches to giving customers VIP status are a sophisticated service package that consists of car-related and adventure-oriented services, an innovative bonus point system, and selected co-operation partners that enrich the broad range of services with further benefits. The figures support the concept: more than 1.2 million members after five years of club activity, more than 95 per cent of Volkswagen/Audi dealers are active partners of the Volkswagen Club and Audi A plus respectively, and there are nearly a dozen prestigious co-operation partners.

## Intensive preparation and implementation

It goes without saying that the implementation of these innovative programmes is not possible without thorough preparation. As early as 1994, the Volkswagen and Audi dealers were informed about the new approach in several information and training sessions, and quickly became enthusiastic about it. These dealers also realized that only additional convenience, fun and car-related services can create real satisfaction for modern customers, with their demand for total mobility. It should be mentioned in this context that, particularly in the starting phase of the two programmes in the spring of 1995, doubts were voiced by some dealers. Like all far-reaching innovations, the Volkswagen Club and Audi A plus programme were met with initial scepticism. Many had reservations regarding the feasibility of programmes of that size. Yet, in constructive meetings in which the comments and criticisms of the dealers were considered, it was possible to clear up most of the doubts and reservations. The most convincing argument was that the Volkswagen Club and the Audi A plus programmes not only serve to attain maximum customer satisfaction, but also form an integral part of the Volkswagen Group's communication. They allow a lively dialogue between the customer, dealer and manufacturer, which in the end also leads to an increase in dealership traffic.

## Initial conditions

Once a company decides to establish a customer club, it has to analyse its own starting points, clearly define the club goals, integrate them into the planning process, and meet the organizational requirements. The general starting conditions depend on the company's market position (regional, national, international supplier), and on the expected number of members of the planned customer club. Although a vast number of German niche companies have established successful customer clubs (IKEA, TUI, Douglas, Steiff), the Volkswagen Group with its Volkswagen Club and Audi A plus programmes, is so far the only global player. This is mainly because of financial and logistical considerations: the smaller the potential target group of members and the more restrictively the club is organized, the fewer organizational duties and the lower costs are for the sponsoring company. The best solution is for the marketing division to manage the club internally.

## A network organizational structure

A special network is necessary for clubs like the Volkswagen Club or Audi A plus that are designed to be national at first, yet plan to gain a more and more international character in the future. Within this network, the Customer Club GmbH has the function of a strategic centrepiece. Its duties are drawing up and managing financial budgets and co-ordinating benefits, including those of several outside suppliers. Specialized agencies have taken over most of the handling and administration of both programmes. The strategic development of both customer relation programmes is driven forward in the operational areas of the manufacturers Volkswagen and Audi. The following comments are focused on the Volkswagen Club.

In a period when even satisfied customers change company and turn to one of the competitors – even simply for 'a change' – it is not sufficient to wait until the customer decides on their own to purchase one of our products again, to use one of our services again, or to keep in touch with us.

It is not sufficient to measure customer loyalty; our task is to redefine it. It will be necessary to monitor the loyalty-consciousness of our customers and their attitude to loyalty in the same way as their loyalty behaviour. This can only be achieved if all information about the customer is stored in a central database. Our target at Volkswagen is holistic customer management.

## Professional database marketing

The mainstay of the two loyalty programmes is professional database management. Increasingly, detailed information on your customers becomes a strategic success factor. Only such precise knowledge about customers allows a target-oriented, customized dialogue. In most cases, however, the huge potential of this address pool is not recognized; or even worse, available addresses and information are destroyed as there is no appropriate computer infrastructure to take full advantage of them. Often, there is no systematic analysis of the existing material. But this is an essential prerequisite for effective database marketing: using all internal sources of sales statistics, information from sales representatives in the field and the results of customer interviews, and additionally from external list brokers.

## Structure of the database

From the beginning, we have directed our efforts towards database management in order to make sure that all relationship management tasks can be carried out without disturbance and all interactions within the network can be clearly assigned to the customer. We have structured our database model as follows:

- *Customer*
    - basic data – such as name, title, form of address and nationality
    - address data – such as postal code, city and street
    - psychographic data – such as hobby and lifestyle.
In this context, however, only those data are stored which support us regarding the development and the arrangement of offers. For example, it is not important to know whether the customer spends their vacation swimming at Lake Constance. However, it is important to know whether the customer is interested in winter sports and travels to such locations by car. Based on this information, we can present to the customer specific offers, such as winter tyres, snow chains, roof racks and a lot more.
    - socio-demographic data – such as birth data and income bracket
    - customer's history
    - other data is marked with exclusion flags, which restricts the use of the customer's address when certain tasks are carried out (such as excluding them from certain mailings they have received before).

- *Customer behaviour*
  - contact data collected by the Customer Service Centre
  - response data taken from orders, from complaint management and customer interviews
  - purchase data, describing the purchasing behaviour of a customer – data are taken from the departments handling the parts sales or the sale of new vehicles, as well as from the computer systems (for example, the new car and used car file)
  - booking of bonus points, showing us when and how often a customer uses our services or purchases parts or accessories within our organization. When the customer uses services of our co-operating partners and collects bonus points, we receive additional information, but this is not yet used.

- *Dealer data*
  - basic data (address)
  - contract data
  - characteristics of the dealer, such as payment and service offers
  - contact data.

## Full service from the beginning

Membership of the Volkswagen Club programme is free of charge, open to drivers and friends of any car brand, and does not place any obligation on members. Membership application forms are available at all Volkswagen Club and Audi A plus programme partners and at the Club Service Centre, which can be contacted 365 days a year from 8 a.m. to 8 p.m. Moreover, the Volkswagen Club takes advantage of modern communication media and also offers information via T-Online and the Internet (<http://www.vw-club.de>).

## Dialogue-oriented customer service

Members of both programmes can benefit from a whole package of car-related and other attractive services, which were selected as a result of workshops with external agencies, several creative meetings with customers, and subsequent market research. The car-related service package includes a telephone-based driver-guide service for all major cities in Germany, individual route planning throughout Europe, a continuously updated traffic hotline for German highways, and a 24-hour breakdown service. Adventure-oriented and leisure time benefits include travel and ticket services that offer tickets to all kinds of events. Exclusive products related to Volkswagen and Audi and the high-quality *Volkswagen Magazine* complete the service package. The club service centres of both programmes are the hub of all customer contacts, and provide information and services concerning the car, traffic and general mobility, as well as all services that are provided by telephone.

## Attractive point systems

Attractive bonus point systems were developed for the two club concepts, and members take full advantage of them. The dealers participating in the Volkswagen Club offer points on all after-sales revenues over €35, including spare parts, accessories and inspections. The points are credited to a personal account. Points can be accumulated without any time restrictions or limits regarding the amount of points. The total score can be redeemed at all Volkswagen Club partners. The equivalent of the collected points – 100 points are worth €1 – can be discounted from the amount due so that the customers pay only the difference. With this concept, the Volkswagen Club offers members real cash value.

## Extended offers involving co-operation partners

Since autumn 1995, co-operative agreements have existed between the Customer Club GmbH and the German railroad company Deutsche Bahn, the German Telecom company Deutsche Telecom, the Hapag-Lloyd Travel Agency, the Volkswagen Insurance company and the Volkswagen Bank. In this way, interesting services can be added to the existing range of offers by Volkswagen and Audi. The Volkswagen Club also has a co-operative agreement with Eurocamp, a family holiday package provider. Club members can also collect bonus points when buying services from these co-operation partners. Moreover, they have the opportunity to supplement their club card with additional functions. Let us take a closer look at the benefits provided by the external partners.

### DEUTSCHE BAHN

In return for buying the BahnCard – a card Deutsche Bahn offers to its customers for a one-time fee and with the benefit of a 50 per cent discount on all tickets for one year – the Customer Club GmbH grants 500 bonus points (1000 bonus points for the BahnCard First Class, 250 bonus points for the BahnCard Junior and the BahnCard Senior, and 500 for the First Class version of the latter cards).

### GERMAN RAILROAD CAR TRAIN (DB AUTOZUG)

Using the car train guarantees the club member a relaxed journey to their destination and while enjoying the independent mobility of using their own car. Bonus points are granted on an invoice amount of €35 or more.

### DeTe CARD SERVICES

The Volkswagen Club Calling Card from DeTe Card Services, German Telecom, allows Club members to phone on particularly favourable terms by using public telephones in more than 75 countries world-wide. This card is free of charge for the first year. Volkswagen Club members benefit from seasonal discounts, and receive bonus points on all transactions.

### VOLKSWAGEN BANK DIRECT

Offers from Volkswagen Bank direct also enable the club member to be financially mobile: the Eurocard and Visa Card (separately or as part of a package), which are free of charge for the first year, the Plus account, savings options with long-term guaranteed high returns, professional investment consultation, and investment fund management.

## EUROMOBIL RENTAL CAR AGENCY

At 2400 Euromobil stations, bonus points are granted on car rentals with an invoice amount of €35 or more.

## HAPAG LLOYD TRAVEL AGENCY

From 450 to 36 000 points can be collected by booking travel through one of the 170 travel agencies in the Hapag Lloyd Group. Points are granted by the Customer Club GmbH for all purchases of €75 or more. This not only includes purchases of Hapag Lloyd sponsored charter packages, but also purchases through other travel providers, airlines, and train tickets.

## VOLKSWAGEN INSURANCE

From 125 to 400 bonus points are granted by the Customer Club GmbH on specific insurance packages purchased at the Volkswagen Insurance agency.

## EUROCAMP

Eurocamp has built a strong reputation as a provider of camping trips for families. Members who book a vacation for over €35 are credited with up to 7000 points, depending on the total price of the trip.

## THE WORLD OF ENTERTAINMENT

### Autostadt
Club members can obtain discounts when visiting this unique automobile 'infotainment' park run by the Volkswagen Group.

### Filmpark Babelsberg and the Bavaria film tour
A look behind the scenes is an experience for the whole family – breathtaking stunt shows, large film sets, the original locations of classic films and intimate experience of current productions. For Volkswagen Club members, this is offered at reduced prices.

### Konzertkasse Wolfsburg
This ticket service for club members gives access to an online booking service offering tickets for rock, pop and classical music concerts, shows, sport events, musicals and theatre events world-wide. Bonus points are credited for every transaction.

# Review of the Club's success

A good source of feedback for the Customer Club GmbH is the *Volkswagen Magazine*, which gives readers the opportunity to ask for information via response cards. The number of cards returned is enormous: for each issue of the magazine, 40 000 information requests are received on car models and several thousand inquiries on car financing, car leasing, credit cards and insurance programmes. The telephone hotlines of the club service centre are also used extensively. Regular direct mailings are very popular. The state-of-the-art database administration allows an up-to-date check of a member's bonus point status and optimal handling of all kinds of database analysis. This again is proof of the high acceptance of the bonus point system.

Market research has shown that club members significantly differ from other customers on all items applied by Volkswagen to measure brand retention, which leads to much higher customer loyalty.

## Conclusion: A successful concept and dynamic further development

The introduction of a sophisticated customer club programme offer has proven to be the right step towards achieving dialogue-oriented customer service. The service modules offered meet the expectations of today's customers, and comply with their high demands for service quantity and quality. The degree of co-operation with external partners is very encouraging. Members and participants make good use of the extra benefits. As a result of these positive experiences, the Customer Club GmbH is constantly seeking new co-operation partners.

Volkswagen has managed to recognize and interpret the change of social values in the 1990s, and it has reacted successfully to the special demands of its customers. Despite the so far encouraging development of the two programmes, a great deal of attention is being paid to a permanent broadening of service performance and securing service quality. Customer satisfaction has the highest priority, and all energies are being focused on this goal. A commitment to the customer will therefore drive dynamic future development.

# 26 *Swatch the Club*

*The original case study for the first edition was written by Patrick Ashworth. It was updated for this edition by the current club management.*

Swatch was instrumental in reviving the Swiss watch industry. In the late 1960s and early 1970s, the Swiss watch industry was facing fierce competition from Asia (primarily Japan). For the first time, the Asians were able to conquer precision with the development of quartz. They were launching high-precision watches at a low price. Switzerland was renowned for its high-quality, high-price watches.

Swatch revolutionized the Swiss watch industry by producing a low-price, high-quality, quartz analogue watch. The main criteria that had to be met by these new watches were:

- a low retail price in order to compete with competition from the Far East
- maintain the high quality synonymous with Swiss brand name watches
- the manufacture of the watch must be possible with a sufficiently high profit margin
- the basic product must be adaptable to a wide range of models
- several requirements must be met, such as water-resistance, durability and at least three years of battery life.

These demands were set high, and were very challenging, especially as for the first time everything was based on and around the marketing objective. Not only was the challenge to act and think innovatively, a large part of the success was due to the communication specialists. These specialists produced one original idea after another, created an image that is unmistakeable anywhere in the world, generated enormous brand awareness in the shortest time imaginable, and positioned Swatch as a lifestyle accessory.

Swatch was revolutionary because it changed the whole paradigm of what a watch is. A watch was no longer regarded as a timepiece, but as an accessory. Swatch brought fashion to the watch industry. It provided a fashionable product that was affordable to all, and it encouraged multiple purchases. People could afford to buy several watches to suit their tastes, clothing, activities and so on. A watch need not be a lifetime possession.

The first Swatch watches were launched in spring 1983, and by 1997 over 200 million had been sold world-wide.

## History of Swatch the Club

Shortage of supply coupled with high demand very quickly made Swatch watches collectors' items. Swatch enthusiasts would queue for hours outside Swatch points of sale to gain the opportunity to purchase rare Swatches. The company had a large number of loyal followers.

In 1990, a club was started in Switzerland to cater to the needs of these loyal customers, called Swatch Collectors of Swatch. A special club watch was produced exclusively for club members. Members were constantly provided with inside information about the life of Swatch. They became part of an exclusive club that catered to their needs. They became part of a group in which all members had similar interests. Swatch opened the doors to its fascinating company, and invited its members to huge Swatch events. Unsurprisingly, the club grew rapidly to over 120 000 members.

Over the years, the club has been introduced to several countries, bringing together a loyal and united group of collectors. The lack of supply created a black market for Swatches which encouraged more people to become collectors. Obviously, some collectors were hungry for information on new products and how they could get hold of these. The club became the most important tool for providing these collectors with the information they required. It worked on a very emotional level, and a personal relationship formed with collectors by inviting them to events and product launches. Informal groups also developed which held private meetings on a regular basis. The club was able to bring people together who had similar interests.

Swatch became a household name, and supply was increased to cater for the increasing demand. This reduced the attractiveness of collecting and decreased the huge monetary gains that had been obtained during the previous few years.

In 1996, Swatch adapted to the changing marketplace and renamed its club Swatch the Club. Two groups were emerging: collectors who love Swatch and are fascinated by the original products that are launched, and the Swatch consumer who likes Swatch and likes the club watch.

The needs of these groups are very different. The collectors want to know as much as possible about the brand. They want to be given the opportunity to purchase special editions. They want to get into contact with other collectors and attend events. The other members are interested in the basic advantages of a club, especially discounts and special offers. These are often related to third parties, such as airlines, hotels or car rental firms.

The launch dates of the club in various countries were as follows:

- Switzerland, Austria – 1990
- Italy, France, Germany – 1991
- Spain, the USA – 1992
- the UK – 1993
- Belgium – 1995
- the Netherlands, and Swatch the Club International – 1996
- Singapore, Portugal – 1997.

## Organization of Swatch the Club

Swatch the Club has a membership of around 90 000, and is being promoted throughout the world. The running of the club is split between Swatch the Club International and local club organizations.

The international club looks after the administration of over fifty countries, such as Canada, Australia, Japan, Spain and Portugal. These countries either do not have sufficient members to set up their own organization, or their organization is unable to handle a one-to-one project like Swatch the Club.

The main Swatch countries, which have a club structure set up locally, are Switzerland, Germany, Austria, the UK, Italy, the USA and Belgium/Luxemburg.

The biggest club countries are Switzerland (around 12 000 members), Italy (around 15 000 members) Germany (around 10 000 members) and Portugal (around 5000 members).

## International club

The conceptual tasks, such as club strategy, product developments, pricing, promotion and merchandising, are all developed at the international club, which gives guidance and direction to the countries. Club publications, such as the *World Journal* (distributed in paper form and via the Internet) and *Swatch News* are published by the international club to inform members what is going on in the world of Swatch. The publications cover products, events, celebrities, offers, competitions, current stories, Swatch Access promotions and many other fun and exciting topics. They give an insight into what Swatch is really about.

The international club is also responsible for the administration of many countries. It takes care of processing application forms, shipping the club watch and/or member card, as well as all mailings during the year. Members can also order merchandise through the international club. It has a hotline which caters to the needs of members. The international club has a sophisticated database which allows it to obtain important information about its customers.

## Club organizations

The club organizations are set up to look after all the needs of their members. They are responsible for all member administration, the running of their database system, sending out membership cards, mailings, merchandise, sale of special offers, local events, distribution of the club watch and promotion of the club locally.

Each club organization adapts the club to local needs, but at the same time must respect the international concept. For example, in Switzerland, the application form for club membership is provided with the watch for the purchaser to complete, whereas in Italy the retailer must complete an application form at the point of sale. Swatch the Club in Italy makes club information available via teletext and at the point of sale, whereas most other clubs conduct local mailings.

## Club package

The membership fee is 140 Swiss francs in the customer's local currency. Members of Swatch the Club receive:

- a club watch
- a membership card
- a subscription to *World Journal* and *Swatch News*
- entry to the club house section on the organization's Web site, where they can find games information in their language and the e-journal

- Swatch catalogues
- VIP invitations to Swatch events
- the opportunity to participate in Swatch events
- Swatch merchandise
- access to limited-edition club special offers
- the chance to obtain Swatch special editions
- access to national meetings
- a great deal of fun!

## Why is it important to have a club?

Swatch the Club is the company's direct link to its customers. There are four main reasons for having a club:

1 *direct marketing and PR* – to promote the spirit of Swatch directly to its main customers, transmitting a positive image of the brand; promotion directly to the customer reduces the waste of traditional advertising
2 *market research* – the club allows the company to obtain valuable information about its main customers
3 *sales* – it can be used as a distribution channel
4 *to reward customer loyalty*.

It is essential to position the club strategically within the company, since it can be either sales- or market-driven. Swatch the Club is not the same as traditional clubs, since it wants to communicate the dynamic and ever-changing character of the company. It challenges traditional theories, and aims to convey the emotions that are created by the brand's products.

Swatch the Club is regarded as a direct marketing and PR tool. It provides an ideal way to reach customers and communicate the real world of Swatch. It is interactive, emotional and is constantly educating members about the philosophy of Swatch. Members, as ambassadors of Swatch, are the company's best salespeople, since word of mouth is a strong means of promotion.

Swatch the Club does not only target avid collectors, but makes the club of interest to any Swatch purchaser who is interested in the life of Swatch and its products.

## Distribution

In most countries, the club watch is available in some of the Swatch retail stores. Swatch customers purchase the watch, and the retailer then completes the application form for the member. The retailer immediately returns the form to the distributor for processing. Retailers are set criteria which they must follow. The club is of most importance to the retailer, since members purchase on average seven or eight watches per year.

It is possible for customers in non-club countries to purchase membership via direct mail. They return a completed application form with credit card details and can become part of the international club.

## Promotion

Swatch the Club does not carry out traditional advertising, since its main objective is to reach Swatch customers directly and provide them with a valuable package of benefits. Since the company is targeting its customers, its greatest exposure is at the point of sale. The retailer must provide adequate window space, the potential to display stickers and posters, and space for counter cards. Thus, Swatch customers are immediately exposed to the club.

All watches include a reply coupon within the guarantee manual. The club then sends information and an application form to these interested customers. All product catalogues and brochures carry information about the club, and a reply coupon.

Public relations is also a strong promotional tool for the club. Many magazines and newspapers are interested in the club concept, and are keen to publish articles about Swatch the Club. New watch concepts are always accompanied by a press release.

Swatch the Club is always present at Swatch events. The club is promoted to those at the event, and all members are also invited to participate. Members are always keen to get together with others who have the same interests.

## Summary

Swatch changed the reason for purchasing a watch: it became a fashion accessory, not just a timepiece. In doing so, Swatch encouraged multiple ownership, and its products became collectable. The club was the perfect vehicle to cater for the needs of these collectors.

Swatch the Club is the most effective tool for getting closer to the customer. It allows the company to reward customers for their loyalty, to gain important market research, to transmit the philosophy of Swatch, and to create a unique way of communicating, providing an emotional bridge to the customer.

# Bibliography

The bibliography is split into two parts: English and German literature. If I am aware that a translation of an article or book is available in the other language, it has been included in both lists.

To enable a publication that has been referred to in this book and published in both languages but in different years to be found more easily, it has been entered in both the English and the German sections under the same year, using the year of the originally cited publication as the guideline. For example, the English article 'Zero Defections: Quality Comes to Service' by Reichheld and Sasser was published in 1990, its German translation one year later. It is therefore included in both the English and German sections as 'Reichheld and Sasser (1990)'. The details of each publication then show its real publication information and year. When cited in the text, in most cases page numbers of both the English and German versions are given.

## English bibliography

ACNielsen (1998) 'Frequent Shoppers Cite Use of Card Over Price and Customer Service', *News from ACNielsen*, 1998.

American Airlines (1998) 'American Airlines Introduces Automated Upgrades for AADVANTAGE Top-Tier Members', *Yahoo!Finance*, 7 October 1998.

American Computer Group (1995) 'Fox Kids Club Database Analysis', in Fox Kids Club information material, 1996.

*Ancillary Profits* (1995) 'How to Boost Profits by Launching a Membership Club', *Ancillary Profits*, September 1995, pp.1–14.

Anon, *What's Working for American Companies in International Sales & Marketing* (1997) 'Building Customer Loyalty Across the Miles', 31 January 1997, pp.1–2.

Anon. (2000a) 'Slippery Slope: Are Online Loyalty Programs Losing Traction With Best Customers?', *Colloquy*, Vol.8, No.4, 2000, available at <http://www.colloquy.de>.

Anon. (2000b) 'The Seven Steps to Designing an e-Loyalty Strategy', *Brandweek*, Vol.41, No.45, 2000, p.2000.

Anon., *The Supervisor´s Guide To Improved Customer Service & Retention* (2001), pp. 1–4.

Ashton, Mike (1996) 'A Step by Step Guide to Planning and Implementing your Customer Club to Guarantee its Success', presentation at the IIR conference, 'Targeted & Dynamic Customer Clubs', London, 14 October 1996.

Band, William (1995) 'Customer-Accelerated Change', *Marketing Management*, Winter 1995, Vol.4, No.3, pp.47–59.

Barlow, Richard (1992) 'Relationship Marketing – The Ultimate in Customer Services', *Retail Control*, March 1992, pp.29–37.

Barlow, Richard (1994) 'Department Stores Move in the Right Direction . . . Slowly', *Colloquy*, 1994, Vol.4, No.3, pp.2–5.

Barlow, Richard (1996) 'Thank You's and Discounts Aren't Enough', *Colloquy*, 1996, Vol.5, No.3, pp.2–3.

Barlow, Richard (1999) 'Exit Lines – How to Close Your Frequency Program', *Colloquy*, 1999, Vol.7, No.3, pp.8-9.

Barlow, Richard (2001) 'One Up, One Down', *Colloquy*, 2001, Vol. 9, No. 1, pp.1–3.

Berry, Leonard and Parasuraman, A. (1997) 'Listening to the Customer – The Concept of a Service-quality Information System', *Sloan Management Review*, Spring 1997, pp.65–76.

*Boston Globe* (1998) 'GM offers loyalty rebates', 15 April 1998.

Bund Jackson, Barbara (1985) 'Build Customer Relationships that Last', *Harvard Business Review*, November/December 1985, pp.120–8.

Butscher, Stephan (1996b) 'Welcome to the Club: Building Customer Loyalty', *Marketing News*, 9 September 1996, p.9.

Butscher, Stephan (1996c) 'Germany Provides Blueprint for Customer Clubs', *Direct Marketing International*, March 1996, pp.46–7.

Butscher, Stephan (1996d) 'Customer Clubs: Bad Planning Can Lead to Financial Disaster', *Direct Marketing International*, April 1996, pp.40–1.

Butscher, Stephan (1997a) 'Customer Clubs: How to Set Up a Value Oriented Customer Loyalty Program that Builds True Relationships', presentation at the AMA/ASQC '9th Annual Customer Satisfaction and Quality Measurement Conference', New Orleans, 16–18 February 1997.

Butscher, Stephan (1997b) 'Brand Battle', *Brandweek*, 10 March 1997, p.18.

Butscher, Stephan (1997c) 'Automating Services Can Cause More Problems than it Solves', *Marketing News*, 24 November 1997, p.4.

Butscher, Stephan and Simon, Hermann (1997d) 'Service Automation – Cost Reduction vs. Customer Loyalty', unpublished manuscript.

Butscher, Stephan (1998c) 'Germany´s Most Popular Radio Station Creates Loyal Listeners', *Colloquy*, 1998, Vol.6, No.3, pp.10-11.

Butscher, Stephan (1998d) 'Customer Loyalty Programmes with Power', *Direct Marketing International*, November/December 1998, pp.38-40.

Butscher, Stephan (1998e) 'German Carmakers Create Loyalty With Innovative Programs', *Colloquy*, 1998, Vol.6, No.2, pp.1, 4–6.

Butscher, Stephan (1998f) 'Loyalty Programs Can Work for B-to-B Customers Too', *Marketing News*, 22 June 1998, p.6.

Butscher, Stephan (1999a) 'Using Pricing to Increase Customer Loyalty', *The Journal of Professional Pricing*, Vol.8, No.1, pp.29–32.

Butscher, Stephan (1999b) 'Quality Databases', *Direct Marketing International*, February 1999, pp.22–3.

Butscher, Stephan (1999c) 'The US and Europe: Loyalty Programmes Compared', *Retail Management International*, 9/10 1999, p.21.

Butscher, Stephan and Simon, Hermann (2001) 'Individualised Pricing: Boosting Profitability', *European Management Journal*, 2001, Vol.19, No.2, pp.109–14.

Bowry, Barbara (1995) 'Can 15 Million Customers Be Treated as Individuals?', *DM News*, 17 April 1995, pp.26, 44.

Carol Wright Promotions (1996) *18th Annual Survey of Promotional Practices*, Naperville, IL, 1996.

*Colloquy* (1994) Vol.4, No.3, 1994 (whole issue).

*Colloquy* (2001) 'The Atlas Effect: How Coalitions Help Support the World of Customer Loyalty', Vol.9, No.1, 2001, available at <http://www.colloquy.com>.

Copulsky, Jonathan and Wolf, Michael (1990) 'Relationship Marketing: Positioning for the Future', *Journal of Business Strategy*, July/August 1990, pp.16–20.

Dawkins, Peter and Reichheld, Frederick (1990) 'Customer Retention as a Competitive Weapon', *Directors & Boards*, Summer 1990, pp.42–7.

Dell, Michael (2000) 'CRM in the Internet Era', *PC Magazine*, 27 June 2000, p.133.

Dolan, Robert and Simon, Hermann (1996) *Power Pricing*, Free Press, New York, 1996.

Dowling, Grahame and Uncles, Mark (1997) 'Do Customer Loyalty Programs Really Work?', *Sloan Management Review*, Summer 1997, pp.71–82.

*European Business Report* (1997) 'Smart Cards: The Wave of the Next Millennium', *European Business Report*, Autumn 1997, pp.46–7.

Fournier, Susan, Dobscha, Susan and Mick, David Glen (1998). 'Preventing the Premature Death of Relationship Marketing', *Harvard Business Review*, January/February 1998, pp.42–51.

Fuerderer, Ralph, Herrmann, Andreas and Wuebker, Georg (1999) *Optimal Bundling*, Springer-Verlag, Berlin, 1999.

Furlong, Carla (1993) '12 Rules for Customer Retention', *Bank Marketing*, January 1993, pp.14–18.

Gofton, K. and Cobb, R. (1996) *Marketing*, Supplement on Direct Marketing Association/Royal Mail Direct Marketing Awards, 12 December 1996, pp.14–32.

Green, P.E. and Srinivasan, V. (1990) 'Conjoint Analysis in Marketing: New Developments with Implications for Research and Practice', *Journal of Marketing*, October 1990, pp.3–19.

Hagel, John III and Rayport, Jeffrey (1997) 'The Coming Battle for Customer Information', *Harvard Business Review*, January/February 1997, pp.53–65.

Hammer, Michael (1996) *Beyond Reengineering*, HarperCollins, New York, 1996.

Hammer, Michael and Champy, James (1993) *Reengineering the Corporation*, HarperCollins, New York, 1993.

Hart, Christopher, Heskett, James and Sasser, W. Earl (1990) 'Profitable Art of Service Recovery', *Harvard Business Review*, July/August 1990, pp.148–56.

Joachimsthaler, Erich and Aaker, David (1997) 'Building Brands without Mass Media', *Harvard Business Review*, January/February 1997, pp.39–50.

Jones, Lynn (1995) 'The Desk Set', *Direct*, August 1995, pp.48–50.

Kiermaier, Raif and Butscher, Stephan (1997) 'Develop Only What Customers Want, At Their Price', *Marketing News*, 17 March 1997, p.10.

Kucher, Eckhard and Hilleke, Klaus (1993) 'Value Pricing Through Conjoint Measurement: A Practical Approach', *European Management Journal*, Vol.11, No.3, September 1993, pp.283–90.

Lee, Louise (1995) 'Warehouse Clubs Gain Amid Strategy Shift', *Wall Street Journal Europe*, 20 November 1995, p.B1.

Liebeskind, Ken (1995) 'Harlequin Launches a Fine Romance', *DM News*, 12 June 1995, p.10.

Long, Pat (1997) 'Customer Loyalty, One Customer at a Time', *Marketing News*, 3 February 1997, p.8.

*Management Review* (1997) 'Interview with Frederick Reichheld', *Management Review*, March 1997, pp.16–17.

Manasco, Britton (1998) 'Here Come the Chatterbots', *INSIDE 1to1*, 30 July 1998.

*Marketing* (1996) 'Safeway To Try Out Tailored TV', *Marketing*, 12 December 1996, p.4.

*Marketing News* (1997) 'Marketing Briefs', *Marketing News*, 3 February 1997, p.2.

*Marketing Report* (1996) 'A Complaint System that Builds Customer Loyalty', *Marketing Report*, 14 October 1996, pp.1–2.

Maszal, Jeff (1996) 'Carrying Out Accurate Cost Benefit Analysis to Make a Solid Business Case', presentation at the IIR conference 'Targeted & Dynamic Customer Clubs', London, 14 October 1996.

Miller, Cyndee (1994) 'Marketers Hoping Kids Will Join Club, Become Lifelong Customers', *Marketing News*, 31 January 1994, pp.1–2.

Murphy, Ian (1997) 'Customers Can Join the Club – But at a Price', *Marketing News*, 28 April 1997, p.8.

Negus, Beth (1995) 'Fox Network's Kids Club Is Plugging Away', *Direct*, September 1995, p.11.

*New Media Age* (2000) 'Attractive Sites', *New Media Age*, 20 April 2000, p.34.

Ovans, Andrea (1997) 'Marketing – Make a Bundle Bundling', *Harvard Business Review*, November/December 1997, pp. 18–20.

Peppers, Don (1999) 'Can Governments Be More One to One? And Should They?', *INSIDE 1to1*, 4 November 1999.

Peppers, Don and Rogers, Martha (1993) *The One to One Future*, Currency Doubleday, New York, 1993.

Peters, Thomas and Waterman, Robert (1982) *In Search of Excellence*, Harper & Row, New York, 1982.

Porter, Michael (1980) *Competitive Strategy*, Free Press, New York, 1980.

Porter, Michael (1985) *Competitive Advantage*, Free Press, New York, 1985.

Poulos, Nicholas (1996) 'Customer Loyalty and the Marketing Database', *Direct Marketing*, July 1996, pp.32–5.

Prada, Paulo (1999) 'Hotels Treat Loyal Patrons Royally', *The Wall Street Journal*, 15 October 1999.

Rapp, Stan and Collins, Tom (1988) *MaxiMarketing*, McGraw-Hill, New York, 1986.

Reichheld, Frederick (1993) 'Loyalty-based Management, *Harvard Business Review*, March/April 1993, pp.64–73.

Reichheld, Frederick and Sasser, W. Earl (1990) 'Zero Defections: Quality Comes to Service', *Harvard Business Review*, September/October 1990, pp.105–111.

Reichheld, Frederick and Schefter, Phil (2000) 'E-loyalty Your Secret Weapon On the Web', *Harvard Business Review*, July/August 2000, pp.105–13.

Reichheld, Frederick and Teal, Thomas (1996) *The Loyalty Effect*, Harvard Business School Press, Boston, 1996.

Reid Smith, Ellen (2000) 'Hit List: Ten Critical Design Factors for Cultivating e-Loyalty', *Colloquy*, 2000, Vol.8, No.4, available at <http://www.colloquy.de>.

Rogers, Martha (1998) 'Ernst & Young´s Online Advice', *INSIDE 1to1*, 27 August 1998.

Rosenfield, James (1996) 'Whither Database Marketing', *Direct Marketing*, July 1996, pp.39–41.

Schultz, Don E. (1999) 'Manage Customers, Not Loyalty Programs', *Marketing News*, 4 January 1999, pp.35–6.

Simmons Market Research Bureau (1993) 'Results of Simmons Study of Fox Kids Club Members', in Fox Kids Club information material, 1996.

Simon, Hermann (1996) *Hidden Champions*, Harvard Business School Press, Boston, 1996.

Sonnenberg, Frank K. (1988) 'Relationship Management Is More Than Wining and Dining', *Journal of Business Strategy*, May/June 1988, pp.60–3.

Steinmetz, Greg (1997) 'German Consumers Are Seeing Prices Cut in Deregulation Rush', *Wall Street Journal*, 15 August 1997, p.Al.

Stewart, Thomas (1997) 'A Satisfied Customer Isn't Enough', *Fortune*, 21 July 1997, p.70–1.

Stone, Merlin (1996) 'Communicating with Business Customers to Keep Them Loyal', *Business Growth & Profitability*, September 1996, Vol.1, No.3, pp.233–4.

Stone, Merlin (1997) 'Organising Mass-market Customers Into Clubs – The UK Retail Way', unpublished manuscript, 1997.

Stone, Merlin and Mounsey, P. (1990) *Managing Direct Marketing*, Croner, London, 1990.

Stone, Merlin and Woodcock, N. (1995) *Relationship Marketing*, Kogan Page, London, 1995.

Stone, Merlin and Woodcock, N. (1996) 'Database Marketing – What Is State of the Art?', *Journal of Database Marketing*, December 1996.

Stone, Merlin and Young, L. (1992) *Competitive Customer Care*, Croner, london, 1992.

Stone, Merlin, Bond, A. and Davies, D. (1995) *Direct Hit*, Pitman, London, 1995.

Stone, Merlin, Woodcock, N. and Jeanselme, M. (1996) 'Managing Customer Relationships Using New Technologies – The Effect on Smaller Businesses', *Business Growth & Profitability*, June 1996, Vol.2, No.2, pp.123–37.

Stone, Merlin, Woodcock, N. and Wilson, M. (1996) 'Making the Change from Marketing Planning to Customer Relationship Management', *Long Range Planning*, 1996, Vol.29, No.5, pp.675–84.

*The Economist* (1997), Trouble at the Check Out', 1 February 1997, p.88.

*The Economist* (1999) 'Direct Hit', 9–15 January 1999, p. 1.

*The Industry Standard* (1999) 'Frequent Flyer', 28 June 1999, pp.96–8.

*USA Today* (1999) 'Waiting for Rewards', 10 September 1999, p.1.

*Volkswagen World* (1996) 'The Volkswagen Club Is Here!', Winter 1996, pp.8–11.

*Wall Street Journal* (1996) 'Merrill Starting Client-reward Program', 27 September 1996, p.C1.

*Wall Street Journal Europe* (1996) 'Free Airline Miles Become a Potent Tool for Selling Everything', 17 April 1996, pp.1, 6.

Weyr, Thomas (1994) 'German Customer Clubs Growing; Help Establish loyalty Programs', *DM News*, 19 December 1994, p.26.

Wittink, D.R. and Cattin, P. (1989) 'Commercial Use of Conjoint Analysis – An Update', *Journal of Marketing*, July 1989, Vol.52, pp.91–6.

Womack, James, Jones, Daniel and Roos, Daniel (1990) *The Machine that Changed the World*, Ramson Associates, New York, 1990.

Wu, Amy (1999) 'In Bid to Survive, Hong Kong Retailers Try Customer Loyalty Clubs', *The New York Times*, 31 January 1999, p.6.

## German bibliography

Albers, Sönke (1992) 'Kundenclub', *Vahlens Grosses Marketing Lexikon*, Hermann Diller (Hrsg.), München, 1992, p.584.

Albers, Sönke und Eggert, Karin (1988) 'Kundennähe – Strategie oder Schlagwort', *Marketing ZFP*, 1/1988, pp.5–16.

Anon. (1986) 'Clubs für Kunden – Dauerdialog mit der Zielgruppe', *absatzwirtschaft*, 10/1986, pp.28–39.

Anon. (1991) 'Zucker für Treulose', *DM*, 2/1991, pp.60–4.

Anon. (1993) 'Dauerhafte Bindung erwünscht', *à la card journal*, 1993, pp.50–2.

Anon. (1994a) 'Im Ikea-Klub sind alle Kunden eine grosse konsumfreudige Familie', *Frankfurter Allgemeine Zeitung*, 3 Mai 1994.

Anon. (1994b) 'Warnung vor der Wollmilchsau', *werben & verkaufen*, 9/1994, pp.116–22.

Anon. (1994c) 'Kundenclubs haben nicht zwangsläufig Erfolg', *Frankfurter Allgemeine Zeitung*, 17 Dezember 1994, p.20.

Anon. (1994d) 'Eine Idee blüht trotz Rezession', *à Ia card journal*, 1/1994, pp.49–52.

Anon. (1995) 'Wie beliebt sind Kundenclubs?', *Markenartikel*, 5/1995, p.212.

Anon. (1996) 'Willkommen im Club', *werben & verkaufen extra*, 18/1996, pp.22–3.

Anon. (1998a) 'Von der Homepage zur individuellen Ansprache', *werben & verkaufen plus*, 10/1998, pp.146–7.

Anon. (1998b) 'Lebensmittel mit Flugmeilen bezahlen', *Blick durch die Wirtschaft*, 30 Juni 1998, p.5.

Anon. (1999a) 'Engagierte Kundenbindung zahlt sich aus', *Frankfurter Allgemeine Zeitung*, 20 September 1999, p.35.

Anon. (1999b) 'Die Kunden sind nicht so loyal wie angenommen', *Frankfurter Allgemeine Zeitung*, 15 Februar 1999, p.30.

Anon. (1999c) 'Dialog schlägt Preisvorteile', *werben & verkaufen*, 8/1999, p.107.

Anon. (1999d) 'Markenbindung in Deutschland niedriger als in Gesamt-Europa', *Frankfurter Allgemeine Zeitung*, 8 Februar 1999, p.28.

Anon. (2000c) 'Mit der Loylitätskarte kann man Angebote attraktiver machen', *Frankfurter Allgemeine Zeitung*, 15 Mai 2000, p.28.

Bauer, Hans, Herrmann, Andreas und Mengen, Andreas (1994) 'Eine Methode zur gewinnmaximalen Produktgestaltung auf der Basis des Conjoint Measurement', *ZfB*, 64. Jg (1994), Heft1, pp.81–94.

Becker, Annegret (1991) 'Unter Freunden verkauft sich's am allerbesten', *impulse*, 11/1991, pp.107–9.

Becker, Annegret (1995) 'Der Boom der Cards und Clubs', *impulse*, 6/1995, pp.92–8.

Becker, Helmut (1996) 'Wer der Erste ist, behält die Nase vorn', in Dieter Lübcke und Raimund Petersen (Hrsg.), *Business-to-Business Marketing*, Stuttgart, 1996, pp.127–36.

Bednarczuk, Piotr und Friedrich, Joachim (1992) 'Kundenorientierung ohne Marketing', *absatzwirtschaft*, 9/1992, pp.90–7.

Belau, Kerstin (1996) 'Ente und Elch bitten zur Club-Party', *werben & verkaufen plus*, 18/1996, pp.190–9.

Berekoven, Ludwig (1990) *Erfolgreiches Einzelhandelsmarketing: Grundlagen und Entscheidungshilfen*, München, 1990.

Berry, Leonard and Parasuraman, A (1997) 'Wie Servicewünsche genau erfaßt werden', *Harvard Business Manager*, 3/1998, pp.80-91.

BGH (1991) Bundesgerichtshof, 22 November 1990 – IZR 50/1989 – OLG Dusseldorf, 'Gewährung einer kostenlosen Transportversicherung', *Wettbewerb in Recht und Praxis* (WRP), Nr. 4/1991, pp.225–7.

Blau, Reiner (1993) 'Erfolgreiche Clubkozeptionen', *MailMarketing*, 9 März 1993, Nr. 307, pp.6–9.

Bohrer, Wolfgang (1999) 'Kundenbindung durch Dienstleistung', *Frankfurter Allgemeine Zeitung, Beilage Geschäftsreisen*, 2 März 1999, p.B7.

Bottler, Stefan (1994) 'Erst im Club wird König Kunde zum dressierten Konsumenten', *werben & verkaufen*, 42/1994, pp.70–4.

Bottler, Stefan (1997) 'Anzug sucht Latzhose', *werben & verkaufen*, 37/97, p.110.

Bunk, Burkhardt (1991) 'Willkommen im Club', *absatzwirtschaft*, 2/1991, pp.42–7.

Bunk, Burkhardt (2001) 'Nach dem Rabattgesetz: Wie das Marketing die neuen Freiheiten nutzt', *absatzwirtschaft*, 3/2001, pp.32–8.

Butscher, Stephan (1994a) 'Freiwillige Bindung', *à la card journal*, 1/1994, pp.46–7.

Butscher, Stephan (1994b) 'Kundenclubs als modernes Marketing-Instrument', *Direkt Marketing*, 3/1994, pp.26–30.

Butscher, Stephan (1995) *Kundenclubs als modernes Marketinginstrument*, IM Fachverlag, 2. Auflage, Ettlingen, 1995, und 3. Auflage, 1997.

Butscher, Stephan (1996a) 'Step-by-Step, Wie Sie eine kundenorientierte Kartenleistung generieren', *Direkt Marketing*, Februar 1996, pp.23–5.

Butscher, Stephan (1996e) 'Die Marketing-Tools müssen greifen – vor allem unter Nutzen- und Kostengesichtspunkten', in Dieter Lübcke und Raimund Petersen (Hrsg.), *Business-to-Business-Marketing*, Stuttgart, 1996, pp.151–62.

Butscher, Stephan (1996f) 'Kundenbindung durch Kundenclubs', *Marketing Journal*, 1/1996, pp.46–9.

Butscher, Stephan (1998a) 'Direkte Kommunikation über institutionalisierte Kommuni- kationskanäle', *Marktforschung & Management*, 1/98, pp.11–15.

Butscher, Stephan (1998b) 'Discounts & More – Bonusprogramme müssen mehr bieten', *Direkt Marketing*, Juni 1998, pp.24–5.

Butscher, Stephan (1999d) 'Kundenbindungsprogramme: Basis für strategisches Database Marketing', *Database Marketing*, 1/1999, pp.22–3.

Butscher, Stephan (1999e) 'Kundenbindung mit Köpfchen', *Direkt Marketing*, Februar 1999, pp.22–3.

Butscher, Stephan (1999f) 'Kundenkarten mit Power', *à la card aktuell*, 16 März 1999, pp.122–6.

Butscher, Stephan (1999g) 'Kundenorientierung als Teil der *Unternehmenskultur*', in *Unternehmenskultur, Frankfurter Allgemeine Zeitung* (Hrsg.), Frankfurt 1999, p.22.

Butscher, Stephan und Müller, Lars (1999c) 'Kundenbindung durch Kundenclubs', in Hans Hinterhuber und Kurt Matzler (Hrsg.), *Kundenorientierte Unternehmensführung*, Gabler Verlag, Wiesbaden 1999, pp.321–36.

Butscher, Stephan und Simon, Hermann (1997b) 'Gefährlicher Spagat – Automatisierung von Dienstleistungen', *absatzwirtschaft*, 1/1997, pp.46–9.

Butscher, Stephan (2000c) 'Marketing mit Kundenkarten und Kundenclubs', in Dieter K. Tscheulin und Bernd Helmig (Hrsg.), *Branchenspezifisches Marketing, Grundlagen – Besonderheiten – Gemeinsamkeiten*, Gabler, Wiesbaden, 2001, pp.775–91.

Butscher, Stephan, Keller, Peter und Litfin, Thorsten (2000a) 'Kundenbindungskonzepte im Zeitalter des Internets', in Jahrbuch Direktmarketing – Trend 2000, IM Fachverlag (Hrsg.), Ettlingen 2000, pp.11–15.

Butscher, Stephan, Keller, Peter und Litfin, Thorsten (2000b) 'Bindungsfähig: Virtuelle Kundenclubs', *Direkt Marketing*, Juni 2000, pp. 22–4.

Cohen, Andreas (1999) 'One-to-One-Marketing im Internet', *ONEtoONE*, 31 Mai 1999, p.8.

Diller, Hermann (1996) *Fallbeispiel Kundenclub*, IM Fachverlag, Ettlingen, 1996.

Diller, Hermann (1997a) 'Was leisten Kundenclubs?', *Marketing ZFP*, Heft 1, 1. Quartal, 1997, pp.33–41.

Diller, Hermann (1997b) 'Preis-Management im Zeichen des Beziehungsmarketing', *DBW Die Betriebswirtschaft*, 57. Jg., Heft 6, pp.749–62.

Diller, Hermann (1998) 'Innovatives Beziehungsmarketing', *absatzwirtschaft*, 6/1998, pp.90–8.

Eichmann, Karsten (1990) 'Industrielles Marketing', in Paul W. Meyer und Anton Meyer (Hrsg.) *Marketing-Systeme – Grundlagen des institutionalen Marketing*, Kohlhammer, Stuttgart u.a., 1990, pp.13–76.

Fournier, Susan, Dobscha, Susan und Mick, David Glen (1998) 'Beziehungsmarketing: Des Guten zuviel für die Stammkäufer', *Harvard Business Manager*, 3/1998, pp.101–09.

Geffroy, Edgar und Zach, Christian (1993) 'Verkaufen heisst heute "Beziehungs-management" ', *Response*, 1/1993, pp.25–7.

Gerling, Michael (1995) 'Frequent-Shopper-Programme in den USA – Neue Wege zur Kundenbindung', *MailMarketing*, 21 Februar 1995, Nr. 354, pp.8–12.

Gruber, Christina (1996) 'Familienbande mit der Karte', *WIOS*, 5/1996, pp.10–11.

Haase, Knut, Salewski, Frank und Skiera, Bernd (1998) 'Preisdifferenzierung bei Dienstleistungen am Beispiel von Call-by-Call-Tarifen', *ZfB*, 68. Jg (1998), Heft 10, pp.1053–71.

Hammer, Michael (1996) *Das prozessorientierte Unternehmen: Die Arbeitswelt nach dem Reengineering*, Campus, Frankfurt, 1997.

Hammer, Michael und Champy, James (1993) *Business Reengineering: Die Radikalkur für Ihr Unternehmen*, Campus, Frankfurt, 1995.

Hart, Christopher, Heskett, James und Sasser, W. Earl (1990) 'Dienstleistungsfehler zur Kundenbindung nutzen', in Hermann Simon (Hrsg.), *Industrielle Dienstleistungen*, Schaffer Poeschel, Stuttgart, 1993.

Helmer, Wolfgang (1999) 'Volkswagen sieht im Internet Chancen für engere Kundenbindung', *Frankfurter Allgemeine Zeitung*, 1 April 1999, p.23.

Herterich, Gerd (1993) 'Der IKEA-Family-Kundenclub', Vortrag auf der Management Circle Konferenz 'Aktive Kundenbindung durch Clubs und Cards', 11–12 Februar 1993, Frankfurt am Main.

Höfner, Klaus und Schuster, Werner (1992) 'Strategien zur Steigerung der Kundenloyalität, *Marktforschung & Management*, 3/1992, pp.123–6.

Holz, Stefan und Tomczak, Torsten (1996) *Kundenclubs – Marktuntersuchung der deutschen Clubs*, IM Fachverlag, Ettlingen, 1996.

Horstmann, Rembert (1998) 'Führt Kundenzufriedenheit zu Kundenbindung', *absatzwirtschaft*, 9/1998, pp.90–4.

Kaapke, Andreas und Dobbelstein, Thomas (1999) 'Kundenbindung im Handel – Empirische Ergebnisse', *Mitteilungen des Instituts für Handelsforschung an der Universität zu Köln*, 51. Jg., Nr.7, pp.133–44.

Kirn, Friedrich Mathias (2001) 'Gute Karten für Kundenklubs', *media & marketing*, 1/2001, pp.28–34.

Kirstges, Torsten (1995) *Erste bundesweite Marktuntersuchung Kundenclubs*, IM Fachverlag, Ettlingen, 1995.

Kowalski, Matthias, Schuster, Jochen und Stadler, Rainer (2000) 'Rabatt – Sieger nach Punkten', *Focus*, 16/2000, pp.236–50.

Kreutzer, Ralf T. (1991a) 'Database-Marketing – Erfolgsstrategie für die 90er Jahre', in Heinz

Dallmer (Hrsg.), *Handbuch Direct Marketing*, 6, völlig überarbeitete Auflage, Gabler Verlag, Wiesbaden, 1991, pp.623–42.

Kreutzer, Ralf T. (1991b) 'Planung – Erfolgsbedingung des Direct Marketing', in Heinz Dallmer (Hrsg.), *Handbuch Direct Marketing*, 6, völlig überarbeitete Auflage, Gabler Verlag, Wiesbaden, 1991, pp.417–46.

Kromschröder, Jan (1990) 'Der Club, der treue Kunden macht', *stern*, Nr.40, 27 September 1990, pp.135–8.

Linke, Klaus (1996) 'Kundenclubs auch für den Mittelstand', *Blick durch die Wirtschaft*, 29 Oktober 1996, p.7.

Lübcke, Dieter und Petersen, Raimund (1996) *Business-to-Business Marketing*, Schäffer Poeschel, Stuttgart, 1996.

Lürken, Jacqueline (1997) 'Finger weg vom Kundenclub', *Direkt Marketing*, 2/1997, pp.20–5.

Mayer, Rainer (1996) 'Kundenbindung online', *Direkt Marketing*, September 1996, pp.32–4.

McWilliam, Gil (2001) 'Online-Communities geben Marken mehr Schub', *Harvard Business Manager*, 2/2001, pp.72–85.

Mengen, Andreas (1993) *Konzeptgestaltung von Dienstleistungsprodukten*, Schäffer Poeschel, Stuttgart, 1993.

Meyer, Anton (1985) Produktdifferenzierung durch Dienstleistungen, *Marketing ZFP*, Heft 2, Mai 1985, pp.99–107.

Möller, Karl-Heinz (1999) 'Die neue Karten-Kaste', *Welt am Sonntag*, Nr.23 13 Juni 1999, p.23.

Neuberger, Stephan (1994) 'Rechtliche Aspekte von Kundenclubs', in Wolfgang Wiencke und Dorothee Koke, *Cards & Clubs*, pp.129–41.

Niedermeier, Ralf (1995) 'Shaq O'Neal als Vereinskollege soll den Konsum ankurbeln', *Frankfurter Allgemeine Zeitung*, 31 August 1995, p.11.

Pellinghausen, Walter (1996) 'Späte Ernte', *Wirtschaftswoche*, 24 Oktober 1996, pp.115–8.

Peters, Michael (1989) 'Der Kundenclub als Selfliquidator', *absatzwirtschaft*, 2/1989, pp.52–4.

Pohl, Alexander und Dahlhoff, Denise (1998) 'Auch zufriedene Kunden werden untreu', *Frankfurter Allgemeine Zeitung*, 14 September 1998, p.37.

Pohl, Alexander und Schmich, Peter (2000) 'Kundenbindung im E-Commerce', Arbeitspapier, Oktober 2000, p.1–20.

Porter, Michael (1980) *Wettbwerbsstrategie*, 5 Auflage Campus, Frankfurt, 1995.

Porter, Michael (1985) *Wettbewerbsvorteile*, 4 Auflage Campus, Frankfurt, 1995.

Rapp, Stan und Collins, Tom (1988) *MaxiMarketing*, Hamburg/New York, 1988.

Rapp, Stan und Collins, Tom (1991) *Die grosse Marketingwende*, Verlag Moderne Industrie, Landsberg am Lech, 1991.

Reichheld, Frederick (1993) 'Treue Kunden müssen auch rentabel sein', *Harvard Manager*, 3/1993, pp.106–14.

Reichheld, Frederick und Sasser, W. Earl (1990) 'Zero-Migration: Dienstleister im Sog der Qualitätsrevolution', *Harvard Manager*, 4/1991, pp.108–15.

Reichheld, Frederick und Schefter, Phil (2001) 'Warum Kundentreue auch im Internet zaehlt', *Harvard Business Manager*, 1/2001, pp.70–80.

Reichheld, Frederick und Teal, Thomas (1996) *Der Loyalitätseffekt*, Frankfurt, 1997.

Rittmeyer, Sabine (1995) 'Clubkonzepte, die Wettbewerbsvorteile schaffen', *acquisa*, 4/1995, pp.47–9.

Schmadalla, Sybille (1996) 'Aus Freunden müssen Partner werden', in Dieter Lübcke und Raimund Petersen (Hrsg.), *Business-to-Business-Marketing*, Stuttgart, 1996, pp.71–8.

Schöttke, Bernd (1990) 'Cards & Clubs sind die Shooting Stars', *Horizont*, Nr.45, 9 November 1990, pp.22–3.

Sebastian, Karl-Heinz und Meyer, Birgit (2001) 'Rabatte, Boni, und Prämien: Dem Affen Zucker geben', *Frankfurter Allgemeine Zeitung*, 19 Februar 2001, p.31.

Simon, Hermann (1988) 'Management strategischer Wettbewerbsvorteile', *ZfB*, 58. Jg., Heft 4, pp.461–80.

Simon, Hermann (1991) 'Kundennähe als Wettbewerbsstrategie und Führungsherausforderung', Arbeitspapier 01–91, Universität Mainz, Lehrstuhl für Bewirbswirtschaftslehre und Marketing.

Simon, Hermann (Hrsg.) (1993) *Industrielle Dienstleistungen*, Schäffer Poeschel, Stuttgart, 1993.

Simon, Hermann (1996) *Die heimlichen Gewinner*, Campus, Frankfurt, 1996.

Simon, Hermann, Tacke, Georg, Woscidlo, Birgit und Laker, Michael (1997) 'Kundenbindung durch Preispolitik' in Bruhn, Manfred und Homburg, Christian, *Handbuch Kundenbindungsmanagement*, 1997.

Stelzer, Josef (1997) 'Wie der Kunde zum Fan wird', *werben & verkaufen plus*, 10/1997, pp.144–6.

Stolpmann, Markus (2001) 'Kundenbindung im E-Business – "Maßnahmen und Erfolgskontrolle" ', *Electronic Commerce InfoNet*, 25 1 Januar 2001.

Stüldeli, Walter (1997) '1:1 Marketing', *Marketing Journal*, 4/1997, pp.240–1.

Thaler, Eva und Rieker, Susanne (1998) 'Müde Stimmung im Online-Club', *werben & verkaufen*, Vol.36, 1998, p.164–5.

Thelen, Michael (1996) Interview von Markus Kreusch mit Herrn Michael Thelen, *Porsche Financial Services*, 12 November 1996.

Thieme, Matthias (1996) Interview von Stephan A. Butscher, 16 December 1996.

Thomas, Falk (1992) 'Der Club-Gedanke ist noch nicht ausgereizt', *absatzwirtschaft*, 5/1992, pp.138–40.

Tluczykont, Ulrike (1997) 'Der Club des SDR3, *Marketing Journal*, 2/1997, pp.112–13.

Tödtmann, Claudia und Froitzheim, Ulf (1994) 'Sehr persönlich', *Wirtschaftswoche*, Nr.41, 7 Oktober 1994, pp.102–18.

Topsiek, Rita (1989) 'Die Wahrheit über Kundenclubs – Entscheidend ist die Kundenpflege', *Das neue Erfolgs- und Karrierehandbuch für Selbständige und Führungskräfte*, 8/1989, pp.93–8.

Vögele, Siegfried (1991) Fremdinterview mit Prof. Siegfried Vögele, Genehmigung für die Verwendung des Interviews erhalten am 10 Mai 1993.

von Usslar, Levin (1993) 'Rechtsfragen in der Clubpraxis', Vortrag auf der Management Circle Konferenz 'Aktive Kundenbindung durch Clubs und Cards', 11–12 Februar 1993, Frankfurt am Main.

Weinem, Ingo (2001) 'Analytisches CRM, Die Basis der Kundenbindung', *Database Marketing Trend 2001*, 2001, pp.32–4.

Westphalen & Partner (1993a) *Cards und Clubs*, Informationsbroschüre der Westphalen & Partner GmbH, Hamburg, 1993.

Westphalen & Partner (1993b) *Aufstellung von Kundenclubs*, Westphalen & Partner GmbH, Hamburg, 1993.

Wiedmann, Rainer und Wörnle, Stefan (1998) 'Müde Stimmung im Online-Club', *werben & verkaufen*, 36/1998, pp.164–6.

Wiencke, Wolfgang (1992) 'Selber stricken oder Kompetenz einkaufen', *à la card aktuell*, 16/1992, 28 August 1992, pp.6–14.

Wiencke, Wolfgang (1993) Interview durch Stephan Butscher, 24 März 1993 in Wiesbaden, in Stephan Butscher, *Kundenclubs als modernes Marketinginstrument*, 2. Auflage, Ettlingen, 1995, pp.95–103.

Wiencke, Wolfgang und Koke, Dorothee (1994) *Cards & Clubs*, Econ Verlag, Düsseldorf u.a., 1994.

Wiencke, Wolfgang und Tribian, Uwe (1996) 'Händler- und Absatzmittler-Marketing durch Business-to-Business-Clubs', *Der Karriereberater*, 7/1996, pp.149–60.

Womack, James, Jones, Daniel und Roos, Daniel (1990) *Der Weg zum perfekten Unternehmen*, Campus, Frankfurt, 1991.

Zorn, Dieter (1991) Fremd-Interview mit Dr Dieter Zorn, 23 September 1991 in Hamburg, Genehmigung für die Verwendung des Interviews erhalten am 10 Mai 1993.

# Index

# Dealing with Customer Complaints

## Tom Williams

Increased consumer protection, government initiatives, changing expectations on the part of the consumer - a number of factors have combined to lead to a marked growth in complaints. At the same time organizations are beginning to recognize the value of an effective complaints handling system. Yet until now there has been no systematic book-length treatment of this significant area published in the UK.

Tom Williams starts by explaining the strategic importance of complaints handling. He goes on to examine how people actually complain and what their objectives might be. He shows how to determine policy and how to set up and run an effective complaints handling unit, considering both the point of view of the complainer and the implications for staff on the receiving end. With the help of case studies and examples drawn from the private and public sector he identifies the principles and practices involved. The book ends with a summary of key points and details of where to find further advice and information. This is above all a practical guide.

It is all too easy to regard complaints as a pain to be avoided or a nuisance to be got rid of as fast as possible. In fact, as Tom Williams demonstrates, they can be a valuable source of information, of customer satisfaction and, ultimately, of improvements in both reputation and profitability.

# Gower

# Gower

For more than thirty years, Gower has published the best in current business practice. Our books are written by leading consultants, professionals and academics, and cover the spectrum of business publishing. They range from practical business guides and textbooks to comprehensive handbooks and research-level business books.

We publish books on all aspects of business and management – such as finance, sales and marketing, training, human resources, project management, quality, logistics… For more information, just call us to request a copy of the Gower catalogue, or visit our website at www.gowerpub.com. You can get full details on any of our titles, or you can search by keyword to find out what books we have on a specific subject. All online orders receive a 10% discount. The website also provides news on our latest releases and special promotions, guidelines for authors on submitting a book proposal, and contact details for our international offices.

Gower is an imprint of Ashgate Publishing, one of the world's leading publishers of academic research and professional practice.

*If you would like to receive regular information on our new books, please let us know the subject areas of interest to you, and we will add you to our **mailing list**. You can also request our **email newsletter**, which will keep you posted on new products, special offers and other items of interest.*

**Contact Gower's marketing department for further information:**

telephone: +44 (0)1252 331551   fax: +44 (0)1252 368525
email: info@gowerpub.com
Gower Publishing, Gower House, Croft Road,
Aldershot, Hants GU11 3HR, UK

# The Author

Stephan A. Butscher is a Partner with SIMON-KUCHER & PARTNERS Strategy & Marketing Consultants in Bonn, Boston, London, Munich, Paris, Tokyo, Vienna and Zurich, and Managing Director of their London office. He spent 3½ years building up the US office in Boston. He holds a business degree (Hons.) from the Johannes-Gutenberg-University in Mainz, Germany.

He has published two books on customer loyalty, and more than 80 articles on retention marketing, Internet strategies and marketing, pricing, marketing and international strategy in various journals in Europe and the USA. In 1993, he received the Alfred-Gerardi-Award from the German Direct Marketing Association for his work on customer clubs. In 1999, he received the Distinctive Pricer of the Year Award from the Professional Pricing Society. Stephan is a regular speaker at national and international conferences.

As a consultant, he has worked for numerous companies in Europe, Asia and the USA, including BMW, DaimlerChrysler, Deutsche Bahn, Deutsche Telekom, DHL, Eurotunnel, Hewlett-Packard, HSBC Lufthansa, Siemens, T-Mobile, Virgin Trains and 3M.

The author can be reached at <sbutscher@simon-kucher.com>.

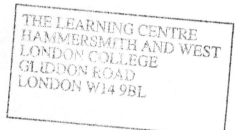
SIMON-KUCHER & PARTNERS
www.simon-kucher.com